PRAISE FOI

MY FATHER'S SU

'Mary Garden roars against injustice to give voice to silent sufferers of sibling abuse. While tugging at the threads of her family in an effort to understand her fraught relationship with her sister, she spares no one, least of all herself. It is a raw and unguarded account of a reckoning, a story a lifetime in the making.'

Michelle Tom

'A heartfelt rendering of the writer's struggles with an abusive sister, and her ultimate journey towards recovery. Mary does an especially good job of describing family of origin dynamics that set the stage for the troubled relationship with her sister, and she points to a path forward for adult survivors.'

John Caffaro, PhD Distinguished Professor, California School of Professional Psychology

'Mary Garden offers an unflinching account of her experience of sibling abuse, a largely invisible form of domestic violence. With searing honesty, Garden combines memoir and deep research to explore the complex nature of sibling relationships, and the uniquely profound impact of abuse, when inflicted by one sibling onto another.'

Nicole Madigan, Journalist and author of *Obsessed*

'From its electrifying opening to its deeply compassionate conclusion, any sibling who's ever had to play happy families will find solace in Garden's visceral battle cry against victim blaming. Writers everywhere will treasure this benchmark book for courageously demanding truth in the face of bothsidesism.'

Michael Burge, Journalist and author of *Tank Water*

'An astonishing life story, containing at its heart a frank, raw and courageous revelation of the reality and long-term effect of violence visited by one sister upon another. Ultimately, almost miraculously, there develops a mood of heroic compassion.'

Carmel Bird

'A fascinating and sometimes shocking story of family trauma and conflict. Writing with insight, restraint and compassion, Mary Garden shines a clear, unflinching light on her own family, and herself.'

Maurice Gee

PRAISE FOR
SUNDOWNER OF THE SKIES

'Beautifully written, *Sundowner of the Skies* is no hagiography. Garden eloquently evokes her father's brief moment of barnstorming celebrity but frames it between his troubled childhood in Scotland and her own troubled childhood during Oscar's long and resentful retirement in New Zealand. This cathartic family history is a profound exploration of inter-generational trauma and its effects on individuals, families and their shared memories.'

Judges, NSW Premier's History Award 2020

'Author Mary Garden travels back through the turbulence of her own startling family history to find her father, Oscar Garden, a legend of long-distance aviation who soared through any sky but crash-landed the one-way journey of his life on earth … A rattling, searing, soulful story that takes flight on the Gipsy Moth wings of the author's relentless search and willingness to pull back every curtain of this extraordinary man's life, sometimes at her own emotional peril. I didn't want this trip to end!'

Trent Dalton

'An important piece of aviation history and a courageous personal story, vividly told. I found it enjoyable in every way. The width of research is astonishing. *Sundowner of the Skies* should find enthusiastic readers – grateful readers in the aviation world and thoroughly engaged readers in the wider one.'

Maurice Gee

'Author Mary Garden writes beautifully and honestly of her father, Oscar Garden, a hero from the golden age of aviation when intrepid men in tiny biplanes crossed the globe in flights that started the world.'

Grantlee Kieza, *Courier-Mail*

'This barebones outline of an aviator's career is simply the skeleton which Mary Garden, with an objectivity rare in a daughter's account of a father's troubled life, fleshes out with solid research into family history, recollections from friends, colleagues and extracts from the files. *Sundowner* is a fine biography and aviation fans will love every mile of it, while the social historian will revel in the stories of how things were so different.'

Jim Sullivan, *Otago Daily Times*

'Mary Garden's portrait of her father could be read as an attempt to retrieve his lost fame, but it's probably read as a daughter's homage to a father who is at once familiar and a mystery. Oscar was born to a dysfunctional family, most of whom moved to New Zealand, where bitter family divisions persisted … Garden's deep affection for her flawed father shines through.'

Steven Carroll, *Sydney Morning Herald*

my father's suitcase

my father's suitcase

mary garden

JUSTITIA
BOOKS

JUSTITIA
BOOKS

First published in Australia in 2024
by Justitia Books
PO Box 306 Chewton Victoria 3451

Copyright © Mary Garden 2024

All rights reserved.

The right of Mary Garden to be identified as the author of the
work has been asserted.

NATIONAL
LIBRARY
OF AUSTRALIA

A catalogue record for this
book is available from the
National Library of Australia

ISBN: 979 8 8849913 6 1 (paperback)
ISBN: 978 0 6468396 7 7 (ebook)

Cover design by Alex Ross
Author photograph by Paula Brennan
Typeset in Adobe Garamond Pro 12/16.5 by Blue Wren Books

'If I live in a world in which my experience is not reflected back to me, then maybe I'm not real enough; maybe I'm not real at all. That is a trauma: to see yourself never in the world.'

Dorothy Allison

'You own everything that happened to you. Tell your stories. If people wanted you to write warmly about them, they should have behaved better.'

Anne Lamott

Oscar Garden (on the left) with Captain Fred Haig, Aviation Manager for
Vacuum Oil Company, during a tour of New Zealand in December 1930.

My father used to keep an old, scuffed leather suitcase under his single bed. He was once a famous aviator and inside that suitcase he stored things related to his flying days: logbooks, photos, newspaper clippings, brass buttons from old uniforms.

After Dad died, the suitcase and its contents were the only things left to remind us that he had once been a hero from the golden age of aviation. Both my younger sister and I coveted this suitcase. My brother was not so interested in it. My mother wanted to hold on to it for a while.

Ōtūmoetai, Tauranga, December 1960.
Robert on the left, me in the centre, Anna on the right.

Author's Note

This is a story about sibling abuse, a spectre that has haunted me for much of my life. Until a few years ago, I did not realise that my sister's ongoing aggression towards me constituted 'sibling abuse'. A psychologist pointed it out. Named it. I began to use this label, although I felt quite uncomfortable doing so. I still do. There is a societal expectation that we should get along with our brothers and sisters. Be friends for life.

I also began looking at the research in this field, which helped me understand more fully what had happened to me. I was surprised to learn that sibling abuse is by far the most common form of abuse in the context of family violence and occurs four to five times as frequently as spousal or parental child abuse.[1] It is significantly more prevalent (as much as three times) than school bullying.[2]

Yet, despite its ubiquity it is the forgotten abuse. It is under-researched and seldom discussed in the media. The 2016 Victorian Royal Commission into Family Violence noted that sibling violence is a form of family violence that receives inadequate recognition and that its seriousness is not recognised.[3]

The problem is that sibling abuse is often dismissed as sibling rivalry. They are different. Sibling rivalry is competitiveness and jealousy between siblings – squabbling and the unwillingness to share things. Sibling abuse is the repeated use of violence (including derogatory taunts) by one sibling against the other.

Like any other abuse, sibling abuse can be emotional, physical or sexual (the most common of intra-familial sexual abuse) and have far-reaching, long-lasting harmful effects on everyone involved. It sometimes results in murder. Siblicide! According to the Bible and the Qur'an, the first murder recorded on earth was Cain killing his brother Abel.

Sibling abuse occurs mostly in a dysfunctional family, such as my birth family, where parents have not learnt to process their own trauma. There may be spousal violence and parental child abuse, including neglect, already occurring. A child can learn that inflicting pain is acceptable and that they can get away with it, just as a parent often gets away with their bad behaviour. A bullying sibling is merely kicking the ball down the generational line.

When I started to tell people my story, I kept hearing over and over again tales of similar abuse. Some had never shared their story before and were relieved. After a chance conversation with a woman at a community lunch in my local town, she emailed me:

> Thank you so much for opening up this incredibly important conversation. As with any trauma, finding out others have suffered similar traumas at the hands of their siblings, and how widespread it is, has significantly reduced my burden. Suddenly it is not just my individual problem because of some defect in me, but a societal phenomenon. That helps a lot.

A journalist who follows me on Twitter sent a direct message to say how valuable my posts on sibling violence and estrangement were.

> It is a topic very familiar to me. It is the cause of my lifetime of living with a major depressive disorder and endless therapy. This stuff has no end, I find. Despite [it] all, I feel an eternal sadness over the family relationships that I never got to experience.

Interestingly, some people make a point of responding by telling me they had very good relationships with their siblings. So what? This is subtle gaslighting as far as I'm concerned, for I'm writing about *my* experience, not theirs. Would they say to a survivor of domestic violence: 'My husband was nice to me'?

I hope my book will help others who have suffered at the hands of a sibling feel less alone, and that it will encourage people to talk about this important issue. There are some confronting themes in this book, including mental illness, suicide and violence. But this story is also one of resilience and healing.

This is a work of non-fiction. In some cases, names have been changed to protect the identities of those who may not have wanted to be written about or chose to remain anonymous. I have also changed the name of a book title and a literary website for the same reason.

getting away with things

CHAPTER 1

Going West

The thought that my sister could fly across the Tasman Sea and kill me has sometimes kept me awake at night. My heart begins pounding, my throat tightens, and it seems as if my brain is shrinking, freezing in fear. I force myself to breathe deeply, think the word 'calm' on each breath and slowly stretch out. Banish this monster that has snuck up on me.

Mum often said I was too sensitive and had a good imagination. My brother, Robert, reckoned I wallowed in the past and that I exaggerated my sister's abuse, even though he was never there those times when she attacked me at night when we were little or when she hurled a compass into my back while we were boarding at Aunt Margaret's, the year I attended Epsom Girls' Grammar School in Auckland.

A part of me believed them, so perhaps this was why I swallowed my fear and flew from my home in Australia back to New Zealand in September 2005 to help Mum, who was going through a difficult time. Even though I knew my sister would be there.

I bet Mum and my aunts and others often chatted about my sister and me over cups of tea. I can see them rolling their eyes, shaking their heads and sighing, 'What a shame they don't get on.' Perhaps I overheard them say something like that. I'd wince when someone would say to me, 'It's such a pity you aren't friends with your sister.' Robert would have felt the same. He was friends with everyone.

We call my sister Anna. Mum and Dad christened her Anna Margaret Garden, but in the 1970s she changed it officially to Annamaria Aurelia Garden. Aurelia is a girl's name of Latin origin meaning 'the golden one'. Mum laughed at the name change: more proof that the Gardens were mad. No one in the family called her Annamaria.

After Dad died in 1997, my sister went back to London, where she had previously worked as a highly paid organisational consultant, and then disappeared for several years. She wrote to Mum to say she needed to be completely alone and would be out of contact for a while. We later found out she went to live in Dad's home village of Tongue, up the top of Scotland, where she agonised and grieved (her words) over Dad for a long time and raged against everyone in the family. I never grieved Dad's passing. I was relieved, as I hoped Mum could have some years enjoying herself after all those years of being Dad's slave, always at his beck and call.

During this time, with Anna out of reach and Mum frantic with worry about her, Robert and I decided to move Mum from Papakura in South Auckland to Orewa, a coastal town northeast of Auckland. It would be a chance to start a new life. We found a lovely brick unit directly opposite the Countdown supermarket and one block from the beach.

An iconic holiday location, Orewa was a favourite of a young Edmund Hillary and his family. His father, Percival, bought a bach (a small holiday house) there in the 1940s and planted the iconic Norfolk pines, which have a Christmas tree shape, along the beach front. The front was also spotted with large native pōhutukawa trees, a species of myrtle, that burst into fiery crimson flowers during the Christmas period. In Māori mythology, its flowers are said to represent the blood of a young warrior who perished while trying to avenge his father's death.

Although the township itself is uninteresting, stretched over a flat area with roads neatly crisscrossed and lined with bland brick houses and units – the poet James K. Baxter once described New Zealand as 'a country where towns are made like coffins' – the best part about Orewa is that it looks out to the sea and has three kilometres of beach with white golden sand. Over the years, I would walk that beach hundreds of times, and sometimes swim or float on my back in its calm waters. I've always loved the beach, a place where my mind and body can relax.

I thought Mum, too, would walk on the beach, dip her toes in the water, but the most she did was sit on a bench on its foreshore and occasionally eat fish and chips there with me. Perhaps when she first moved there, she'd wander down and stare blankly out at the water, wonder where Anna was and if she would ever hear from her again. It was something of a shock when Anna turned up at her doorstep at the end of 2000, not in the best mental state, and seemingly without a cent to her name, and expecting to live with Mum indefinitely.

A few years later, Mum wrote to me:

> I have a lot of time to think about my time with your father. I really do not want to think of him except that Anna is showing some of that weird side of him. It could drive me crazy if I had to have a repeat performance. I sometimes think there is an improvement in Anna, then she has a day when she really is out of this world talking madly and loudly to herself. I have a heavy heart when I think of the future if I have one – and also if I haven't, she will have to go into some sort of home.

After Mum moved to Orewa, Robert often called on me to help Mum even though he lived not far from her. He was about to fly with his partner to Europe for a cycling holiday and wanted me to look for a place for Mum to rent. Mum had mentioned in several letters and phone calls that she was 'in dire straits financially' because

Anna had been living with her on and off for about five years and not contributing in any way. Robert and I decided to sell her unit to free up some money for her.

I wonder now why my brother didn't help. He was wealthy. Why didn't I suggest this? I should have put my foot down. Mum had already had enough upheaval as Dad had been unstable and restless throughout their marriage, always on the move. She was almost 88 and had endured significant stress from putting up with Dad all those years and then Anna landing back on her doorstep, penniless and homeless. My brother suggested that while he was overseas, I look in Helensville, a town northwest of Auckland, about 30 kilometres from Orewa. Robert lived just north of Helensville, on a large farm, where he had established mountain bike trails on the hills and in the bush at the back of his property. He and his partner spent a lot of time away at various events, orienteering or mountain bike riding, not only in New Zealand but all over the world.

At Robert's behest I flew over to New Zealand but instead of staying with Mum, I stayed with my Aunt Ola, who was 92. After Mum had moved to Orewa, Aunt Ola and Uncle Pat had decided to move from Wellington and bought a unit just around the corner from Mum's place. Pat died a few years later at the age of 100.

Anna and I were estranged, so now I don't know why I agreed to go with the three of them in Mum's little two-doored grey car to look at a rental property for Mum in Helensville. Maybe I hoped things would be better now, my sister and I could be friends, she would not turn on me. Anna was friendly before we set off. She was driving while Mum sat in the front. I was in the back with Ola, who had recently come out of hospital after suffering a heart attack.

Ola was smartly dressed as usual. Although she was on an aged pension like Mum, she got her nails done regularly and bought beautiful clothes, sometimes even designer wear when they were on sale, from my favourite clothing shop in Orewa. I don't recall exactly what she was wearing, but she probably had on the white-grey faux-fur Russian Cossack–style hat that often crowned her face in the cooler months. Perhaps her purple satin blouse and a necklace with large lime-green baubles, which she would wear with a smart taupe mid-calf skirt, and wedge-heeled shoes. I loved Aunt Ola. She had not been able to have children and doted on her nine nieces and nephews. She was a big sturdy upright woman, whereas Mum was thin and slight and strained and a bit frozen.

Mum would have been wearing her usual grey slacks and perhaps a fawn jersey (she liked the colour fawn), along with a cardigan and lace-up black shoes. In recent years she had been buying her clothes – bargains she called them – from second-hand shops around Orewa.

My sister was also big and sturdy, and stronger than me. I don't recall what she was wearing but Mum said that since her mental breakdown Anna had resorted to wearing odd outfits, a hodgepodge of clothing, things flung together, nothing matching and usually either too thin or too thick for the weather.

My hopes were up as we headed west. Once we got off the Hibiscus Coast Highway, there was a meandering country drive across the island along Kahikatea Flat Road. It was a weird feeling sitting in that small car, bobbing along with forced smiles on our faces. I remember looking out the window at one stage, opening my eyes wide and shaking my head a little, thinking *what the fuck* and wishing I was back home.

Anna and I chatted a bit and we both laughed at something I said. Apart from a short phone call after Dad died, it was the first time I'd spoken with her for many years. I was now 55 and Anna was 53. I felt excited, relieved – did I finally have my sister back? I had thought we were the closest of friends until 1980, when she sent me a nasty letter, in which she blamed me for all the problems she'd had in her life. That was the beginning of our long estrangement.

As we reached the township of Helensville, Anna turned her head a little and asked for directions. I had the map on my lap and told her to take the next turn right. Suddenly she slammed on the brakes. The car skidded and jerked to a stop in the middle of the road.

She turned around and began to scream at me – I can't remember her exact words, but she said something about me being bossy and that I was a fucking bitch. Her freckled face was bright red, her bulging blue-green eyes wide and blazing. She looked deranged. She flung open her door, stormed around to the other side of the car and yanked the front door open.

Mum scuttled out like a praying mantis. Anna bent down and, reaching through the small gap between the seats, grabbed my arm and tried to drag me out. She began to bite and scratch me. My heart was beating so quickly I thought it might explode. My ears started popping, drowning things out. I was unable to utter a single thing, not even a wordless cry or a shout. Was she going to kill me?

A man rushed to help, shouted something at Anna and she backed off. I pushed the seat forward, scrambled out and began to run up the road. I heard Mum calling out, 'Come back, we'll sort it out.' I yelled back, 'I am no longer playing happy families.' That was a strange thing to shoot out of my mouth. I'd never stood up to any of them before.

I slowed down when I reached the shops at the crest of the hill and waited for Mum to catch up with me. I told her I was going to the police station, which was a few blocks away. She did not object, which was strange. While we were walking, I rang Tom, a friend of Robert's, who I had met a few times. He kept an eye on Robert's property whenever he was away. I told Tom briefly what had happened, and asked if he could bring me one of Robert's cars.

At the police station, a female officer took down notes, and said she would be in touch with the Orewa Police and the mental health crisis assessment and treatment team (CATT). She seemed unsympathetic; she may have thought it was just a family tiff. She advised me to go to hospital, which was odd as I wasn't badly injured.

I'm wondering now, writing this, why I didn't ask the police to check on Aunt Ola and see if she was safe. Maybe I just assumed Anna would take off back to Orewa with Ola still sitting in the back, which she did. I didn't have much space to worry about anyone else, to tell you the truth: I was in too much shock myself.

Things are blurry here. I vaguely remember Tom arriving with Robert's car, then perhaps I drove him back to his place, about 15 kilometres away. Also, I've always had a memory of going to a hospital. Did we drive to North Shore Hospital, a good 40-minute away from Helensville? If not, where to? We went somewhere, I'm sure, as I remember a doctor saying the visit would be covered by accident insurance. I don't remember what Mum and I said on the way to wherever we went. She felt sorry for me. That I do know. That was unusual, a first. I don't think she mentioned Anna the whole way.

After I'd been checked over – just bruises and scratches and bite marks – I dropped Mum off and then popped into Aunt Ola's to collect my bag. She was sitting in her armchair, radio in her hand, listening to the news. She was still shaken up. I gave her a big hug.

'Oh, Mary dear, I can't believe the way Anna attacked you. Absolutely priceless. You did nothing, absolutely nothing.' Ola was one of the kindest, most generous people I've ever known, but she, too, had always made excuses for Anna.

I drove to my brother's place. As soon as I got there, I rang him – he was somewhere in Europe – and burst into tears. Deep racking sobs. He'd never heard me cry like this before. He was concerned and sympathetic. That was a first too. He was also relieved. He reckoned that because of the assault my sister would be helped at last. We would be able to get her sectioned into a mental health facility, possibly for a lengthy period, as opposed to the one- or two-day stays she'd had before. She could be diagnosed and treated properly, and Mum's nightmare would be over.

Even though I was alone, I thought I'd be safe there in that lovely big house my brother had built on top of a hill at the edge of his farm but I stayed awake most of the night. I feared my sister would turn up, stab me to death. I spent the night on the lookout for headlights coming up the long driveway.

The next morning I drove down to the Orewa Police Station, around the corner from Mum's place. An officer said CATT had interviewed Anna and assessed her as being in no danger to herself or others. They said she had presented to them as being clear and articulate, and emphasised that she was *very* intelligent. Evidently my sister told them I had provoked her. They did not interview Mum or Aunt Ola, let alone me. I was shocked. My sister, unmedicated, *was* dangerous to others. She had assaulted me!

The officer said mental health crisis teams in New Zealand were completely hopeless. He told me about an incident the previous week where they had not intervened when a man went ballistic, threatened to kill his parents and smash up their house. CATT palmed it off as a police matter, whereas clearly the man needed help, needed to be sectioned. The police hadn't signed up to be caretakers of people suffering psychotic episodes! The officer said I could take out a civil case against Anna but added how lucky I was to be living in Australia. 'Go back there and to try to forget your family,' he urged.

It was a typically cold, grey and overcast day. I changed my air ticket and flew home that afternoon. I did not see Mum or Ola before I left. In my rush to leave, I forgot all about a suitcase Mum had said I could have. It was an old leather one that Dad had used when he was a commercial pilot for British Airways in the 1930s and for Tasman Empire Airways Ltd (TEAL) in the 1940s. Later, he kept it under his bed and stored precious things related to his aviation days, unless they were valuable and he could pawn them. The suitcase was at Mum's place but I did not want to go near there.

I ached to get back to the warmth of Queensland. The 2016 census recorded 201,202 New Zealand-born people living in Queensland,

40 per cent of the total New Zealanders in Australia.[4] Some have fled the ghosts of their childhood, others have been lured by the warmer climate and higher wages. I found Australians, especially Queenslanders, to be more open and friendlier, more relaxed, than New Zealanders, but maybe that's because of what I escaped.

My home at that time was a small fibro cottage in a beachside suburb 18 kilometres from Bundaberg. I'd just spent a year renovating it, painting it in light blue, aqua and orange, and had added a deck across the front. The cottage was at the back of a long narrow block that led right onto the beach.

For the next month, I spent most of my time on the couch in the front room that faced the beach. I did not feel well. My head ached as if it had been punched repeatedly. I lay on the couch listening to the sound of the waves, letting the sound seep through my brain and drown out Anna's screams, which kept reverberating. I couldn't bring myself to read or even watch television. Before dawn, I'd wander down to the beach and go for a walk. I did not want to see anyone, as I felt I'd have to smile and say hello or have a chat.

I didn't tell any of my friends I was back from New Zealand. I didn't ring Peter, who I'd recently broke up with but who I was still good friends with. (We'd been in a relationship for almost six years – at last, a decent guy who did not mistreat me in any way.) I didn't ring my son or daughter, even though I was very close to them. I did not want to burden them. I was too ashamed to tell them that violence had again re-entered my life. Bundaberg had been a new start for me, after some dark years in an abusive relationship in the 1990s in Maleny, in the Sunshine Coast hinterland, one of those little-bit-hippy places for so-called creative types. They were both now at university, finding their own way in the world. They'd never had anything to do with my sister; she had rejected them because they were mine.

Eventually I dragged myself into town to see my doctor, who referred me to a psychiatrist. She said I'd probably have to wait some weeks for an appointment, but luckily there was a cancellation for the next day. I'd never seen a psychiatrist before. I'd been to therapists and psychologists over the years, but not a psychiatrist. Would they lock me away? Make me have electric shock treatment?

I was expecting someone stern and aloof, but the psychiatrist was kind and friendly. He did not sit on a chair but perched himself on the front corner of his desk, his long legs swinging slightly as he sipped from a can of Diet Coke. I told him about Helensville. Blurted out bits and pieces from my life. The long sad story of my sister that went back so many years. I cried at times and dragged tissues from a box on a small table next to my chair. Wept about my weird, fucked-up birth family.

Towards the end of the session, he announced that I had post-traumatic stress disorder (PTSD) from the assault and other traumas from my past. Sustained trauma. He said I should 'divorce' myself from my family. Cut myself off from all of them, even though he said it was the hardest thing to do. Family bonds are the strongest ties, he added. The rest of the family were enabling my sister and always had been, from what I'd told him.

Cut off from *all* of them? I was taken aback. Wasn't that a bit harsh?

*

I thought the psychiatrist might have been exaggerating about me having PTSD. But my sister's attack haunted me for years; the fear stayed with me. I couldn't understand why I couldn't just ignore it all and get on with life. That's the sort of thing my brother would say: 'Stop wallowing in the past.' But then I did some research and discovered the psychiatrist was right.

There *are* psychological consequences of being physically assaulted. Georgina Fuller, from the Australian Institute of Criminology, points out that assaults may have ramifications that extend beyond direct consequences such as physical injuries and lead to a disruption across a wide range of functions.[5] As well as the resultant fear, anger, sadness and stress, the impact of violence can lead to the development of mental health conditions such as PTSD, with studies showing that females are at an increased risk of developing this disorder in response to physical assault compared with males. Studies have shown that the experience of victimisation results in fundamental changes in the way the individual perceives and interprets the world around them, including the way they view their own capabilities and self-worth.[6] It can lead to self-blame and negative thoughts about oneself. In other words, victims can blame themselves. And I was good at that.

CHAPTER 2

A Lot of Running

There was a lot of running in my childhood, and it was not for pleasure.

My family was not healthy, psychologically or emotionally. You could describe it as a toxic island, my father at the centre, as in many ways he had cut himself off from the world.

I knew we were not 'normal'. I knew we were not like other families. We were nothing like Mum's parents or my Aunt Alice and Uncle Brian (Mum's younger brother), who lived in Westport on the West Coast of the South Island. It was like going to heaven when we had holidays down there. It was obvious to me, even as a child, that there was something wrong with our little nuclear unit.

Dad had a violent streak and his anger leaked out in all directions. Maurice Gee, a much celebrated New Zealand author, described Dad as 'a sort of archetype of the damaged man, a strange and lonely and self-defeating man, and one who inflicts damage'. (Maurice married my half-sister, Margareta, in 1970). He was also very odd. Ironically, that's what had appealed to Mum when they first met. He was different from all the other blokes.

My father, Oscar Garden, had been a famous pioneer aviator in the early 1930s and ended up at the helm of Tasman Empire Airways Ltd (TEAL), the forerunner of Air New Zealand, during World War II. In March 1947 he resigned and bought a citrus orchard in Kerikeri, up in the Bay of Islands. He'd met Mum (Helen Lovell) in 1945, although they didn't get married until August 1948 as Dad had to wait three years for the divorce from his first wife to come through.

He'd met Greta Norlén when he was a pilot for British Airways doing night flights, mostly carrying mail from Heston to Stockholm. Greta was a receptionist at the hotel in Stockholm he stayed at. They married in December 1937 and their daughter, Margareta, was born in May 1940. The marriage was tempestuous – Margareta remembers her mother screaming and crying a lot – and they separated in early 1944. Margareta told me that when she was older our father would tell her, 'Your mother was mad, of course, quite mad. I don't know if she ever got better.' And Greta would say to her, 'Your father was quite mad of course, I don't suppose he'll ever be quite right in the head.'

Mum said she was attracted to Dad because he was so unusual. 'Oh boy, did I have to pay for wanting to be with someone different from the usual run of the mill. Serves me right.' Wasn't she worried about his baggage? A former wife and a child he'd have to support and look after from time to time?

It wasn't until after they were married that he showed his true colours. Within weeks Mum realised she had made a mistake. She was trapped. She said Dad had warned her that she would have to keep an eye on him as he was very impetuous. Indeed, he was. A few days after they returned from their short honeymoon, Mum was shocked when a real estate agent appeared at the door to put their house on the market! Then, without discussing it with Mum, Dad bought a milkbar with small living quarters at Paeroa, a small town at the base of the Coromandel Peninsula, a midway point for those travelling between Auckland and Tauranga, a seaside town in the Bay of Plenty.

This venture lasted only a few months. During this time my mother fell pregnant.

Dad then sold up and they moved south to Whakatāne, pronounced Fuk-a-taw-nee,[7] in the eastern Bay of Plenty region. He was back to being a horticulturist. Willowbank Nurseries had a shop, a small tumbledown house and a nursery on a couple of acres; the house was meant to be temporary as the plan was to build a new one. Mum recalled rats the size of cats coming through the holes in the floor, and Dad keeping a spade by the side of their bed to bash them on their heads.

Robert was born in Whakatāne in June 1949. I arrived one year later. My mother was loading boxes of oranges onto the back of a truck when she fell off and went into labour. She said that as soon as she reached hospital, I rushed out. This was a story she told often over the years, adding 'and Mary hasn't stopped rushing since'. Mary on the run.

Six months after I was born, we moved north to Papatoetoe, a suburb of South Auckland. Ivy and Henry Lovell, my mother's parents, came to visit, and Henry accompanied my father to look for a business to buy as he was prepared to put money into it. Dad found something wrong with every place they looked at and eventually Henry gave up, said it was a waste of time as 'there was no satisfying this man'.

Within the year Dad had sold up again and headed north to Kumeu, a small town northwest of Auckland. It was here my mother became pregnant with my sister, Anna, but soon afterwards the Kumeu house went on the market and it was sold before my father had found another house. My brother and I were shunted off to relatives. I was lucky as I went to stay with Aunt Ola, while Robert got farmed out to Aunt Rose, one of Dad's older sisters, who I always found a bit stern and uptight. Mum went to stay with her parents at Westport. By this stage both her mother and father were worried sick about all the moving around.

Mum said that in all the time she was in Westport waiting for Anna to be born Dad wrote her only one letter:

Dear Hel,

Where's the ink?
Nothing much happening here.

Oscar

I stayed with Aunt Ola for about four months, which created a lifelong bond between us. She was heartbroken when I had to leave. Years later she would say she would have kept me if she had only known then what my father was like.

Eventually Dad bought a house in Tauranga (pronounced Toe-rrrung-a), 90 kilometres northwest of Whakatāne. Behind the house was a glasshouse. He'd decided to try his hand at growing tomatoes. Tauranga was a town of about 14,000 people, situated in the Bay of Plenty, a wide scoop of sandy beaches stretching for 250 kilometres on the northeast coast of the North Island. Its name is Māori, meaning 'safe anchorage', and our house was in the suburb of Ōtūmoetai (pronounced Ou-two-mo-tie), Māori for 'peaceful waters'.

The house in Tauranga was Mum and Dad's sixth in three years. Mum recalled, 'Nothing was ever right for Oscar. Soil no good, so let's move.' Move somewhere else, even around the corner, and feel better for a while. Mum hated moving. She said she had no choice but to follow Dad wherever he went.

In their first 35 years together, my parents moved more than 23 times, selling and buying, only occasionally renting in between moves. After Dad retired in 1973, he became even more restless. For the next 10 years they moved every year, sometimes within nine months. Once they moved next door. That was an easy move, Mum said, as they simply chucked stuff over the fence. Dad seemed to lose money with each sale, so by then he could only afford small two-bedroomed units, plain drab brick-boxes.

17

All this moving struck many readers of my book *Sundowner of the Skies: The Story of Oscar Garden, the Forgotten Aviator*, published in 2019.[8] Historian Robyn Annear told me, 'What fascinates me about Oscar in his later years was his restlessness – all those changes of address.' Some commented they thought there had to be something wrong with my father. Was he mentally ill? When I was married and a young mother living in Queensland, I'd feel ashamed, sick inside, when Mum rang to say they were moving again. I don't know why I felt like this. They were the ones doing the moving, Mum doing all the packing.

Interestingly, New Zealand author Alison Jones, who was born three years after me, suggests in her award-winning memoir *This Pākehā Life* that her father moved the family every few years, trying, she now believes, to outrun his depression.[9]

Dad was definitely depressed; that had been documented in his medical records I obtained after his death. I believe he was outrunning his depression, like Alison's father, as well as running from other things, such as traumatic things that happened to him during his childhood.

We stayed at Ōtūmoetai Road for five years, which was a record! However, despite their names, Tauranga was no safe place for me and there was little peace living in Ōtūmoetai. I have a few good memories from this time. There is Dad roasting chestnuts in the fireplace in the lounge. He seems happy. That's unusual. We had chooks. I remember feeding them wet warm mash. There was the free-ranging play. In the 1950s and '60s children were allowed to roam free with no adult supervision, as long as we were home by nightfall. Robert, Anna and I, along with friends we had made in the neighbourhood, explored the countryside, waded through creeks, scaled large trees, swung on ropes we looped over high branches. Mum would sometimes pack us a lunch of Marmite and chive sandwiches, slices of homemade date loaf, an apple and a glass bottle of lime cordial. We would stack this in the front baskets of our bikes and head off to the Tauranga Wharf, where we would sit for hours, legs dangling over the edge. Once my brother pulled up an octopus.

Then there are the bad memories, or things that stand out as strange, such as this one. When I was about five, Mum dressed my sister and me in identical dresses. Dad was angry for dressing me like that as men might take notice of me. He said nothing about Anna.

I had large dark-brown eyes, olive skin and dark curly hair, with an easy big smile. I got more attention from adults than my sister did. They would make remarks about how pretty I was – wasn't I cute, wasn't I gorgeous – and ignored or overlooked Anna, who had fair skin and mousy brown hair, and a face speckled with freckles. She seldom smiled.

What were these adults thinking? This favouritism, the way I was singled out, may have planted the seed of my sister's rivalry, which would soon turn into a deep-seated hatred. If the tables had been turned, perhaps I'd have hated her.

Here's another memory from my second year at primary school. Our house was just down the road from school. One day I was sent home as I was feeling sick and vomiting. I can still see Mum there on the front porch, apron over her dress, with a frown on her face. She wiped my mouth with a damp facecloth and sent me straight back. This may seem heartless, but from a very young age Mum had decided she did not want to have to worry about me. Perhaps she couldn't stretch herself any further. At the end of my primary school years, the only prize I received was for having no days absent. The headmaster presented me with a handkerchief.

Mum and Dad were worried about Anna for as long as I can remember. They suspected there was something wrong with her, that maybe she had a mental illness. I definitely knew there was something not quite right with her. She was moody, sulky and volatile. We all had to walk on eggshells to avoid upsetting her.

Not only did Mum worry about Anna, but she had to put up with Dad and try to shield us from him. Some of the diary entries of my half-sister, Margareta, who stayed with us during school holidays, are telling.

> 15 January 1956: Dad expected me to pick tomatoes today. I think he is positively horrid. The way he treats Helen is appalling.

> 16 January 1956: I picked tomatoes and found it heavy work. I really don't like Daddy that much and I would hate to work for him for any length of time. If Mum should die heaven help me.

> 17 January 1956: I picked tomatoes all morning and Daddy wouldn't let us go for a swim ... Daddy is very unfair and I just find myself hating him.

It was a cold environment to grow up in: there was an absence of music, laughter, conversation and hugs. Dad was not only authoritarian, but puritanical, and even recoiled from human contact. I never saw him kiss or hug my mother or put his arm around her. However, I don't remember ever hearing them fighting, yelling or screaming. There was none of the volatility that marked his relationship with Margareta's mother Greta. Nor do I recall them not speaking to each other. And yet, years later, Mum told me they were always falling out and wouldn't speak for days.

Mum said after she got pregnant with Anna that was it: they got single beds and never had sex again. His only show of affection was to clutch her by the wrist. I have a photo of Dad holding me as a baby, but I don't remember him hugging or kissing me. When I visited him during his last years, each time I went to hug him to say goodbye he'd recoil.

No wonder Mum was depressed ending up with a man like that, and with him home all day, wanting lunch at precisely 12, morning tea on the dot of 10. At least he wasn't interested in sex, so he didn't force that on her. But she was his slave. She was powerless. Back then, it was a man's world. The home was his castle. Dr Fraser McDonald, medical superintendent of Auckland's Kingseat Psychiatric Hospital and keen supporter of the women's liberation movement, made headlines in 1968 when he told *Thursday* magazine that 'Women are the Negroes of New Zealand society'. In her book *Fifty Years a Feminist*, Susan Kedgley writes that Dr McDonald later explained to the media that 'most women were so totally at the mercy of their husbands, and in such a state of financial and emotional dependence on them, that they were literally slaves.'[10]

When I was little, I'd catch sight of Mum's reflection in the mirror of her dressing table. She would be weeping, thinking no one was looking. She would sit there every morning to 'put on her face' – her lipstick, foundation, powder and rouge – a half-burnt cigarette resting on an ashtray. When Susan Kedgley interviewed Dr McDonald in 1973, he claimed that most married women suffered from depression and took tranquilisers or 'mother's little helpers' as they were called. Did Mum ever seek help? Did she take these pills, I wonder?

We did not know it at the time, but Mum was depressed for another reason. This was a secret we would not find out about until after her death in 2012. In 1944, before she met Dad, she'd had a child out of wedlock. The father was an American service man who Mum went out with while she was nursing at Wellington Hospital. (She began nursing there in April 1938.) At that time, it was generally agreed that adoption was *in the child's best interests*. The mother was *bad* and *irresponsible* to have had sex when she was not married. The child's adoptive parents called him Michael McLennan. He became a famous New Zealand rugby league footballer and a leading coach. (There is more about this story in Chapter 14.)

I can't imagine carrying around a secret and a grief like this. It has been said that mothers who give up their children for adoption can suffer chronic bereavement for the rest of their lives. The pain, shame and secrecy can profoundly affect their future marriages and relationships with children.

I'm pretty sure Dad did not know about Michael. Mum sealed off this part of her life in an underground compartment of her memory bank in the hope she could pretend it never happened. She ran from that trauma for the rest of her life.

My heart breaks to think of her sad life. Smothered by shame, the emotion that makes people keep secrets, feeling unable to speak the truth not only about her first child but also about what was going on with Dad. She told me that once, on the train to Wellington, she considered leaping off onto the tracks, dragging us three kids with her. Although she wanted to leave, Mum felt trapped. In the 1950s and '60s there were no services, counselling or refuges, and there was no single parent's pension.

Neither of my aunts liked Dad. Mum told me her other sister, Margaret, who died in 1986, kept asking her, 'Why did you marry him?' Mum would laugh, 'Now that's a bloody good question.'

Ola told me, 'Your father had plenty of intelligence but was damn odd as well. I'd have hated to have him. I'd hate all men to be like that.'

I wish Mum had run away from him.

CHAPTER 3

Violent Streak

My father's violence was erratic, to say the least.

One of my earliest memories is of him giving my brother a hiding because he heard his urine hitting the side of the toilet bowl. The toilet was just off the kitchen, near the sink where Mum used to wash our hair, rinsing mine with vinegar and Anna's with lemon juice.

I got my first hiding when I was about four. I'd gone outside with a glass to fill it up with water from an outdoor tap. The glass slipped out of my hand and smashed on the concrete path and a shard flung up and cut me on the wrist of my right hand. My father was enraged and belted me before taking me to our doctor to get the wound stitched. The scar remains visible on my wrist today. I'm always telling people, 'I haven't tried to kill myself.'

I had another hiding about a year later. I'd chucked an apple core with a bit of flesh still on it down the side of a shed and Dad had found it. He screeched in his throttled high-pitched voice: 'What about the poor children starving in Africa?'

Remarkably – because she did not stand up to him about anything else – my mother told Dad not to hit us girls, and he complained about this to other men at Turners & Growers, the local market in town where he sold tomatoes. 'The wife doesn't let me hit them.' However, he kept on belting my brother.

Although we got off lightly compared to other children of that era – in the 1950s corporal punishment was meted out regularly in homes and schools – the threat was always there. There was a part of me that was terrified of him much of the time. That fear and anxiety would have altered my brain as it was developing. For some reason though, Dad never hit or yelled at Anna. It's unlikely Anna would've felt the same fear as me around Dad, but it's difficult to believe she would not have been anxious to some degree.

One sports day at Ōtūmoetai Primary School, we were standing under a long line of fir trees at the edge of the field watching the games, when suddenly Dad appeared and rushed onto the field like a madman. He'd seen a boy hit another boy. He walloped him several times on the bottom, then strode out the gate and went home. No one said anything afterwards. Most of the kids were watching, as well as teachers and parents. I was mortified, ashamed of my father, ashamed to be me. I don't think Dad ever went back to the school again.

I didn't know Dad had been physically violent towards Mum until after he died. I was horrified when she told me Dad used to choke her and this was why she had to have part of her thyroid removed. Others knew about his violence, including Alys Ingrid Wicksteed, the daughter of Mary Revfeim, one of Mum's closest friends. They had lived around the corner from us in Tauranga, in a beautiful historic homestead called 'Maungawhare', built in 1878. After Mum died, while researching *Sundowner of the Skies*, I got in touch with Alys.

Alys remembers my mother visiting them in our small green station wagon used to carry boxes of tomatoes to the local markets. She said Mum was always beautiful to look at because of her lustrous shoulder-length curly locks, but life was far from easy for her living with my father, having to work in the glasshouses and look after three young children. She said they looked after us on a few occasions when were young, including once when my mother became severely depressed, and another time when my father was violent.

> Late one afternoon, after dinner was over, Helen arrived very distraught, with Anna in a pushchair. Luckily, the back door was open as she just rushed inside. We were all still sitting at the dining table. All I recall is Helen crying, 'Mary, Mary.' Immediately my mother rushed and hugged her. We children were ushered outside onto the veranda by our father. Helen and Anna stayed the night in one of the upstairs bedrooms. The next day Oscar arrived at our back doorstep. You and Robert were crying in the green station wagon. My mother went outside to talk to Oscar. A heated conversation occurred. My mother said, 'No, no, Oscar, she's not going back with you. You can leave Robert and Mary with me. They need their mother.'

Dad was controlling in other ways, including money. He was miserly. He gave Mum £10 a week towards all household needs. Luckily, her father, Grandad Henry, paid her about the same and also paid for our fares to go to Westport for holidays. Grandad gave her an allowance right up to his death in 1984.

Although Dad was frugal, he didn't hesitate to spend money on horse racing. When they lived at Whakatāne, he'd take off on the weekends to the racing circuits in Thames or Paeroa, but in Tauranga he'd find his way to the nearest TAB. While Dad was courting Mum, Margareta would spend weekends with him at this flat in Mount Eden. As she recounts in Maurice Gee's memoir *Memory Pieces*:

> I do remember once finding a sack full of chits. Tickets, cards, bits of printed stuff. I took some back to Mum [Greta] – she told me it showed Daddy was gambling. I didn't know what gambling was, but I found out later. Any spare cash he had he spent betting on horses. He was always broke.[11]

Mum told me Dad was the meanest man she had ever known: 'If only I had some money to leave him.' However, Greta, his first wife, *had* left him. She had no money and no family in New Zealand; they all lived back in her home country, Sweden. Mum *could* have left and got help. Her parents would have helped her. Her father was a solicitor and was reasonably well off. Ola and Margaret had no children; they would have helped as well. Was it shame that stopped Mum? Was she too depressed to leave?

Meera Atkinson, author of the critically acclaimed memoir *Traumata*, says she still holds her mother, a victim of domestic violence, accountable 'for failing to seek help', despite the lack of support facilities at the time. 'However economically, emotionally or otherwise trapped an adult may be by their abuser, whatever fears they hold for their safety, they have power, options and abilities that a child does not.' She explains that her rage towards her mother is perhaps the part of her that says, 'I don't care how much he broke you down; you were the mother and you should have protected me.'[12]

A year after Mum and Anna spent a night at the Revfeim's, we moved again. Dad bought a house on acreage on Levers Crescent at the end of the Ōtūmoetai Peninsular, about 12 kilometres away. Alys told me she always thought Dad wanted Mum away from Mary Revfeim's influence and her meddling in private family affairs. Perhaps he also wanted us to get away from the neighbour.

CHAPTER 4

Mountain out of a Molehill

I remember running out of a henhouse, through an orchard and through long paspalum grass, its sticky seeds clinging to my legs, down a long dirt driveway and screaming at the top of my voice.

Later that day I pulled apart my favourite doll. Its legs. Its arms. Its head. Buried the pieces in the soft earth under the pine trees on the edge of our property, covering it with a blanket of pine needles. I was six.

I have another clear memory of the recurring nightmare I had afterwards. Of siren-like creatures, attractive from a distance with long blond hair and sweet smiles, but as they loomed closer I saw they had horns sticking from their heads and blazing yellow-red eyes. They made screeching and snarling sounds as they crawled over me, their slippery hands sliding up and down my legs and playing in between them. I'd wake up in terror and think God had sent the devil to punish me for something dreadful I'd done. In the dream the creatures were called cannas. Were they named after the canna lily flower with its probing stamen?

I remember sitting up in bed, talking to my sister, who said she had the same nightmare. Her bed was close to mine. Our bedroom was about three metres by three metres, beds along each wall with a narrow space between them. The wallpaper was ugly – yellow and green and khaki flowers from memory – and Mum let us draw all over it with crayons.

This memory was buried for many years. When I was 36 – happily living in Brisbane, Queensland – I was watching a television program about child sexual abuse and had this strange feeling I'd been abused by a neighbour, who had been about 16 or 17 at the time and whose name I suddenly remembered. I rang Mum, who laughed and said I always had such a good imagination.

I did not ring my sister, who was by then living in London. However, a year later, in 1987, I sent her a copy of my first book, *The Serpent Rising: A Journey of Spiritual Seduction*, a memoir of my years in India in the 1970s when I was searching for 'spiritual enlightenment', in the hope it would heal things between us. I thought she would be sympathetic about all the awful things that had happened to me at the hands of an abusive yoga guru.

In 1973, I'd visited a yoga ashram in Henderson, on the outskirts of Auckland, out of curiosity. A swami, a Hindu monk, the first to visit New Zealand apparently, was to perform a special ceremony. I was sitting on the floor at the back of the room, when my eyes were drawn to a large ornate picture of the Hindu deity Lord Siva on the alter at the front. He was sitting in full lotus position in the snow, his back erect, his head held high. Long matted hair fell over his shoulders, snakes were entwined around his neck and upper body, and a large third eye gleamed from his forehead. At his feet was a strange black object that looked like an erect penis embedded in two lips, resting on a curved base. While sitting before this picture in a semi-trance state, memories of the henhouse and the nightmares surfaced. I mentioned this in my book, but made no mention of having been sexually abused, as I had no concrete memory of this occurring.

Anna's letter, in response to receiving my book, floored me. She showed no sympathy at all. It was the worst letter I've ever received in my life. This is some of what she wrote:

> Another thing I want to comment on is your 'memory' of being sexually molested. I remember exactly what happened. You really do exaggerate. You self-glamorise and then wonder why you fall into the trap you do.
>
> What happened was as follows. I had been sexually playing with him a number of times. (I was four and you were six.) I certainly wasn't molested by him – I thoroughly enjoyed it – he used to have an erection and I would play with it and tell him how beautiful it was and I remember it as a really wonderful experience. One day I bought you along too. You were horrified and petrified and ran away crying. He tried to get you to touch his erection and you freaked.
>
> You may call that sexual molestation, but I think you are glamorising for your own ego reasons. I think you are making a mountain out of a molehill – are you calling an erection evil for Christ's sake?? You always were more sexually repressed and trying to compensate for it. It becomes another hook for others to use against you.

I had not even suggested that we had been sexually abused. And what did she know about my sex life? I'd never spoken to her about it. I knew nothing about hers either.

Mum, when I rang her, now had a different story. Yes, it had happened. We had come running back to the house and were laughing hysterically. She and Dad were going to call the police but decided against it as we didn't seem that upset. So much for it being just a product of my good imagination.

I would have seen the neighbour's sister at school. And presumably would have continued to see him from time to time. We moved to a new house two years later.

My sister's letter unhinged me. A part of me believed her. I exaggerated. It wasn't abuse at all. I was sexually repressed. There was something wrong with me. It was my fault I made such an issue about something so minor.

I don't recall being distressed as a child about whatever happened in the henhouse. I suppressed my feelings and buried all memories of it. The fact that I remembered the nightmares and not what the neighbour actually did is an example of traumatic amnesia, or dissociative amnesia – being unable to recall information about oneself that cannot be explained by typical forgetfulness. Despite therapy, and even hypnosis, no memories have ever surfaced. Did I touch his penis? Did he make me touch it? Was it pushed into my mouth?

Whatever happened in the henhouse to Anna and me, it was sexual abuse. The neighbour was grooming Anna. Today he'd be charged. We've come a long way. Because of the inaction of my parents, I had no model of how to assert and protect myself in the face of abuse in later years. They were no models themselves, with their own behaviour at home. My father was not a positive role model for how to treat women.

When I visited Tauranga in 2019, to launch my book *Sundowner of the Skies* at the Classic Flyers Aviation Museum, I mentioned this incident to two of my male classmates I met up with. They said that would be right. They'd heard rumours of other girls who'd gone to the henhouse.

CHAPTER 5

The Hut

Things got worse between Anna and me after we moved in 1958 to the end of Ōtūmoetai Peninsula. Our new house – a plain white stucco building – had only two bedrooms. One was for my brother, the other for my parents. My sister and I had to stay in a hut about 100 metres away from the house. I was now seven, Anna five. Robert wasn't happy about us having our own 'house'. Mum went into his bedroom the first morning and found him sitting up in bed with some small scissors. He had cut off all his eyebrows and eyelashes as a sort of protest.

The hut was an ex-army hut, relocated there by the previous owners. It was wooden with no lining or insulation, a cheap malthoid roof with strips of bitumen-impregnated felt. There were no internal walls or doors, only curtains. My bedroom was at one end, my sister's bedroom at the other; the room in the middle had a door leading outside. The bedrooms were small, with space for a single bed, a chest of drawers and a narrow wardrobe. My bedroom had a bench and sink at one end.

Outside the hut, at one end, was a dunny that stunk and was shrouded with spiderwebs. It had a deep hole in the ground, and no bucket to remove or empty. There was just a big pile of crap building up. Dad would not let us use toilet paper, only newspaper or the tissues that had been wrapped around apples he bought in wooden crates from the markets.

At first, I thought living in the hut would be fabulous. A home of my own, how grown-up! But sleeping there during storms was terrifying. I'd hide under the bed covers listening to the sound of the wind shaking branches of the large willow tree hanging over the roof. Some nights I'd curl up under the sheets and weep for what seemed like hours. I have no idea what I was crying about. My mother often said I was too sensitive and too emotional. I'd also pray to Jesus to *please, please, help me*, but he never came.

I can't remember when Anna started lashing out at me. Perhaps when we were at Ōtūmoetai Road, but it was often in the hut. She would attack me when I was in bed reading or trying to go to sleep. She would lunge at me, bite me, scratch, pull my hair. I'd fight back, try to defend myself, and scream out loud. The noise would bring Dad striding down the concrete path. He'd have a furious look on his face, and screech at me. What had I done now? It was always my fault, as my job was to look after my sister.

It was the blame that hurt the most. Shame began to build up deep inside. My sister's attacks were my fault. I deserved it.

I wonder now why my parents didn't separate us, let Robert sleep in the hut and Anna in the house, since they were so worried about her all the time. That would have made sense. I suspect Mum wanted a break from worrying about her youngest daughter and handed her over to me, instead. It was as if she wanted me to co-parent Anna.

Dr John Caffaro, an expert on sibling abuse and author of the seminal book *Sibling Abuse Trauma*, says that parents who fail to intervene appropriately inadvertently encourage conflict. In troubled families, parents frequently scapegoat one child, indirectly favouring another.[13] This is what happened with Anna and me. She kept on attacking me and I kept on being the scapegoat.

Australian author Amani Haydar was also the scapegoat in her family. In her multi-award-winning memoir *The Mother Wound*, Haydar mentions her difficult relationship with her younger brother. Once when they were children, Amani had been playing with her brother's ball when he grabbed her around the waist from behind and flung her to one side. She hit her head on the sharp corner of a dressing table. Her father took her to the doctor where the wound was sealed with glue and strips. Afterwards, her parents blamed her, reminding her not to provoke him. 'You know what he's like.'[14]

Her brother's abuse became a regular occurrence. Her mother would say things such as 'Just stay away from him.' Her father would say 'It's just a phase', 'All boys are like this' or 'He will grow out of it.'[15] Such abuse by a sibling is a result of a deeply dysfunctional family, with both parents failing to intervene appropriately, just like my parents.

For a while I developed what could have been obsessive compulsive disorder. I can't remember whether it lasted a year or two or longer. My room always had to be neat and tidy. I could not sleep at night unless the folds of the curtains were exactly equal or the plastic figurines that I collected from the cereal boxes were all in neat rows, standing up and the same distance apart on the bench. Sometimes I'd sneak into my sister's room and begin to tidy hers. If she woke up, she would lunge at me, scratch and bite my arms, pull my hair.

Despite her bullying, my sister and I were best friends and talked a lot. I've discovered that this is called the 'friend' response. We often hear of flight, fight and freeze responses to our body's response to fear, but there is another response, the fawn repose: befriending the person who is attacking you. So, although I usually fought back, my long-term response was to appease her, be friendly with her and try to forget about the abuse.

There are echoes of this in Robyn Davidson's memoir *Unfinished Woman*. In Davidson's case she was bullied by her sister, who was six years older: 'She turns and I know what's coming, because it has come so often before. Her nails dig into my arm, the air goes into my stomach, and the sneering, loathing refrain pours down: "useless, ugly, stupid".' [16]

During fights, Robyn recalls, 'I would be left doubled up, wondering if, this time, I would die before breath came back', but admits that playing with her sister, for all its hazards, was the 'ultimate of play'.[17] This sounds to me like a 'friend' response. Later she mentions the relief when her sister was sent to boarding school, as there would be no more bullying.

At least I was older than my sister, which meant I was given more work and could be away from her. I worked a lot for my father: in the glasshouses, mowing lawns, clipping hedges. I loved working, although I'm sure I was at times a little on edge, fearful that I'd make a mistake. Once I accidentally broke a tomato plant and spent the next few days in a state of panic, waiting for the explosion to occur. Although he never mentioned it, it is hard to imagine he never discovered it.

I wanted to please Dad. He'd wait for me to come home from school to find things he'd lost, even his false teeth, which I found buried in the soil in one of the glasshouses. He'd get me to disentangle twine he had inadvertently knotted up. I had nimble fingers and did not give up. I was also the label remover. My father would recycle wooden boxes to pack the tomatoes and these needed soaking at one end to remove the old labels. I'd come home from school to find rows and rows of boxes stacked in my bedroom. I'd stand them upright one by one in the sink and pull the labels off after they softened.

There were times when life got too much for me. When Dad yelled at me, I'd crawl under my bed and curl up tight with my head in my arms. Or I'd run away, hiding under bushes or running down to the back paddock and crouching behind a log. I'd climb a tree and hide up there: sometimes I'd take a knife and dig it into my wrist, make little indentations. I'd sit up there and mutter: 'I want to kill him.' Sometimes I'd hear my mother's high-pitched voice calling,

'Mary, Mary, where are you?' She would never come to look for me. She would never ask why I was upset. I'd climb down, put on a brave face and go back as if nothing were wrong. Whatever my father had done to make me so upset, I'd have forgotten about it shortly after.

That's what happens when you're young. Children aren't aware that the way they're being treated is wrong. This is just the way their family is: it's the only thing they've known. And when bad things happen, they often forget about them shortly after or they don't dwell on them. They have to, in order to cope and survive. But I sometimes wondered whether I would be carted off to the loony bin. Someone would realise there was something wrong with me. After all, I was made to feel that way often enough.

When I wasn't working, I'd often go down to the beach. At the end of our property there was a path down a rugged craggy cliff to the Matua Estuary. My brother, sister and I would swim, sit on the jetty and hang our fishing lines over the end, float into the channel on large logs and dig out caves in the tall cliffs.

There were no Māori living on the Ōtūmoetai Peninsula, although I'd see them down the beach. They would walk over from the western side of Tauranga. They taught us to spear flounder, how to gently shuffle our feet on the sand when the water was shallow and the tide out, and thrust the spear down, taking care not to spear our toes. I used to wish I'd been born a Māori, been part of a Māori family, a Māori iwi (tribe). I thought they were warm and friendly and relaxed emotionally, not frozen like Mum and Dad.

The late Ans Westra, regarded as one of New Zealand's most important documentary photographers, was fascinated by the rural Māori way of life in the 1950s, and saw them as free, natural and spontaneous, although in an essay on Westra, Talia Marshall regards this as a 'simplistic, homogenous view of Māori'.[18] Perhaps I was being simplistic too, and generalising, but I was only a young girl and this was how I felt about Māori I met. They were freer emotionally and more open than us Pākehā.

I got along with my brother; I don't remember us ever arguing. But he was the reason I broke my leg when I was about nine. It was an accident, but he never apologised for it, not at the time, nor years later when it came up during a conversation. He was a little annoyed I'd mentioned it, and said I was stuck in the past. I suppose that was easier than saying, 'I'm sorry that happened to you. I'm sorry I did that to you.'

The accident happened when Mum and Anna were away. Anna had developed tics in her shoulder and face and was getting teased at school. The headmaster advised my parents to take her to see a psychologist or psychiatrist. They wouldn't consider it. Instead, Mum took her to Westport for a holiday, leaving me to look after the house, do the housework, make the meals and wash up. I can't remember much of this time. Looking back, no matter how hard I try, there are huge blanks in my memory bank. Memories do fade with the passing of time, and I have lived quite a full life, in many different places across three countries. However, there is no doubt that sustained psychological and physical trauma, especially when young, can result in loss of memory. I still don't remember what happened in that henhouse.

But I do remember this. My brother and I went out one afternoon and were riding our bikes home. Coming down a small hill near our place, he cut in front of me. He had a big grin on his face. The wheel of his bike hit mine and I crashed, falling onto the bitumen road and landing on my right knee. The pain was excruciating. There was skin scraped off, bits of gravel embedded in the flesh and blood streaking down my leg.

I can't remember Robert's response – did he help me get up? – but I do recall hopping and limping home, using my bike as support. My only fear was Dad's reaction: Robert would get into trouble. Dad saw me coming up the driveway and although I told him it was just an accident he gave Robert an almighty hiding.

That night my father took us to the movies, 'the pictures' as we called them, but I had to sit on the end of the row and have my leg stretched out as I couldn't bend it. The pain was excruciating. It might seem strange that my father took us out when I was injured. But going to the movies was his *only* entertainment. In the 1950s, New Zealanders loved going to the pictures. We were among the most regular cinemagoers in the world. Even though Dad never socialised and seldom went to church (his devout mother had taught him everything he said, so he did not need to go), he enjoyed going to the pictures.

Despite the pain in my knee, for several days I continued to do all the household chores while hopping on my leg or dragging it around. And slept alone in the hut. Finally, Dad took me to the doctor, who sent us to Tauranga Hospital, where an X-ray revealed a break. My leg was put into a plaster cast for several months. I loved it. It was so cool being on crutches. I got attention from the kids at school, some sympathy at last!

I got none from Mum. I heard her groan on the phone when I told her about the accident. It was too much for her. She had enough to worry about. Same old pattern. I was the one they did not want to worry about.

I felt crushed. I needed my mum. I needed *a* mum. When she was in her late eighties, I told Mum I felt I'd missed out on being mothered, that I shouldn't have been expected to act as though I was grown-up when I was only a child. She was taken aback and said that I was her friend. I was her ally. I told her I had needed to be a child, not her friend. I had needed someone to look after me. She did not reply – I don't think she understood.

A few years later, when I was 12 years old and had begun high school, Robert began punching Mum and me on our upper arms, leaving bruises. The sleeves of my uniform just covered them. Mum would say, 'Just ignore it, dear. He needs to take out his frustration on someone,' meaning his frustration with Dad. Robert got the brunt of

Dad's rage, that's for sure. There was only a one-year age gap between Robert and me, which is probably why he used me as punching bag and not Anna, as she was three years younger.

There is no other way to describe it: this is sibling abuse. I think Mum was negligent and irresponsible not to say anything to Robert or feel sympathy for me. What on earth did she think I was? A stoic who puts up with pain?

Perhaps she thought it was normal behaviour? A recent Australian study of family violence found that sibling violence among adolescents is often dismissed as 'normal sibling behaviour or minimized within families due to feelings of shame and guilt'.[19]

I've come to understand that the abuse I experienced is a symptom of a dysfunctional family. Darlene Lancer, an American author and a marriage and family therapist explains that it involves a complex dynamic between the victim, perpetrator and the home environment.[20] There may be spousal violence and parental child abuse, including neglect, already occurring. When there are strict gender roles, differential treatment of siblings, lack of parental supervision and parental unavailability, as there were in my family, the risk increases.

We were each treated differently by both Mum and Dad. Dad made it clear that I wasn't allowed to pluck my eyebrows, shave my legs, wear make-up or go out with boys until I was 21. When I asked Mum if I could get some stockings, as all the other girls in my class had them, he was furious. He said men might become attracted to me. Mum went and bought some anyway. That same day Dad drove into town and got some for Anna, who didn't even want them.

It was a similar story with Robert. Dad did not want Robert to have long pants (a big deal in those days – long pants meant you were no longer seen as a child). Mum told me that she remembered clearly the day she went into town to get long pants. She was crying, and thought, 'Damn him. I'm going to get them anyway.' All the other boys in his class wore them, and he was still in shorts.

Luckily, we were able to have a break from Dad during the summer school holidays as we would go to Westport to stay with Mum's parents. Music, laughter and warmth filled my grandparents' beautiful two-storeyed house in Queen Street, which was built in the 1860s and is now protected under the New Zealand Historic Places Trust. We would have picnics at Carters Beach and Cape Foulwind.

Westport is a town built on coal extraction from remote places on the wild west coast. The sulphury smell of coal is the thing I remember. It was in the air, floating through the small town from the port and from people's houses, as they used coal as fuel for fires. The smell was comforting; I'd feel snug; I was somewhere safe.

I was happy in Westport. There was no tiptoeing around in fear. I loved riding my nana's bicycle around the streets, bringing her groceries in the front basket. As I was an early riser, my job was to take her a cup of black tea with a slice of lemon, along with the newspaper, to her bedroom upstairs. I never ran away when I was down at Westport. I never hid under a bed or under a table or under a bush or up a tree. I don't recall Anna lashing out at me when we at Westport. She also seemed happier down there.

Wherever I was, I was the good little girl. The pretty one, the happy one, the responsible one, the grown-up one, the one they did not have to worry about, the one always ready to please, to help. These things made me feel good about myself. This would not help me in the long run, mind you. Why didn't I scream instead? Cry? Howl in rage? Have a tantrum? Lash out? Like Anna.

Instead, I pushed all my rage and sadness down, deep inside. Buried it. Put on a happy face. In all the family photos I'm the one with the big smile, Anna is often scowling, and Mum is sometimes tight faced, like she is forcing her mouth to widen a little.

CHAPTER 6

The Stab in the Back

Although Dad had ostensibly banned me from wearing make-up or going out with boys until I was 21, I did both from the age of 13, determined to grow up as quickly as I could. In 1963, after I began secondary school, we moved into town to a two-storey house. My bedroom was upstairs. I hid my make-up and high heels in the garden and at night I would climb out the upstairs window, scale down the wall and take off. As well as the Down Under coffee lounge in the next street, there was the Inferno coffee lounge on the waterfront, where Tauranga's top rock and roll band, The Four Fours, would play. The flame-walled club was the hottest spot in town. Mum would say, 'Don't let your father catch you!'

That year, Margareta began working as a librarian in Turnbull Library, Wellington; in a letter dated 6 July 1963 I wrote that I hoped she was enjoying herself in her new job. I told her about school, how I was enjoying Latin and French, and that most of the teachers were young and had just come from training college. Although I was in a class called 3 Academic, the highest level, we were the noisiest and often played up, and hardly any teacher could control us. 'We are always throwing paper ships around the room …[and] the head mistress storms into the room to tell us to "shut-up".'

Margareta was ten years older than me. Growing up, I held her in awe, looked up to her. From a young age, I used to write letters to her. I don't recall Robert or Anna doing this, except perhaps a note to thank her for a birthday or Christmas present. Margareta had a cheerful personality and had clearly fared better than us, even though her mother brought her up single-handedly. Maurice Gee said in an interview about his 2018 memoir *Memory Pieces* that even though Margareta had a divorced foreign mother and moved from place to place and school to school, 'she grew up happy and undamaged'.[21]

Soon after working at Turnbull Library, Margareta began going out with another librarian, Stuart Hickman, who she married in November 1964. They must have visited us in Tauranga, as my letter sent in January 1964 is addressed to 'Marg and divine Stew'. I tell them I was having 'the most fab holidays' and I'd been going over to the Mount [Maunganui] with a friend, where we had met some fabulous boys from Australia who were surfers. They were both 17, had 'piles of money', a couple of cars, and boats and surfboards. As well as learning to surf, we went to parties and got home after midnight.

I also mention that I'd gone to several shows at the Tauranga Soundshell, including the Howard Morrison Quartet (Howard Morrison would become one of New Zealand's leading concert performers) and Lou and Simon, a musical comedy duo who became much loved entertainers. I don't recall either of these shows. But I do remember The Beatles. When Beatlemania hit New Zealand and shook the uptight conservative nation.

As part of The Beatles' Far East tour, the group landed in Wellington on 21 June 1964 and were greeted by 7000 hysterical fans. They had flown from Sydney in a propeller-driven TEAL Electra plane. The tour was described as 'seven days of pandemonium' as thousands of New Zealanders flocked to hear the 'Fab Four'. In the back-to-back concerts in Wellington, Auckland, Christchurch and Dunedin, the screams of the fans drowned out the music. This kind of hysteria had never been seen before and it was said that everything changed after The Beatles came. It was 'the moment that young New Zealand plugged into an international youth culture'.[22]

I wrote a letter to Margareta at the end of that momentous week. 'I suppose you won't believe me but Mum and Dad like the Beatles. Mum thinks Ringo and Paul are gorgeous. We have been listening to their interviews on the radio for the last week in different places in their tour.' Evidently Dad was always wanting to listen to my Beatles records, which is difficult to imagine. I loved The Beatles and would spend hours listening to their music, as well as that of Elvis, Leonard Cohen and other musicians. I don't recall Anna being swept up like I was. She wasn't yet a teenager and was still at primary school. Always top of her class, she often had her head stuck in a book.

I also told Margareta about my job during the holidays. At Tauranga Library!

> I absolutely adored working in the library. I worked for a week and I got six pounds. It was sure worth it. From the day I started I began to work on the counter issuing books and putting books way etc. Some of the time I sorted cards and tidied shelves. I really loved it. The boss is really mad. I think he's rather dotty. He was always coming out of his office and mumbling something.

After I'd spent two years at Tauranga Girls' College, my father suddenly had the idea of moving to Papakura, south of Auckland, and try his hand at being a real estate agent, which was a rather odd decision considering his anti-social personality.

Anna had just finished primary school and Mum and Dad decided she would go up to Auckland and attend Epsom Girls' Grammar School, a leading girls' school in New Zealand. Anna would board with Aunt Margaret, who lived in Remuera, which was only about four kilometres away from the school. I'm not sure why they made this decision. Perhaps Mum needed a break, but it is also likely that, considering Anna's academic achievements, they thought this school would be better for her than the one in Papakura.

Papakura is one of the poorer suburbs of Auckland and for some reason I felt right at home there. I settled in quickly at Papakura High School and made new friends. It was a co-ed school and I was clearly happier around boys. I wrote to Margareta:

> It's absolutely fantastic being here in Papakura. It is miles better than Tauranga especially the school and the boys – the only thing that counts ... The kids up here are really nice and awfully friendly. The boys at the school are quite terrific, especially some of the prefects. Co-ed is far better; you seem to work harder with boys in the same class but you have a lot of fun. The teachers are awfully good – much better than at Tauranga.

I explained that on Tuesday nights I went to gym classes and had become infatuated – 'goofy' was the word I used – with one of the instructors. On Friday nights, I'd go with a group of friends to ballroom dancing classes at the Ardmore Teachers College. Margareta and Stuart had sent me a pair of diamond-patterned stockings for my birthday, which I said 'went terrifically with my groovy red hipster skirt, a gorgeous black, red and white Fair Isle jumper, and my black suede boots.'

For all my memory blanks of much of my childhood and teenage years, I do remember wearing this outfit one Friday night and also remember the good-looking gym instructor and my fantasy of us falling madly in love despite the fact that I was too nervous to talk to him.

Not surprisingly, Dad loathed being a real estate agent and at the end of the year decided to sell up, return to Tauranga and grow tomatoes again. Robert went back there with Mum and Dad. I was sent up to Auckland and Epsom Girls' Grammar School to join Anna. I suspect that my aunt had found it difficult to handle Anna's mood swings and probably couldn't cope with the extra housework as she worked full-time. Aunt Margaret trained dental nurses, the first woman in New Zealand to have such a position. She and Mum would have known I'd be good at helping around the house and looking after Anna.

It was such a wrench for me to leave Papakura. I loved the school and had formed some close friendships. I've always looked back on that year as my best year. Many years later Mum would say she made a mistake sending me to Auckland; she wished she had found someone for me to board with at Papakura.

Aunt Margaret wasn't married – in those days she was considered a spinster – and lived in Remuera, one of Auckland's oldest suburbs. It was affluent and a few kilometres from the city centre. It was a leafy suburb, with tree-lined streets and many large houses, often Edwardian or mid-twentieth century. My aunt's house was a very cute wooden, two-storey house with a steep pitched roof, nothing like the plain, drab brick-boxes Dad bought. The only rooms upstairs were the two bedrooms that my sister and I used.

I hated Remuera from the outset. I thought it was snobby and I felt out of place. A caption on a photo of Remuera in the 1940s on Te Ara, the online encyclopedia of New Zealand, notes that the suburb had become the domestic hub of Auckland's wealthy, who lived in 'large houses with well-tended gardens', and it is a favoured address for the business and professional elite.[23]

I hated Epson Girls Grammar too. It was my third secondary school in three years. It was more rigid and formal than my other two schools. Some mornings, after assembly, we had to kneel on the floor and if our skirts did not touch the ground we were slapped on the hands with a ruler.

Aunt Margaret was kind to us, although a heavy drinker (probably an alcoholic), and a heavy smoker. Ashtrays full of butts were scattered around the house. I'd do most of housekeeping and preparing meals while my sister spent a lot of time in her room. She was often sullen and sulking and had few friends. I was more outgoing, pretending to be happy on the outside. I was becoming like my mother, pushing everything underground. Over the years I'd sometimes overhear my aunts and Mum saying, 'I wish Anna was more like Mary.' Perhaps Anna heard them too.

The worst thing about living with my aunt is that I was again subjected to my sister's rages. My aunt, as did everyone else, treated her with kid gloves: the cossetted child, as if there was something wrong with her. Once she smashed my bedroom door with an axe, splitting it open in the middle. I was lying on my bed reading a book. Her assault came out of nowhere and was terrifying. Nothing happened to her as a consequence. I'm sure I was blamed.

Another time on returning from school, I went into her room to ask how she was. She shouted at me to get out and as I was walking away I felt something enter my back. It was the spike of a metal compass, an instrument we used in Maths for drawing circles. These compasses had two parts, joined by a hinge. One part had a long spike at one end, the other was for holding a pencil. The spike lodged deep in my back near my spine. I might be dramatising here – I was often told I exaggerated – but I think I told my sister to get an ambulance. She just curled up on her bed, sulking, and did not say a word.

I stumbled down the stairs and across the road to a neighbour, who drove me to hospital, me sitting in the front seat, bent over, blood dripping down my blazer. I remember nurses yelling out, 'She's been stabbed!' I remember people rushing towards me. An X-ray showed it had just missed my spinal cord.

Surely someone would feel sorry for me now? Afterwards, however, my parents and aunt were worried about Anna. I was bewildered when I was told: 'You must have done *something* to upset her.' I had to go to school the next day and told one of my friends about it and somehow – presumably through Anna – this got back to my aunt and then Mum. They were angry. 'How could you have done that?' they asked.

I'm furious just thinking about this now. Why the fucking hell wasn't anything done to help me? Why didn't my parents get any help for her? Why didn't they take her away from me, to keep me safe?

When parents or caregivers don't protect the victim and give them little or no support, it constitutes a second wound – first inflicted by the sibling, then by the parent. Their responses and reactions can be emotionally damaging. This pattern of being blamed and shamed for abuse, which began when I was little, would have disastrous consequences in the life ahead of me.

After the stabbing, I continued being the good responsible daughter my aunt and parents did not have to worry about. I don't recall feeling any animosity or resentment towards Anna at all. I find this puzzling. Why didn't I feel angry towards her, furious at her treatment of me? As I mentioned in an earlier chapter, I realise now that behaviour of mine is what is known as the 'friend response'. I hate to admit it, but a part of me felt a bit embarrassed to have her as my sister, in much the same way I was embarrassed of Dad. They were both socially awkward and, in my mind, 'not normal'.

The fact that it was my job to look out for Anna, even look after her, could have contributed to her hatred of me. Psychiatrists call this hostile dependency. I was everything she wasn't. In his most recent memoir, *Two Sisters*, the award-winning author Blake Morrison describes his relationship with his troubled younger sister: 'And Gill was taught to look up to me, which meant she learnt to look down on herself.'[24] This is a perfect encapsulation of what happened to Anna and me. She looked down on herself and her self-hatred spilled out on me.

I felt out of place at school and living in Remuera. I was traumatised by the axe shoved through my door and the stabbing, and retraumatised for being blamed for both. I wrote two letters to Margareta that year but I made no mention of Anna, what she had done to me or what it was like living with my aunt and having to do most of the housework. In the second letter I wrote that I was happy and relieved we had finished accrediting exams as they were easily the worst exams I have ever done. I did less than a week's swot. I told her that 'school is an absolute bore and I can't wait to get out of this mouldy hole'.

It was a difficult year at Epsom Girls. I hung around with a group of girls but wasn't particular close to any of them, and I made little effort in the subjects I'd selected, which is reflected in my leaving certificate:

> A student of quite good ability, Mary took time to settle into a new school ... She is quiet and reserved yet reveals at times a liveliness and a sense of humour and gets on well with all her contemporaries. She is pleasant in conversation but has not, we feel, fully revealed as yet either her personality or her capacity though she has been quite cooperative.

In the 1960s, New Zealand high schools had lower and upper sixth forms, the latter being optional. At Epsom Girls Grammar I did not consider doing the second year.

Unlike my sister, I'd party when I could and fortunately my aunt let me do what I liked. At the end of year there was a school dance that finished at 10 pm and afterwards we headed off to a party at a large house of one of the girls, whose parents were overseas. We had invited about 150 boys, most of them from university. The party finished at five the next morning. No sneaking in, like I had to do back home in Tauranga.

Over the years no one in the family ever mentioned the compass incident. I never spoke about it. It became another 'family secret'. I buried it deep in my memory bank, but it came up years later in therapy. It whooshed out, on waves of rage and grief, along with other scars and bruises.

Decades later, when I was about 56, I mentioned it to Anna. I was helping Mum move house and in a moment of courage blurted it out, hoping for an apology. She had charmed Mum out of yet another $1000 for a flight back to London so she was in a good mood. 'Oh that,' she laughed. 'I thought I had apologised.'

My aunt's old house at Remuera is still there. I found it on a real estate site. There is the staircase I stumbled down. The bedroom door my sister thrust an axe through. There is her old bedroom where I was stabbed. Looking at the images now gives me shivers up my spine.

Back then, I'd covered the entire ceiling of my bedroom with photos of Elvis. I would lie in bed and gaze up at him, dreaming of falling in love for ever. On the walls I'd stuck photos of The Beatles and The Rolling Stones and other bands, but Elvis was my idol. I was excited for the future. It was going to be thrilling. There was something in the air in the swinging sixties. The world was shaking and rocking, and my generation was going to be free.

CHAPTER 7

You Want the Whole World
at Your Feet

After leaving school, I felt on top of the world. Still 16 years old, I considered myself all grown up, and so did everyone else it seemed. I no longer had to look after Anna. That was a load off my back. I spent the summer holidays at Tauranga (it would be my last holiday there for 53 years) but spent little time at home. In a letter to Margareta and Stuart, I tell them all about it:

> I've had the most fabulous holiday – best I've ever had. Robert persuaded me to go over to the new hot pools at the Mount [Maunganui]. I met this boy Mike Rutherford, or should I say, man. He is 28 years old ... well he took me to this fabulous party that night at their bach where Mike and seven other boys were staying over Christmas. Well after that I hardly had any time to breathe. Mike lives about a mile away from our place. Mum and Dad didn't exactly approve of the relationship, but do you blame them! I went out with him every day and every night for the next week and got home early in the morning every time.
>
> We used to go to the Anchor Inn pub every day about 3 o'clock. It is the most gorgeous place right by the beach. Modern

49

> as anything – everyone used to go there straight off the beach. I met so many people it's quite unbelievable. Well then I met this gorgeous boy – Darrell Innes who is 25 years old. He is a stock agent from Te Awamutu. He was staying in a colossal bach with six other really divine boys. We hit it off right from the start. He has got pots of money and a big flash latest Zephyr.

I went out with that gorgeous boy for over a year. Luckily, Te Awamutu was only about 30 kilometres south of Hamilton, where I'd enrolled to go to Waikato University and also Hamilton Teachers' College, which was on the same campus. There was no expectation from Mum or Dad for me to go to university – or do anything for that matter. They did not care what I did. I was now financially independent and received no money from them. They were back to worrying about Anna, who'd moved back to Tauranga to finish her high school years at Ōtūmoetai College.

Initially I'd enrolled to do nursing training, but Aunt Margaret put her foot down, saying 'no niece of mine is going to be a nurse', even though she had been a dental nurse and Mum had been a nurse. She insisted I go to university. And since I'd loved working at Tauranga Library so much during the school holidays, why didn't I consider doing a library certificate, as Margareta had done? She had done a New Zealand Library School certificate course, which was three years of study done largely by correspondence. A job as a librarian would have been perfect for me.

Waikato University opened in 1964 with 100 students and was touted as being innovative and experimental. Hamilton Teachers College, which had been temporarily housed on another site until the buildings were ready in 1965, was on the same campus, on a hill overlooking Hamilton. There were still cows grazing in the paddocks, the old cow shed had been converted to a café.

Student accommodation was yet to be built and so for the first year I boarded, and after that lived in share houses with other students. The sixties were a dream time for students. You could chuck in a job and get another one the next day; houses and flats were readily available and no rental bonds were required.

I spent a year with Darrell. He was a football player and had a wide circle of friends. We saw each other most weekends and often went away to football matches. The night when his team won a big national Catholic tournament he drank too much and I drove him home to Te Awamutu, even though I did not have a licence. I ended up scraping his car on a concrete post going up the narrow driveway. Darrell was a good guy, easy to be with, and towards the end keen to marry me.

I don't remember smoking – when did I start? – but it is there in a letter to Margareta. 'I broke off with Darrell. We used to fight the whole time over my smoking, but I'm not going to change for him. He can accept me as I am or not at all. It's a filthy habit really but it's not up to him to say.'

In 2019, Darrell got in touch. He was living in Australia and had met his future wife in Dubbo the year after we broke up. When he was living in Brisbane in the 1980s, he'd read some articles about my book *The Serpent Rising*, but was hesitant to reach out. He changed his mind in 2021, after reading about *Sundowner of the Skies*; by then he was living on the Sunshine Coast, a 40-minute drive away from my house. I met up with him, his wife and their two daughters after a book event at Annie's Books at Peregian Beach, and we've kept in touch ever since. Looking back on our relationship, he said he was 'besotted' the moment he saw me. 'I absolutely fell head over heels in love with you.' When he first met me, he thought I was over 20 years old. 'You were very mature. You were terribly special to me. There is always a place in my heart for you.' He acknowledged we were not right for each other. 'You were very intellectual. I only have positive memories of our relationship despite you bashing up my Zephyr.'

After breaking up with Darrell, I threw myself into university life. I wrote to Margareta: 'I'm having the wildest, and most absolutely fantastic year ever. Hamilton is just mighty.' I go into detail of my courses and the lectures I attend: ten at the university and ten at the training college, a gruelling workload. 'I've never worked so hard in my whole life'. I was also getting little sleep, going to bed most nights at 11 pm and getting up around 4 am. I mention I'm doing Maths and there are only seven students in the class. I tell her it's double-Dutch. It turned out to be my best subject.

In 1968 my friend Barbara Tew (now Hill) and I were Waikato University's entrants in the Miss New Zealand University Pageant held in Dunedin. It was a bizarre experience. Much of it is a blur except that I was so nervous at the prospect of being interviewed I got drunk and could hardly walk up onto the stage. Barbara says it is something she tries not to remember: 'I just felt out of my depth.' She recalls that after the event she heard a story that one of the judges, a male professor, detested 'inertia' in people and had remarked that the 'Waikato girls' (meaning Barbara and I) 'were the only ones who *sat back* in the chair during their interviews; the others perched on the front edge of their seats. I was probably slumped not only in terror but because of my inebriated state.

Susan Kedgley recalls this contest in her book *Fifty Years A Feminist*. 'It was a humiliating ordeal. We were treated like sex objects in every sense of the word.'[25] In the *New Zealand Women's Weekly* 1993, Susan is reported as saying she believes the roots of eating disorders such as anorexia and bulimia were from women succumbing to the pressure of the images represented in these pageants.[26] Susan told me recently she saw these pageants as a real statement of the times and the overwhelming sexism of the era.[27]

I wonder what Anna thought of me going in this beauty event. I even wonder why I went, especially as it was the mid '60s and there was a hippy revolution going on.

The bohemian culture of the hippies had infiltrated universities. Like most students, I went to a lot of parties and experimented with drugs (mainly pot, but a few acid trips). We smoked pot with some of our lecturers and tried to seduce them into having sex with us.

Despite my inadequate social skills, I managed to seduce a politics lecturer and we had an unmemorable one-night stand. I'd often get drunk and behave recklessly. Once I woke up in bed with some guy and had no memory of how I ended up there.

In her memoir *Fifty Years a Feminist*, Susan Kedgley writes about the darker side of life at Victoria University and says she was often sexually harassed and twice assaulted:

> Men would routinely get plastered at parties and seek to 'lay' as many women as they could ... They took it for granted that they were entitled to have sex with whoever they pleased. Sex was a minefield; a power struggle between men who wanted it and women who didn't. I don't think I knew a woman who wasn't sexually molested or chased around rooms at student parties by drunken male students. For the most part, however, we didn't discuss these horrific encounters. We kept them to ourselves and assumed that if sex had gone wrong or went too far, it must have been our fault.[28]

This wasn't my experience. Perhaps we were lucky because Waikato was new and a misogynistic culture was yet to emerge. Several female students I'd studied with said they did not encounter this sort of harassment. One went on to Victoria University as a postgraduate student in the 1980s and found that university, in comparison to Waikato, 'a Victorian, male, stale, Freudian institution'.

Although I appeared happy on the surface, I began struggling at times. When I got drunk, I'd sometimes plumet into a place of despair and wander around the streets of Hamilton alone, and weep for hours. I was lucky not to be raped or bundled off to the loony bin. It was if a monster was chasing me and I kept trying to outrun it.

I'd long feared being locked away, like the famous author Janet Frame. She had been training to be a school teacher but couldn't cope and attempted suicide. In 1940 she was admitted to Dunedin's Seacliff Mental Hospital and spent years in and out of mental hospitals, and endured numerous bouts of electroshock treatments. A lobotomy was cancelled after her book of short stories was awarded a national literary prize.[29] Would I end up like Janet Frame, locked up, receiving electroshock treatments?

Coincidentally, Janet Frame also lived for a while in a hut like the one I'd lived in as a child. When released from psychiatric care, she accepted an invitation from author Frank Sargeson to live in an old army hut in the garden of his Takapuna home. It was during her 15 months there that she wrote her famous novel *Owls Do Cry*.

Luckily yoga came to Hamilton and I went to the first class – yoga was yet to become popular in the Western world. I loved it and began doing it regularly. It was a way of soothing my mind and relaxing me. I also joined the university tramping (bushwalking) club and in weekends went off and explored the bush in the Waikato region. I cut down on drinking and partying.

I don't remember seeing much of Anna during these years. She was working hard at school and, according to Mum, spent most of her time at home in her bedroom. She never snuck out or partied like I'd done at her age. I'd occasionally make short visits back to Tauranga, putting over the Kaimai Range on a little Honda motorbike I'd bought when I was 17 years old.

During university holidays I travelled or worked. I hitchhiked around New Zealand twice. One summer I flew to Australia with a friend and went to the Gold Coast where we saw the world-famous cabaret revue 'Les Girls' performed by drag queens, and then hitchhiked down to Canberra. Hitchhiking was a common and accepted way of getting around; we never waited long for a lift and never considered the dangers.

I worked at various jobs, including modelling, housekeeping, childminding, strawberry picking and waitressing. Once I worked for six weeks at a hotel on the waterfront of Napier, and often went to the Albion Hotel to hear the Ernie Rouse Trad Band play. One summer I worked as a nurse aid at Porirua Mental Hospital, near Wellington. I don't remember much of that as it was the worst job I've ever had and I've blotted out all memories except that in one of the locked wards patients screamed for hours and smeared their faeces up the wall. A report in *Stuff*, New Zealand's largest news site, in 2015 revealed horrific stories from former patients, alleging they had been beaten, raped or given electroshock treatment as punishment during the 1960s and '70s.[30] With my ongoing fear of being dragged off to the loony bin, I'm not sure why I decided to work there. Perhaps the pay was good.

In the 1970s, my sister got a holiday job at Kingseat Mental Hospital in Karaka, south of Auckland. Susan Lea, who lives in the United States, was an exchange student at Ōtūmoetai College in 1969 and befriended Anna that year. In January 2015, Susan got in touch with me to say she enjoyed reading my articles on my father. She recalled him being severe, and there was 'a lot of trauma and frustration'. She had visited Anna when she was working at Kingseat. 'While she pretended to be hardened against the disaster there, I could see Anna was deeply affected by the state of the patients.' They had a friend at Ōtūmoetai College who was subjected to electroshock therapy three times. 'She became a disaster from what was done. It was a terrible fear for Anna that someone might overpower her in that way.'

During their last year at school, Susan and Anna spent a lot of time together, 'We had so much fun, we would stay up all night, singing and laughing, and would hit the bakeries at 5 am. Anna had no interest in the guys in our class but most of them were interested in her.' I was surprised to hear this. I wonder what they found interesting about her. Perhaps her intelligence? Or did she have some sex appeal I was completely oblivious to?

In my fourth and final year for my B.Ed. degree, things began to change for the worse. I began to isolate myself, focused more on university studies and spent a lot of time in the library. The Black Dog began to tap on my shoulder and I started to feel I was wading through a fog of depression and anxiety, although I had no names for these things.

In one course, Philosophy and Education, I had to write an essay on 'The Status of Mathematics Truths Synthetic a Priori'. Even though I told Margareta I loved doing this and 'got lost in it for months', it sounds like mumbo jumbo to me now and I wonder what the relevance of such a topic was to teaching primary school children.

One of my former classmates emailed me after *Sundowner of the Skies* was released in New Zealand. She said she had been reading with interest the articles in the newspapers about my father. 'Just in case you didn't know, at university when we were still so young, you were viewed as beautiful, interesting, vivacious and confident.'

I was taken aback that she saw me as confident. I remember being very anxious and dreaded talking in tutorials; being attractive got me nowhere. I may have inherited my father's good looks, as well as his intelligence and perfectionism, but a part of me felt cursed and as if I'd inherited his ghosts. I told her about my depression, and she replied:

> I think a lot of us were suffering depression, with the pressure of studying for four years and having to pass *all* our subjects at Teachers College or we would fail, as well as doing double majors at university. We all should have been awarded double degrees. But we didn't know back then; we were guinea pigs.

My depression and loneliness were not just from the excessive workload, they were caused by what I was running from. It was as if my past was catching up with me. Survivors of childhood and sibling abuse can struggle with shame, depression, low self-esteem, PTSD, loneliness and hopelessness. Tanya Whitworth and Corinna Tucker, researchers at the University of New Hampshire who focus on sibling dynamics, parenting and mental health, have found that sibling aggression is 'linked to worse mental and physical health' across the life span of a victim. Even just 'one incident of victimisation at the hands of a sibling' is linked to worse mental health in childhood and adolescence.[31]

According to therapist and author Darlene Lancer, when you are betrayed by a sibling and a parent (through lack of protection) then you can be distrustful, emotionally unavailable and seek self-sufficiency and independence, which can lead to 'intimacy problems, loneliness, and isolation'.[32] All those things were happening to me.

In all the letters I wrote to Margareta, there is no hint of how I was struggling. I pretended everything was fine. I pointed this out to my daughter, Natalya, and described how I was completely split off and felt frozen inside. She said, 'Maybe not split off or frozen – maybe surviving. And the culture of the era you were in. There was no dialogue or awareness of the impacts of violence, whereas in my generation so much has changed.'

Living in Hamilton didn't help. The city, surrounded by hills, lies in a basin of rolling land and extensive swamps. The Waikato River runs through its heart. According to the World Atlas it is one of the foggiest places in the world. During the wet and cold winters misty fogs would hang around until midday. I hated the greyness and dampness.

Despite my personal struggles, my hard work paid off. I was one of the top two students in my year, scored an A+ in Philosophy and Education, and won a scholarship to do a Bachelor of Philosophy degree – a one-year Masters degree. Anna had always been a top student. I don't recall there ever being any competitiveness or rivalry between us academically. She was the undisputed brains of the family.

However, I was tempted to completely drop out. The 1960s was a turbulent time. Award-winning music writer Nick Bollinger argues in his book *Jumping Sundays* that the counterculture movement, which embraced alternatives to politics, culture and sexuality, and rejected the values of the previous generation, transformed New Zealand society.

> It was a pretty grey place, New Zealand. In some ways they just wanted to liven it up … but they were also questioning the morals of the previous generation. You had this nuclear threat hanging over the world, the potential to destroy the planet, and I think there was a lot of blame thrust on the pre-boomer generation for that … It was a period of questioning. Their parents who had gone through the austerity of war years, made a lot of sacrifices and wanted the best for their kids. And their kids turned around and, to a large extent, rejected what they were being offered.[33]

I was hugely influenced by this movement and have had a foot in the alternative world ever since. Although I never dropped out to live in a commune, I came close. In 1970, the famous long-haired, bearded, barefoot and shabbily dressed poet and playwright James K. Baxter, who was awarded the Robert Burns Fellowship in 1966–67, visited Waikato University. I was captivated. His radical and alternative views appealed to me, and in a letter to Margareta I wrote that he is a really beautiful person.

(Margareta's marriage to Stuart only lasted a few years. She began her relationship with Maurice Gee in late 1967 and they married in Hastings in July 1970. She, like Dad, had to wait for her divorce to come through. My letters were now usually addressed to both Margareta and Maurice.[34])

I also mentioned that in August I'd be going down to stay a few days at Baxter's commune at the remote rural settlement of Jerusalem, on the Whanganui River. I have no memory of this visit, if I ever went. I do, however, have vague memories of staying at several hippie communes and being put off by the dirty dishes and the lounging around. I had a need to have things clean, tidy and organised.

Baxter wanted his group to centre on spiritual aspects of Māori communal life. *New Zealand Weekly News* journalist Mervyn Dykes and photographer John Pettitt visited the commune in December

1970. Dykes found Baxter to be 'a strange mixture of patriarch and guru', with his followers describing themselves as 'refugees from a sick society':

> James Baxter detests materialism, scorns senseless pursuit of the dollar and believes that modern society is so sick it needs a spiritual transplant ... [He] has a passion for mental health and he is convinced that the aroha and kōrero of pure Māori life hold the keys to a saner society. Aroha, with its open displays of esteem and love, and kōrero, a deeper, more relaxed form of communication, are principles he holds to be vital.[35]

In January 1971, I went down to the Summer University Congress at Curious Cove, Marlborough Sounds. These congresses were yearly camps run from 1949 until the 1970s by the New Zealand University Students Association. Leading speakers from various fields gave talks, and political ideas and issues discussed. Some amazing photos of this congress were taken by photographer Ans Westra and can be seen on the National Library of New Zealand website.[36] These include photos of parties held at night, students swimming and rafting in the bay, and even an encounter group.[37]

I hung out with James Baxter and his close friend Jim Kebbell, a Catholic priest, who was chaplain at the congress. Although I don't appear in any of Westra's photos, I have photos of me sitting on the grass with James and Jim. In one I'm frowning and my arms are crossed tightly over my chest. I'm wearing a scarf over my long hair and a paisley-patterned blouse.

James and I found the talks boring and we would wander away and go for long walks on the beach. I'd show off yoga positions, standing on my head or doing shoulder stands, twisting and stretching. We argued a lot about religion. He insisted I was spiritual; he could see it in my eyes. I'd laugh, say that religion was a lot of bullshit.

While I was down at Curious Cove, my sister worked for two weeks as a waitress and housemaid at Paeroa Hotel, a holiday job I'd done previously. She hated it. Mum told me that Anna never saw Paeroa, as she 'locked herself in her room every spare minute'.

Anna had enrolled to do a Bachelor of Social Science (Economics) at Waikato University and I'd agreed that she could live with me. The week before the term began, she arrived with a girlfriend from Tauranga. They were wearing expensive new clothes. Anna said they'd both won wardrobes in a raffle, clothing worth $1000 each, a staggering amount at the time. I believed her. Mum later told me this was a lie. They'd been on shoplifting sprees, with Anna the ringleader. But Mum laughed it off as just another case of the Mad Gardens. The clothes were not returned, nor were the police involved. This theft and lie – with Mum the bystander – were perhaps the roots of her extraordinary theft to come later in her life (which we will get to).

Weeks after university had commenced, I knew I'd made a mistake. The classes and assignments were overwhelming. Having my sister live with me did not help. One day, I was in the library and had just pulled a book off the shelf to read when I began to feel dizzy and the words started swimming around on the page. I felt overwhelmed with fear, and negative thoughts raced through my brain: I'd been fooling everyone; I wasn't that intelligent; I'd just been lucky so far; I was going to be exposed.

To top things off I came home to find Anna in bed with a guy I'd been dating. The bedroom door was open. I can still see them sitting up in bed resting against pillows and looking at me as I walked past. I said nothing afterwards. *What the hell. What was wrong with me? Why wasn't I enraged? Why didn't I say anything?* I was turning into my mother, my anger buried and hidden.

My sister was also struggling. Although she had been somewhat wrapped in cotton wool, our shared childhood would have damaged her: she had witnessed Dad's violence and cruelty, she would have been aware of Mum's suffocating sadness, and she had been sexually abused by that neighbour. I discovered she had bulimia (bingeing food and then vomiting), although it wasn't named as an eating disorder until 1979. This unnerved me and added to the weight on my shoulders.

The dark clouds of depression returned. I dealt with it the only way I knew, by running. I decided to drop out. I can't remember what story I came up with, but the dean, Professor Peter Freyberg, was furious and said I wanted the world at my feet.

CHAPTER 8

Turning East

I moved to Auckland and spent the rest of the year teaching at Grey Lynn Primary School. The class comprised mostly Pasifika and Māori children; they were a sheer delight after having taught mostly Pākehā children when I was on teaching practice. Māoris always seemed to be happier, more relaxed, less uptight than us white people. In one university essay I'd argued against Māoris being labelled 'culturally disadvantaged'; instead, they were 'culturally different'. In fact, I thought they were superior.

To tell you the truth, I was a pretty hopeless teacher, especially in the traditional education system. I remember thinking at the time that not one thing I'd studied at university or teachers' college was of any use to me. During those years I'd been drawn to the alternative methods of teachers such as A.S. Neill, who established the independent school Summerhill in England, and Sylvia Ashton-Warner, who had remarkable success teaching Māori children in rural areas.[38] Ashton-Warner believed learning must be real – it must start from a child's experience and relate to their world.

For my year of teaching, the headmaster gave me permission to do what I wanted. I jumped at the chance to try some of Ashton-Warner's methods and rearranged the classroom with my desk at the back and set up learning corners: dress-up here, drawing there, reading over here, and so on. The children chose what they wanted to do. Those who could not write would draw or paint pictures and I'd write their own stories underneath, which they would read back to me. There was a tree outside the classroom, which I called the poetry tree. If the children felt like writing a poem, they could take a piece of paper and pencil and go sit under the tree. There was an empty storage room underneath the classroom which the headmaster said I could use as a carpentry room. The children could go there, unsupervised, to build things with hammers and nails and glue. My approach worked. An inspector who came in mid-year was incredulous at the children's progress in maths and reading and was impressed by some of their poems.

Despite the joy the kids brought me, I was still struggling, my depression still hanging around. One morning I was trimming sheets of paper on the guillotine outside the classroom and cut off the tip of my finger. I remember the headmaster running down the stairs from his office, yelling 'Where's the tip?', before rushing me to Auckland Hospital, where they managed to reattach the top of my finger. When I got out of hospital, I rang Mum. I can't remember what she said, but there was not a single word of sympathy. I remember the awful sinking feeling in my heart, the feeling of being abandoned, yet again. How was it possible for her not to even have a tiny space for me?

Sadly, for the next year at Grey Lynn it was back to traditional methods. I was frustrated and the Black Dog roared back into my life. I decided to return to university and enrolled in a Master of Education degree at Auckland University. It was one of the darkest years of my life. Depression became a constant companion. Even though it happens within the brain, it feels as if it comes from the outside: dark thick clouds that close in until the world shrinks. I spent hours not under the bed covers but actually under the bed, curled up in a foetal position, just as I had done as a child. I didn't believe in God or the Devil, but the only explanation I had for what was happening to me was that the Devil was punishing me for something I'd done.

I kept moving house, just like my father, not because I needed to but because it gave me a short-lived reprieve from feeling down. I was trying to outrun my depression. Dad was soon to finish growing tomatoes and retire and would enter a really crazed period when he was on the move at least once a year – over six years he'd move house eight times, buying and selling and losing money on each move.

It helped that houses and flats were readily available to rent and usually furnished. I moved to Browns Bay for a few weeks, then to a little wooden cottage out in the dark green lush bush of Titirangi, where I thought I'd stay for the rest of my life it was so beautiful. But I lasted less than a week before moving back to Ponsonby, which was then a colourful working-class suburb that attracted hippies and bohemian artists along with many Māoris and Pasifika migrants, so I felt right at home, but even then did not stay long; here, there, everywhere, chucking my possessions into the boot and back seat of my little grey Morris Minor car. My brain hurts digging up these memories. Only now can I see the parallels between Dad and me in trying to outrun the trauma monster.

I was also lonely. What had happened to all my friends? I'd had many over the years but I seemed to have abandoned them all. Barbara Hill, who I lived with in Hamilton for two years and who had also lived next door to me in Auckland for a few months, recently got in touch: 'Welcome back to my life. I missed you! I worried about you for so many years.' Why didn't I reach out to her, back then? She recalls: 'You were unstable, depression wasn't a word back then, and I also remember you being terribly worried about your sister who'd ring you up from time to time and tell you she wanted to kill herself. You'd come over crying and wouldn't know what to do.'

There is a paragraph in *The Serpent Rising* on my year in Auckland in which I wrote: 'In the past year my closest girlfriend had made several suicide attempts. I felt helpless and guilty because I did not know how to help her.' After my old friend and I reconnected, I sent her a copy of this book. After she read it, she told me she knew I meant my sister, not a girlfriend.

While at Auckland, I certainly wasn't going to burden either her, Mum or anyone else with what was going on for me and what was happening inside my head. I was adrift on a sea of trauma, with no roots. I was turning into both my mother and my father, the two people in the world I least wanted to resemble: depressed and emotionally frozen like my mother; unstable like my father. If only I'd got into cycling back then or if someone had whispered in my ear, 'Let it out, have a good cry or a scream.' That would have helped for sure.

Judith Herman in her book *Trauma and Recovery* explains that traumatised people feel utterly abandoned and alone.[39] There is a sense of alienation, of disconnection, that pervades every relationship. Luckily, I wasn't suicidal. Strangely, for as long as I can remember, no matter how tough things got there was always this little voice in my head, whispering, 'You are going to be okay.'

In 1945, Janet Frame was working as a probationary teacher in Arthur Street School, Dunedin. She describes in her autobiography how she pretended to be happy, had woven a visible layer, when in fact she felt completely isolated, knew no one to confide in, to get advice from, and there was nowhere for her to go.[40] That is exactly how I felt.

I don't recall depression ever being discussed. It wasn't a term we used. Around university there was no mention of mental health support in the way of counselling or psychological help, except for one person. There were flyers around the campus advertising workshops conducted by self-appointed therapist Bert Potter. I was tempted to see him but was too shy. Potter would go on to establish Centrepoint, an infamous commune at Albany, Auckland, with Potter a guru-like figure at the helm. The group imploded after a string of convictions for drug dealing and underage sex, with victims as young as three years of age. Centrepoint has left a dark stain on New Zealand's landscape.

What sort of society spawned a place like Centrepoint and many more in its wake, such as Gloriavale, a secretive fundamentalist Christian cult located at Haupiri on the West Coast of the South Island, near Westport? Its leaders were recently charged with underage sexual assault, and there are ongoing court cases around labour and servitude.[41] My theory is that groups that morph into dangerous cults, as well as families that implode and fracture like my birth family, often stem from what a society represses or denies.

On 22 October, James Baxter died of a heart attack in Auckland. He was only 46. His body was taken to Jerusalem, near Whanganui, where hundreds of mourners attended a full Māori tangihanga. I've recently learnt that this person I idolised sexually abused several young women at Jerusalem, including Ros Lewis, a psychotherapist and writer now living in Melbourne. Lewis shared some of her story in an article for *Stuff*.[42]

On reflection, I was lucky. In the six years I'd spent in Hamilton and Auckland, riding through the hippy and counterculture revolution, nothing bad happened to me, nor during my holiday adventures. No one raped me. No one forced me to do anything I didn't want to do. No one assaulted me. No one bullied me. My experiences of sexual harassment and assault would come later, in India in the 1970s, and in Maleny in the 1990s. And how lucky I was not to have become pregnant. All those times I had sex with men who did not use a condom – they were thick and rubbery back then – and me not taking the pill as it wasn't available to unmarried women. Why wasn't I ever worried about getting pregnant?

In the 1960s, according to Susan Kedgley, 'there was still a clear, though unspoken, assumption that a girl's only purpose in life was to get married and spend the rest of her life looking after her husband and family.'[43] I never felt that was my purpose. No one in my family expected that of either me or my sister. Since my parents' marriage was so miserable, it was no wonder my mum had no expectation or ambition for me to get married. She often said: 'Just don't do what I did and get trapped like me.'

In many ways the late 60s and early '70s were an exciting time, and full of hope. The world was changing. Some of New Zealand's dour conservativeness was lifting. In 1973, the traditional family unit was shaken, for good. A benefit to support sole parents, who were mostly women, was introduced. The divorce rate soared. Women could now leave toxic marriages and violent husbands. It was sadly too late for Mum.

These huge changes in the world did not help my own internal world, my mental anguish. During the final exams at Auckland University, I stood up and walked out. I'd been too depressed to study well and was overcome with anxiety. In the only subject that did not require an examination but relied on coursework I got the top mark. I rationalised my actions to myself, and my lecturers, with a plan to repeat the three examinable subjects the following year *and* do my thesis at the same time. I wanted to be assured of getting First Class Honours! My thesis supervisor thought it was a great idea.

At the end of that year, I found the perfect drug to escape it all. Religion! God! My conversion to Eastern mysticism was sudden and unexpected, and happened during a ceremony of worship conducted at a yoga ashram, on the outskirts of Auckland. This ashram, run by an eccentric yoga teacher, Lou Postlewaight, called 'Guruji', was a branch of the Sivananda organisation, whose headquarters are in Rishikesh, India.

I still can't understand fully what happened to me that night. It was as if I was transported into another world during the hour or so that I sat there. I remember there was incense burning, candles lighting up the darkened room, some very strange pictures of Hindu gods and goddesses on the altar at the front of the room, and a Hindu swami was chanting prayers. Within minutes my mind seemed to 'explode' into ecstasy and bliss. I felt the region of my heart grow warmer and warmer and then it was as if it was opening and all these feelings of love were pouring outwards. My forehead felt ablaze with white light. I had dropped acid a few years previously and in many ways this experience was similar, except that here I felt in complete control and this enormous sense of peace came over me.

Over the next few days, I abandoned my studies, burnt my thesis (my supervisor said he'd never seen me so happy), got rid of most of my possessions and moved into the ashram. I began to meditate and chant Hindu mantras and read books such as Herman Hesse's *Siddhartha* and Paul Brunton's *Search for Secret India*. It was as if I'd entered an enchanted kingdom, as it was so very different from the dreary Christianity of my childhood.

I'd found a family at last, a place where I felt at home. We all shared something in common: we were on a spiritual journey. I seemed to be on a permanent high: the depression and loneliness that had haunted me throughout the previous few years had vanished; in their place were calmness and joy.

Within months I was off to India in search of enlightenment and my true guru. I wasn't alone. In the 1970s, tens of thousands of us went to India. Eastern mysticism was new and exotic to Westerners and we were in the vanguard as we traipsed from guru to guru ready to surrender our critical thinking and our hearts. How ironic that many of us who'd been part of the counterculture movement, with its anti-establishment and anti-authority stance, turned eastward, where many of those gurus, who claimed to be enlightened or God, turned out to be more authoritarian than anyone we had encountered in our lives.

There'd been no exposés or warnings of the damage that gurus could do to our minds and bodies. Most of us were still running from our past, the damage done to us in our childhood, which pot and flower power could not heal. Childhood abuse isn't something you 'get over'; what we actually needed was psychotherapy, not yoga, meditation or a guru.

Fifty years later, despite all the exposés, people still go looking for a guru, seek 'spiritual enlightenment' (whatever that means) or do lengthy meditation courses as a way to heal unresolved trauma.

Anna, Dad and I all grabbed hold of religion as a salve, and were ardent believers, but I eventually chucked it away.

CHAPTER 9

Estrangement

With our history, is it any wonder that my sister and I eventually became estranged? Estrangement means to decide to impose distance. It is rarely linear and can be short or long, temporary or permanent. The Merriam Webster Dictionary's definition is, 'to arouse especially mutual enmity or indifference in (someone) where there had formerly been love, affection, or friendliness'. Sibling estrangement can take various forms, from having no contact at all, to having infrequent contact, to being emotionally distant and having a superficial relationship.[44]

In an article she wrote for *The Australian* in 2021, Anna claimed that Mum told her she and I were 'rivals' even as children and that she separated herself from me 'increasingly' when she went to live in London for 20 years.[45]

First to the rival bit. Perhaps my mother said that to her, but she never said it to me. My recollection is that Anna harboured resentment towards me, was jealous of me. As I've said, I was prettier in a conventional sense. The adults would often praise my looks, ignoring Anna completely. Not that beauty or prettiness helped me much –

it did not ward off depression and anxiety and loneliness, and it sure doesn't matter now that I'm in my seventies.

Mum often compared us. I'd hear her say to her friends and my aunts 'If only Anna was more like Mary'. In a letter to Margareta in 1974, she wrote: 'I must say I am a little worried, Anna doesn't fall on her feet like Mary, nor has she Mary's initiative.' (She *should* have been worried about me. By then, I was caught up in a religious cult in India and sending very strange-sounding letters home.)

She would also say to me, 'You have a fine bosom, dear, much bigger than your sister's.' I'd roll my eyes and reply, 'For fuck's sake, Mum. Not *bosom*. It's breasts, boobs or tits. And who cares?' She kept saying I had a lovely or fine bosom, even in her later years when she was stuck in a nursing home in Orewa.

Comparing siblings is unhealthy and creates rifts, leading to feelings of superiority and inferiority. Many parents in poorly functioning families place children in comparative categories, such as the 'smart child' or the 'responsible one'.[46] Anna was the smart child and I was the responsible one. Also, I was the pretty child, Anna was plain-looking.

Is it any wonder that Anna came to hate me? A study by researchers Alex Jensen and Susan McHale found that parents' beliefs about their children – and the comparisons they make between them – may cause differences to be magnified. They suggest parents should focus on 'recognising the strengths of each of their children and be careful about voicing comparisons in front of them'.[47] Psychologist Wasim Kakroo argues that such comparisons can have a negative impact on children's confidence and self-esteem, and cause envy and jealousy among siblings, even leading to mental health issues.[48]

As for my sister saying she separated increasingly from me when she went to live in London, I have a different recollection. The truth is that Anna cut herself off from me suddenly and unexpectedly in 1980.

After graduating from Waikato University, Anna went to Auckland University where she obtained a Master of Philosophy degree in Economics in 1977, and then began working as an economist in the New Zealand Treasury in Wellington. In 1980, she left New Zealand and went to London to work in the treasury there.

During all those years we sent letters to each other. We were on very friendly terms. There was no hint of animosity, although some of my letters were completely loopy, as I was living in the ashram in India and off the planet. Yet she made no comment about the strange things I wrote. Here's an example from a letter I wrote in 1975 from Rishikesh, in the foothills of the Himalayas. The name I'd been given was 'Archana', meaning adoration of the divine, which sure fed my delusion of being spiritual. Note the lower case i to signify my lack of ego! Like many so-called 'spiritual aspirants' who raced off to India, I was arrogant and thought I was superior to those caught up in a worldly life.

Beloved parents, Brother Robert and Sister Anna,

Never have i been so happy – everything is given to me when i humble myself and serve those deserving to be served – the saints and sages who have all the secrets. All one needs is faith – faith in one's Self – then everything will be provided to the one who has no want. Never will i need money again, never do i need to think of returning to the world to earn money – through surrendering everything is provided – including peace and joy. I can see Anna here and you, Mother – it's remarkable beyond words – heaven on earth – so much unity, so much joy. The cerebrum of the earth, so close to Heaven. May you soon reach that Peace within.

Lots of love

Archana

Fortunately, I have this letter (my mother kept a few) as I would never have believed, 50 years later, that I was capable of such hogwash. I was clearly under a spell and brainwashed. I never thought to ask my mother if she was ever worried about me. If either of my children wrote letters like this, I'd jump on the first plane to kidnap them. I can imagine my sister wanting to distance herself from me during these years, as I'd apparently turned into another person, morphed into a strange new personality. But she said nothing, and even knitted me a jumper, which she posted to Rishikesh.

Luckily, I managed to escape the guru I was entangled with and eventually gave up on the search for spiritual enlightenment, which had all been very enlightening in an entirely different sense. In 1980 I landed back on earth, with even more trauma weighing me down. I settled in Brisbane, where I'd spent some time in 1976 between trips to India. I loved this big open-hearted subtropical city with its lushness and summer rains.

Out of the blue, I received a letter from Anna to say she wanted to kill herself and could I help since she believed I was connected to God in some way. It was odd she thought this after my strange letters, where clearly I'd denounced the Christian God and embraced Hinduism and its pantheon of gods and goddesses. I wrote back that I didn't believe in God, had given up on religion and was traumatised by my own experiences and could not help her. I begged her to get some help, to go and see a psychiatrist. I had no idea what else to say and meant no ill will.

(I'd changed my mind about psychiatrists and psychologists and therapists after being at the Rajneesh Ashram in Pune in the late 1970s. I had started getting help from a number of therapists while I was there.)

If my sister was increasingly distancing herself, why out of all the people she knew did she reach out to me for help? Her friend Susan Lea was actually in London at the time. She had a boyfriend, Ralph Lewis, a leadership development consultant, who would later write endorsements for some of Anna's books. Why couldn't she have asked them for help, instead of me, who could not be of any assistance being so far away?

Anna's reply stunned me. It was angry and vitriolic. I no longer have the letter, as I burnt it soon afterwards; the only thing I remember is that she wrote *I* was the reason her life had been such a torment. It made no sense. What had I done except help her, put up with her, be pleasant to her? At first I was angry, but later I was distraught.

I sent a copy of the letter to Mum and Dad in the hope they'd persuade her to get help. I expected them to be sympathetic towards me and say how awful it must have been to receive such a missive. But they did not want to discuss it and were angry at me for suggesting Anna see a psychiatrist.

I felt abandoned. They blamed me and had sided with Anna, again. This is what happened when Anna stabbed me in the back when we were living with our aunt at Remuera. It had been my fault. I must have done something to upset her. It was the pattern established in our childhood.

Over the next eight years, I kept trying to reach out to my sister. The letters I wrote would be returned with nasty comments scribbled on the outside of the envelopes such as 'nasty bitch' and so forth, and the occasional 'fuck you'. I wonder what the people at Maleny Post Office thought as they sorted out the mail.

During this time, Anna was having extraordinary success in her career. She gave up on economics and completed an MBA at the Cranfield School of Management. There she discovered 'organisational behaviour', which would interest her for the rest of her life. She embarked on a Doctor of Philosophy degree at the Sloan School of Management, Massachusetts Institute of Technology, one of the world's leading business schools, and in 1983 won their award for the best PhD student. Her research was on the dynamics of burnout. Returning to London, she worked at London Business School for several years.

In 1989, Anna helped establish the British Association of Psychological Type (BAPT)[49] and was its first president. BAPT promotes Jungian psychological type systems – mainly the Myers-

Briggs Type Indicator (MBTI), the most widely used personality test in the world. Despite its popularity, the MBTI lacks scientific support and is considered an inaccurate and unreliable psychological instrument.

Sally Campbell met Anna in 1989 and was part of the group of people behind the establishment of BAPT. Sally recalled that Anna was 'a bright light and hugely intelligent'. One of her strengths was her ability to stand up and be counted. 'She did not suffer fools gladly and had a deeply creative and often spiritual side. Her knowledge of type and leadership was inspirational.'

In late 1990, Anna left the London Business School to run her own consultancy business and ceased involvement with BAPT, although continued to be a MBTI supporter.

The rest of the family were in awe of her. I had no interest at all in her career – academia was a waste of time in my book and I'd never regretting burning my half-finished Masters thesis before flying off to India. I was only interested in restoring our relationship, but Mum would not discuss Anna with me. In a letter to Margareta and Maurice I wrote: 'I have no idea what Mother knows about why Anna hates me so much and I've given up trying to squeeze it out of her.'

Now I see that the way my mother treated me, the game she played, was insidious. It is all very well to say parents do the best they can with what they know – and yes, they were damaged, too, by their parents – but they can still be incompetent. And Mum was playing a toxic game. She had from the time I was a child.

Even though Anna was having success in her professional life, Mum told me that on several occasions Anna said she was suicidal and Mum flew over to the UK try to help her. She didn't tell me much except to say there were screaming matches and things broken, especially photos in frames. From the sounds of things, a psychiatrist or a psychologist was exactly what Anna needed, not Mum playing the rescuer. I assume she thought she knew best as she had once been a psychiatric nurse herself, even though that was in the 1940s and the era of straightjackets and lobotomies.

In another letter to Margareta, I mentioned that Anna was returning to New Zealand soon but there was still no communication with her. 'Not that I get any from Robert but in his case it's just plain laziness, not unresolved hostility or whatever Anna's deep-rooted problem is.' In another letter later that year, I wrote that Anna still refuses to have any communication with me. 'Presumably she still believes that I am the reason her life has been such a torture.'

It was reassuring to receive this response from Margareta: 'I am puzzled by your remark in your letter about Anna, as I had no idea you were incommunicado. I thought it was me she was so angry with. I used to get on so well with her and then it all went phut.'

This ghosting by Anna crushed and hurt me deeply. It left me wondering what was wrong with me. Fern Schumer Chapman, who has written widely on sibling abuse and estrangement, explains that a sibling cut-off without explanation often leads to profound grief, as 'the estranged mourn the living', and that 'not knowing the reasons for the cut-off can be its own form of torture'. The choice to cut off is 'a weighty club of control' and can generate feelings of self-doubt, anxiety, rejection and powerlessness in those left behind.[50] This tactic, she argues, is often used by siblings with narcissistic traits and is a form of emotional abuse. They may have resentment or deep feelings of jealousy, or they may be hiding something such as an addiction or symptoms of mental illness. That description fits my sister to a tee.

Kipling Williams, a Professor of Psychology at Purdue University, who has studied ostracism for 20 years, argues that 'excluding and ignoring people', such as giving the cold shoulder or silent treatment, is a way to punish and manipulate, and 'people may not realise the emotional or physical harm that is being done'.[51]

In 1986, I threw myself into writing a book about my years in India. In 1981, I'd attended a short TAFE writing course in Brisbane and had written a short story called 'Ripped off by ants' describing my escape across India from Sai Baba and chucking my passport and money out the window of a train. I'd hidden them in a paper bag full of nuts and raisins, which overnight had attracted long lines of large biting ants. The teacher, Rolfe Bradley, wrote that 'this is exceptionally well written and I believe you should write a full-length book of your experiences and your detailed reactions to India. This could be straightforwardly factual or spiced here and there with a little invention. I'm sure this would find a ready market.'

I was thrilled to read this. No one had ever praised my writing before. But it was too soon to write my story. I was still shell-shocked from some of my experiences. However, over the years the idea of a book hung around, and occasionally I'd write down snippets and chuck them in a folder in a bottom drawer.

I mentioned my new project to Mum. 'It's been a little bit freaky getting into this book again and pouring over old correspondence. I didn't realise how hypnotised I was by India and by Eastern religions – all religions, in fact, are hypnotising. At least I was lucky to get out of it all.' However, I don't recall my mother showing any interest in my project.

In a letter to Margareta and Maurice in 1987, I told them I was sending them a draft and asked if they could forward it onto Mum when they had finished, as she had insisted that she read it. 'She thinks she has a right to request deletions,' I wrote. 'But I'm not changing much, irrespective of what she says.'

This was quite odd, in hindsight, considering Mum insisted I write a 'warts and all' account of Dad in *Sundowner of the Skies*: she wanted all his flaws included. Regardless, I hardly mentioned Mum in *The Serpent Rising* and the only feedback I can remember getting is that I'd given an 'exact' portrayal of her and Dad.

Margareta's response was wonderful. 'Maurice says it must be published because there is so little written about your experiences. He found it gripping, interesting, very moving and beautifully written in parts. That's high praise from him. We both – at separate times

– flew from page to page, chapter to chapter.' She added that she needed to say something that sat slightly uneasily on her as she did not use 'that vocabulary that includes "sharing", but I want to say I actually feel privileged to have been allowed to read this.'

How lucky to receive this, to have their encouragement, whereas I received none from other family members. In my letter back, I wrote, 'I don't know what I'll do when this book is finished. Though there is always the story about the sundowner of the skies that should written by someone!'

After years of ignoring me, I finally received a letter from Anna in February 1989. *The Serpent Rising* was published in November 1988 and I'd asked Mum to send her a copy (she wouldn't give me Anna's postal address). I was pretty sure the book would heal things between us, that she would feel sorry for me for what I had been though in India and at what I had endured at the hands of the abusive yoga guru. She would realise why I'd not been in a fit state to be able to offer her emotional support when she wrote to me and asked for help, after she'd gone to live in London.

However, the book made things worse. The letter was a blast of hatred, with no ounce of sympathy. As well as confirming we had been sexually abused by a neighbour, she lectured me about the 'truth', pointing out she had been 'psychically blazing' since she was born.

The sneering voice of my sister is similar to that of Robyn Davidson's sister, Margaret, described in *Unfinished Woman*: 'When she spoke her voice was cold, bitter – the tone of one who has been wronged. That voice vibrated with … What? Rage? It was more like loathing – the longing to crush something loathsome.' Margaret asks Robyn if she remembers the dog that killed her pet duckling Auburn, and says, 'I willed death to that dog. And the next day it took a poison bait and died … That's when I first knew my own psychic power.' [52]

Anna's letter reveals her contempt and loathing of me:

I feel like I need to instruct a naive innocent in the spiritual and psychic reality, but I don't have the time and energy to do all of that. Of course, evil exists and Satan exists. Did you know that (!!!). Very specifically: there exists an evil force called the Isauri which has languished underground for a very long time (ever) and periodically surfaces dramatically. The energy is unbelievably clever and has been working primarily in New Age circles and gurus. It manifests psychically in the form of revolting lizard-like creatures – what we called cannas as children. At present, they possess people who are outwardly are healers-saviours etc. such people get a lot of power particularly healing power and people think they are 'good' and 'wonderful'. You need spiritual discrimination which seems to me to be the thing you most need. (Use the Psalms for protection against evil.)

At the time I thought her writing was the deranged ramblings of someone who was mentally ill. While writing an earlier draft of this book I'd done a search of Isauri and could find no mention of this 'evil force' anywhere, but I've recently discovered she was talking about the reptilian conspiracy theory. Her friend Susan Lea told me she herself had seen reptilians. She suggested I read up on David Icke. Icke used to be a footballer but now is considered the father of conspiracy theories and believes he is the son of God. He is a prominent advocate of the belief that the world is run by reptiles and the royal family are lizards. This is complete rubbish. I wish I'd known that this was an actual belief, as it would have been less unnerving than thinking the reptilians were a result of a deranged mind and that Anna had gone completely nuts.

Anna recommended in the letter that I take my book into a Catholic church and get a priest to bless it and sprinkle it with holy water. Then she chided: 'You need to stop deluding yourself about being the nice, good child – you were a nightmare to my mother as a child as well as to me. You won't get ANYWHERE unless you finally cut the crap and look yourself eyeball to eyeball.' She said I was 'full of crap' about my childhood.

Nowhere in *The Serpent Rising* do I mention being a nice, good child, even though I was. I barely mention our childhood. I have a few paragraphs about going home to Tauranga to say goodbye to Mum and Dad before leaving for India.

As with the first letter, I sent a copy to Mum and Dad. They would not discuss this one either, which was upsetting. I wanted them to stand up to her for being a bully, tell her it was a nasty letter, tell me they were sorry she had done this and agree she needed professional help. But after their non-reaction to the first letter, why did I expect them to behave any differently this time?

I sent a copy of the letter to Margareta and asked her to burn it when she had read it, and not to tell Mum and Dad that I'd given her a copy as 'I would be cast out of the family network.' I said I was already in disgrace 'for daring to humiliate and embarrass the family because of the publicity of my book.' I mention that I'd originally planned to go over to New Zealand that year to promote my book but that is now out of the question. 'I've been told in very definite terms not to let it into retail shops in NZ. Mum has said, "What will ALL her friends think!!!!" Hmm. Families. It's partly why I escaped to India.'

I've forgotten I'd planned to go over to New Zealand to promote and sell my book, but it is there in this letter to Margareta. Remarkably, Margareta kept all my letters. In late 2007, I'd been given a grant which enabled me to go on a research tour of the South Island of New Zealand.[53] For a month, I visited museums and libraries, and interviewed pilots, aviation historians and a handful of people who had known my father. At the end of the tour, I visited Margareta and Maurice in Nelson and spent many hours going through Margareta's collection of photos, letters and news clippings. While sitting on the floor in the garage of their house, looking through boxes of archival material for stuff on Dad, I found a large folder containing every letter I'd written to Margareta since I was eight years old, and later, after they married, to both she and Maurice.

I cannot remember Mum ever congratulating me on my book. Instead, she seemed ashamed of me for writing it. I discussed this with my cousin, Gillian, who said that in the main that generation preferred not to talk about things that were considered 'unsavoury' in case it reflected on them as parents and bought 'shame' to the family. 'Ignoring, emotional coldness and discarding were the tools they used to enable this.'

The Serpent Rising was to have enduring appeal and has helped many. Writing it was cathartic and helped me make sense of what I'd been through. Norwegian writer Karl Ove Knausgaard, who wrote a bestselling, deeply exposing memoir called *My Struggle*, says 'writing is a way of getting rid of shame. When you write the whole idea is to be free.'[54] That's what *The Serpent Rising* was for me: freeing. Out of the hundreds of letters I received from readers, and emails after the book was republished in 2003, the only negative feedback I've received was from my sister and my mother. (I don't think Robert ever read my book, or if he had, he never mentioned it.)

Trying to connect with my sister to repair our relationship was pointless and destructive. She had a pattern of cutting people off who were close to her, much like Dad. He cut himself off from all the friends he made during his flying years, and turned his back on them.

The hardest thing was no one in the family condemned Anna's behaviour. I was sidelined and felt out on a limb. When I visited New Zealand in 1990 all my father could talk about was how dreadful my hair looked. I had long wavy hair at the time, ironically just like the hair my mother had when she first met my father. It was what had caught his attention!

I wrote to Margareta and Maurice that it had been 'an appalling trip', and that 'I have absolutely nothing at all in common with any of my family.' Evidently, we only saw Dad for about half an hour in three days, and I was beginning to wonder why I'd spent $2000 dollars and stayed in motels, when 'the only thing Dad had to talk about was my dreadful hair and how I should get it all cut and straightened and off that good Garden brow. They all make me sick at times.'

I can feel my sadness and my loneliness in these letters. I felt like an outcast. Writing about Prince Harry, journalist Nikki Gemmell writes that there is nothing 'quite like the loneliness felt within a dysfunctional family, the loneliness of feeling you don't quite belong'.[55] This could equally be applied to me. Families like mine and Harry's use non-communication, emotional bullying and exclusion as weapons.

If only I'd taken Anna's letters and sought professional help, seen a psychologist myself, instead of just sending copies across the ditch to my parents hoping for some support. It could have saved me a lot of heartache. I could have healed some of the shame that hung around, the perpetual feeling it was my fault. Instead, I got sucked into a toxic family game.

I wasn't the only one to receive nasty letters from Anna. Susan Lea also received her share. In June 2017, Susan emailed Anna: 'I found another pile of your early, wild letters. Let me know if you'd enjoy reading them and I will send them on to you! Hugs.' Anna replied, 'I don't want any of my terrible letters. Throw them in the rubbish bin.' Nevertheless, Susan must have sent them to her, as a few weeks later Anna tells Susan, 'Got those insane letters of mine from you. Many thanks. They are revolting.' This response shows that Anna had some insight, at least at some stage! I wonder if she realised how terrible and revolting the two letters she sent me were, the ones that destroyed our relationship.

I had things back to front. I should never have tried to sort things out. I should have just cut off from Anna in 1980, run a mile and not looked back. That realisation only came a few years later though, when I began to have extensive therapy. I'd done a little therapy in the late 1970s and during the 1980s – mostly gestalt therapy or the controversial rebirthing therapy. But this was not enough or good enough. These workshops were sometimes provocative and confrontational, and I was sometimes stung by feedback from participants and even therapists.

What I needed was regular, sustained and safe psychotherapy. I needed help for many things. There was trauma building up in layers: from my childhood, from the years in India, from my sister's abuse and her vile letters, from my parents' enabling her and not supporting me and, if that wasn't enough, from my relationships with men.

CHAPTER 10

Unravelling

My sister's abuse and violence has had lifelong repercussions. It has clearly influenced my relationships with men and the dynamics that played out, especially the blame game: *it is all your fault*, men would tell me. And not surprisingly, I was attracted to men like my father.

A recent Australian study sought responses from siblings who'd experienced abuse when they were adolescents.[56] They found there were 'ongoing and serious impacts' from this violence, including the ability to sustain intimate relationships.

American author and family therapist Darlene Lancer, explains that intimate relationship dynamics can mirror the dynamics in their sibling relationships. This pattern is known as the repetition compulsion. If the victim is socialised to the use of violence – they have learnt to tolerate or accept it – they may find themselves in similar situations as adults and unknowingly repeat the cycle of violence. 'They can develop co-dependent and pleasing behaviours, repeating their accommodating, submissive, victim role.'[57]

That is exactly what happened in both my marriage and the disastrous one-year-long love affair that followed in its wake. It was after this that I realised I really needed help.

In 1990 my marriage ended. By then I had two children, Eamon, born in 1981, and Natalya, born in 1983.

I had met Kevin in 1980. On returning from India, I managed to get a short-term job as a research assistant at James Cook University in Townsville. One weekend, I participated in a gestalt therapy workshop, which I enjoyed so much I decided to do a training course that was to take place in Melbourne in January 1981. While waiting to begin this new chapter in my life, I went to Brisbane for several weeks to manage the Taringa Healing Centre – a place that offered Riechian psychotherapy and other therapies – while its owner was in Bali.

One evening this tall, slim, rather good-looking man with slightly greying hair came in for a massage. He seemed very direct and self-assured. The masseur assigned didn't show up, so I said I'd do it, even though I'd never given a massage in my life. Kevin recalls the massage as being very soothing and transporting.

We felt an instant attraction to each other, and I felt at ease with him, finding him easy to talk to. Afterwards we decided to have a soak together in the outdoor spa and ended up spending the night together. He thought I was very interesting and exotic: I was still wearing Indian-type clothing, sandalwood beads around my neck, and had a ruby nose-stud, a rare sight in Brisbane in those days. The thing that had special appeal to me was his *car*, even though it was just a Ford station wagon. Perhaps it represented stability after all my years roaming around India, homeless and often barefooted. A few weeks later, I moved into his small old Queenslander house in the leafy suburb of Bardon.

Kevin and I had ten good years. He was a businessman, an importer and distributor of bicycle parts, with a warehouse in Fortitude Valley. He'd been a racing cyclist, and would put on cycling events around Queensland. I'd cycled everywhere as a child, and now suddenly I was cycling again. Kevin built me a bike, with drop handlebars, that I'd often ride around the neighbourhood before he went to work.

I adored being a mum. I realised it was what I'd always wanted. My bible was Jean Liedloff's 1975 book *The Continuum Concept*. Liedloff argued for a return to more natural rhythms and advocated co-sleeping, breastfeeding on demand, carrying a baby in arms for six months. I became an instant convert. Kevin had no objection to putting our mattress on the floor so the children could sleep next to us; when little I carried them around on my chest most of the time, even when doing housework. This method seemed to work for me, as I had no problems breastfeeding or getting my babies to sleep.

After my history, it is a miracle I was such a good mum – not perfect, but pretty damn good. Mum never flew over to help me for any significant period of time: she merely paid a flying visit on several occasions, staying in a motel nearby and spending a few hours with us. She was too embroiled looking after Dad and his ongoing health and mental problems, while also worrying about Anna and trying to help her.

During those years in Brisbane, I was struggling with the fallout with my sister, and feeling abandoned and unsupported by Mum and Dad, and even Robert, who showed no interest in being an uncle. Also, Kevin's parents, who lived in Sydney, cut off from us when they discovered I did not change my name when we married. It never occurred to me for a second to change my surname. Kevin wasn't bothered by his parents' behaviour, and over the years had little contact with them, even after we separated.

Kevin spent a lot of time away for work, sometimes weeks at a time. I was very focused on the children – two healthy beautiful children, whom I adored – while he was consumed with the business and worked long hours. We neglected our relationship and cracks began to appear.

In many respects I'd married my father. I'd picked an odd and eccentric man who could be self-absorbed and expected me to be strong, capable and organised. If I became sick it was invariably 'not his reality'. He was also a strong advocate of corporal punishment, which was only formally banished in Queensland state schools in 1995. Once, he washed Natalya's mouth out with soap, justifying it because his mother did it to him. Patriarchal in his attitudes, he thought my place was in the home. I was the homemaker; he was the breadwinner.

I struggled living in a city – I could not cope with the traffic and the noise – and longed to be in the country. I persuaded Kevin to sell up and move to Maleny, in the Sunshine Coast hinterland. I'd spent a weekend with the children in Maleny and loved its hippy, alternative lifestyle.

After we moved, it was clear Kevin and I were moving in different directions. He'd relocated the business to north of Brisbane, so the commuting time wasn't much different to what it had been when we lived at Indooroopilly. Rather than our lives becoming simpler and less stressful, Kevin threw himself even more into work, and we hardly saw him.

In spite of getting counselling, I could hang on no longer. It was a heart-wrenching decision. It took a lot of courage to leave. Some people, like my mother, stay trapped in toxic relationships for years, for decades, for their whole life.

Although I had a fantasy of us co-parenting, this was not to be. Kevin moved back to Brisbane and I became a single mum with no job. The next few years would be a struggle for me financially – we had an acrimonious divorce and I naively relinquished my share of the family business.

After taking that leap, I went from the frying pan into the fire. It was all rosy for the first six months with my new partner, who I thought was the love of my life, and then he turned on me and the children. This included physical assaults, and the killing of our pet cat: he put it in a sack and asphyxiated it on the exhaust on his motor-bike. I had the trauma of going to court to obtain an intervention order – he even applied for a counter order, which was dismissed – and fortunately he moved away from the area. Eamon and Natalya remember him even today as 'the monster'. This lived experience led Natalya to later train as an art therapist and work for some years in the family violence sector.

My dream of a better life in the country had turned into a nightmare. I knew I needed help. My past had caught up with me. What was my part in these nightmares that life kept throwing at me? The love that turned to hate? Weeks after the end of that disastrous relationship, I went to see someone who'd trained with American-Swiss psychiatrist Elisabeth Kübler-Ross, author of the bestseller *On Death and Dying*, published in 1969. I began unravelling my life.

Kübler-Ross developed ground-breaking 'Life, Death and Transition' workshops. These used a therapeutic technique of 'externalisation' of emotions – expressing bottled-up or long-forgotten emotions, such as anger, sadness, fear, love or joy – and helped people find parts of themselves that had been buried, or cut off, by trauma and neglect. This is what Elisabeth called the 'unfinished business' that impacts our current life.

The room was soundproofed and on the floor was a mattress, which Brian, the facilitator, said was my *safe* place. There was a pile of fat telephone directories neatly stacked at the end of the mattress. He handed me a piece of reinforced hose (to use as a truncheon), gave me some gloves to put on (to prevent blisters) and placed an open telephone book in front of me. 'Put him out there,' he suggested. 'Talk to him. What do you want to say to him? Show him your anger.'

My words soon turned to the most shattering shouts and screams I had ever heard. The rage that I'd pushed down most of my life erupted. It was like a spewing torrent of emotional pus that gushed out of me in wild bursts. I was completely taken aback. Was this me? In me? At times I was so enraged I dropped the hose and began to furiously tear the phone books up as I howled and screamed abuse at my ex-partner. How dare he. Wild shouts of 'No, no' shot out of me.

How dare he do those things to me and to my children? How dare he. I also beat up some of his friends who had supported him and called me a liar. They'd said he wouldn't hurt a fly and I was on a power trip.

The therapist hardly said a word, just a few whispers, sometimes reiterating what I'd shouted. 'How dare he.' Suddenly, with no prompting, I found myself beating up my ex-husband for things he'd done, and then my father: that mean, miserly man.

Exhausted, I collapsed into grief. Why had I allowed it? Why didn't I protect my children? What had I done?

Spontaneously, some memories of my childhood came tumbling to the surface. Me as a little girl, often terrified, who seldom felt safe and who shut down emotionally. Hiding under my bed, away from the world. Running away, crouched under a hedge where no one could find me; curled up in a cave down on the cliff or up the tree with a knife. Running inside, always running. Deep sobs rocked me. I clung to a pillow and dragged tissues by the handful from several boxes. There at the bottom of the well was a sense of the deepest loss. I'd been running from my childhood most of my life. But this is where it all began. The reason why it was so hard to leave, decades later, when I had grown up and thought I'd found 'true love'. This is often where it all begins, for the abused and the abuser.

Elisabeth Kübler-Ross trained doctors to continue her work and over the next few years I did a number of these workshops in Australia, New Zealand and even Arizona. The work was life-changing. I began to become friends with my emotions – my rage, my sadness, my fear, my joy – instead of stuffing them underground.

I began to see my sister more clearly, the harm she had caused me. I realised I should have cut off from her many years ago, as soon as I was on my own and at university. Oh, to have had that insight back then, when I was 16. I realised I should now have no contact at all with her, that I'd had enough. Her behaviour was toxic and harmful and there were no signs it would change.

Cutting ties with family members is a hugely difficult decision. It is seen as a taboo, because the family is considered a sacred institution. People who do so are often labelled as 'bad' or selfish.

Alison Croggon writes about the vicious fights she had with her sister when they were children, and their painful estrangement as adults, in *Monsters: A Reckoning* (2021).[58] Croggon veers away from who is to blame (although one senses her sister is the chief villain), and instead digs deeper. With echoes of my relationship with my sister, Croggon sees that she and her sister were torn apart by a shared past, especially the volatile marriage of their parents, damage handed down through the generations.

Dr Lucy Blake, a developmental psychologist in the UK and a leading expert on family estrangement, says there is stigma surrounding estrangement and a view that a person who rejects a family member must be awful. One respondent to a survey she conducted in 2015 remarked that people treated her with 'tension, awkwardness, distance – as though I'm odd or broken, and should be kept at arm's length'. Another said, 'The saying blood is thicker than water seems to be the view. Never mind you're being abused and destroyed it's somehow your responsibility or duty to take it because it's family.' Interestingly, 80 per cent of respondents said their lives improved due to cutting family ties.[59]

Sherrie Campbell, a California psychologist and author of the book *Loving Yourself: The mastery of being our own person*, argues that if an abusive sibling were not family, we would not have anything to do with them:

> We spend years sacrificing our mental and emotional health in abusive relationships under the notion that we have to because these people are our family … the facts are that family members are just people and not always healthy people, and if these people were not family, we would never choose them to be a part of our lives due to their poor treatment of us.

> When the relationship is based on any kind of abuse, mentally, physically, sexually, verbally or emotionally, when you are living in constant anxiety never knowing or being able to predict how any engagement is going to turn out, it is time to love yourself enough to let go.[60]

Despite the subtle pressure from other family members, I managed to avoid having contact with my sister for decades and keep myself safe. I was able to do this because I sought help, underwent therapy and began to shed some of the shame that had shrouded me since early childhood. Therapy has been beneficial for me, as it helped me understand why I seemed to have attracted so much violence into my life, like a repetitive switch, on and on, over the years, over the decades. The patterns established in my childhood, unconsciously repeating themselves.

I now realise that *none* of the violence was my fault. None of my sister's violence and her abusive letters were my fault. I am not to blame. It is not my shame. I may have overreacted, inflamed situations, said things I now regret and used way too many words, but I got help and began to heal the pain at the bottom of it all.

Therapy is not for everyone. Sometimes therapy may be ineffective or not even needed; there are times when talking therapy or emotional release work do more harm than good. Someone with a mood disorder may be better helped by medication, for example. There are also incompetent clinicians. I've run into a few.

I don't think my sister found a way to heal the pain of our shared childhood. She did not believe in therapy. According to her friend Susan Lea, Anna did not feel psychologists could be trusted. She only believed in Lord Jesus Christ.

Although she mentioned her belief in the rituals of the Catholic church in the letter she wrote to me after receiving *The Serpent Rising*, she told Mum she first became a Catholic in 1989, when she was in north Scotland. Maybe she was just dabbling before then.

It is one of the best things that has ever happened to me or that I have ever chosen to do. I love it and love going to Mass and praying the Rosary. It is one of the most important things in my life. I would love to hear that you had gone along to Mass yourself, Mother – it is almost certainly different than when you were younger. Please try it once or twice.

Fifteen years later, she told Susan Lea:

I do no sport. Sit on my bum. I am much more preoccupied with being a Catholic/Christian. My highest priority in my life for a long time.

I love the Holy Spirit and the Mary the Holy Mother. I remember a white witch I used to frequent who said if I ever become a Christian, become a Catholic. So, I did. I spent a year praying to Isis and Horus. I had their statues in my living room. I gave up on Isis for some reason – forgotten. Might be for discovering Jesus Christ. Now I have the Virgin Mary in my living room. I have a big picture of her dominating the room and lots of small statues on the bookcase. The white witch I told you about said that there were two reasons to choose the Catholic faith and one of them was the Virgin Mary – especially if you are a woman.

I don't believe Roman Catholicism did Anna much good. It did not help her heal the trauma of our childhood, which she acted out on others and hurt those close to her. Hinduism and Buddhism didn't help me, either. John Bradshaw, an influential writer on emotional health – his book *Healing the Shame that Binds You* has sold millions of copies – cautioned against religion or spiritual teachings, often rooted in patriarchal worldviews and scriptures, to heal chronic trauma. What is needed, he says, is to do the 'pain work' and allow previously repressed emotion to surface.

Religion didn't help Dad either. He never was able to throw off the cold, repressive force of Scottish Calvinism. On one visit to New Zealand, a few years before he died, Dad and I talked about religion, which he always said he never had to study as his mother taught him everything. He said he believed in the coming 'rapture' and that Christ would return and take him away on a flying saucer. I told him I thought that was nonsense. He was very surprised when I told him I was an atheist and said he thought that I, out of all his children, would be a Christian and believe in Jesus.

Mum told me that when he was dying in hospital, he piped up, said he'd never done anything wrong so he would be a candidate for heaven. Mum thought that was laughable, after all the harm he had caused.

Dad loathed Catholicism. When he heard we were calling our son Eamon (Kevin chose this name in honour of the Irish politician Eamon de Valera), Dad fired up, 'You can't give him a Catholic name.' I pointed out that he had called me 'Mary'. To appease him we chose Charles as Eamon's second name. If I'd known then that Prince Charles would be a bystander to his older son William's bullying of Harry, I'd have chosen another name.

Mum also loathed the Catholic religion. When she became pregnant with her first son Michael, she went to Auckland to St Vincent's Home of Compassion for unmarried mothers. Presumably she was taught there that she had done a shameful, if not evil, thing and needed to seek forgiveness from Jesus. When Mum was in the nursing home, Anna would sometimes try to get her to see a priest but she wouldn't consider it. She and Aunt Ola had no time for religion.

Nowadays I only seek help when I need it. The last psychologist I saw suggested I should just keep writing, that I seemed to make sense of things that way. As well as being somewhat cathartic, writing this book has helped me reach a deeper understanding of my brother and sister. Memoirist Blake Morrison writes in *Two Sisters* that his wife sometimes tells him he is 'stuck in the past', which is something my brother sometimes told me. Wallowing was his word. Morrison does not see himself as stuck.

The point about revisiting the past is that you find new things each time you go there – things that you missed or didn't understand or failed to see the significance of, which as you get older you begin to grasp. If I'm addicted to the past, I tell her, it's because it hasn't passed. I'm still there, still working things out.[61]

I suspect I'll always be spending some time in the past, working things out.

CHAPTER 11

Days of Anna's Life

After I left New Zealand to fly to India in 1973, I did not see my sister for 24 years. I had no communication with her after her toxic letter sent in 1988 following the publication of *The Serpent Rising*. And I didn't want any.

I didn't see much of my brother either. Although we were on friendly terms and never argued, there was an emotional estrangement. We had a superficial relationship. He had not been an uncle figure to my two children, despite my urging. No cards. No birthday gifts. No phone calls. When he was in Australia taking part in a mountain bike event, even when close by, once at the Glasshouse Mountains, he didn't ring. I felt hurt but learnt to accept it. He was caught up with business pursuits, earning money, and his orienteering and cycling. For many years he rang each Christmas Day. We would chat mostly about cycling and the family bicycle business in Australia that I run with my son.

Robert was also emotionally estranged from Margareta and Maurice (our half-sister and her husband), as well as cousins on both sides of the family. Since leaving home, he'd had no contact with any of them except occasionally with a cousin who was sporting and competed in long-distance running events.

My brother and his partner had no children. When they were trying to have a child, my mother told me she hoped they wouldn't succeed. I was shocked to hear her say this. It was quite out of character for Mum to be mean and nasty. Was Mum worried that my brother would turn out like our father? But what about me? Didn't she worry that I might turn out like her? Sad, frozen and repressed, a martyr unable to leave a toxic marriage. Wasn't she afraid I might treat my children like she did, put them in situations where they were not safe, not stand up for them if one of my children was bullied by the other? What if I attracted men like my father? Why didn't she consider that?

Dad died in hospital, in the early morning of 2 June 1997, dying in character: no one was with him. My daughter and I flew over to Auckland just hours later. We were the only ones with Mum that first day. My sister was on a plane, flying out from England, and my brother would arrive a day later, as his partner had broken her leg orienteering in the Manawatau.

Fortunately, Dad had gifted his body to medical science so there was to be no funeral. Rather than being sad, Mum was relieved he had finally gone and hoped she might have some peace at last. That night I had panic attacks and heart palpitations at the thought of seeing my sister the next day after such a long period without contact. In tears I told Mum I would change my tickets and go back home early. She wasn't upset with me. I think she almost got it, my fear of my sister.

The next day Robert collected Anna from the airport and brought her to Mum's place. When my sister got out of the car, she said hello to me with a big smile as if nothing had happened between us. I barely glanced at her as I put my suitcase in my brother's car and got in. My daughter ignored her as well. Robert drove us to a hotel near the airport, where we stayed overnight before flying home the next day.

Anna rang me a few months later. She was still in New Zealand. It was the oddest phone call. She spoke as if we were close friends, as if we hadn't been estranged for over 17 years. Mum had gone to look after my brother's partner with her broken leg, as Robert was away for some weeks. My sister said she was very worried about Mum being with Robert's partner and was convinced she was possessed. She went on and on about her behaviour. Evidently Robert's partner was frustrated being unable to work, but it all sounded quite normal to me. I had no idea what to say. In the end I didn't say much. My words were frozen, a scant bit of hope trying to poke through.

Anna then went missing for two years. Robert went to great lengths to try to track her down. I just hoped she had disappeared forever. I had begun therapy by then and had come to the realisation that – for the sake of my mental health – I should not seek any contact with her.

Finally, in July 1999, Anna contacted Mum. In her letter she explained that she moved from London to live in Dad's home village of Tongue for a year. During this time, she finished her first book, *Reading the Mind of the Organisation*.[62] She told Mum, 'I agonised and grieved over Dad for a long, long time. I raged against everyone in the family and hated everyone for a while. I needed to be alone to get many things out of my system. I was a mess.' After a year, she moved to Inverness, about 70 kilometres from Tongue. She told Mum she wouldn't be able to return home to scatter Dad's ashes that November.

I flew over with Natalya to scatter Dad's ashes at Mechanics Bay with Mum and Robert. Mum picked us up from the airport and on the drive to her place she mentioned casually that Anna was actually arriving the next day. I was furious and felt I'd been tricked. I'd been reluctant to go over in the first place as I was packing up my house to move. In two weeks, I would be moving up to Bundaberg, 400 kilometres away from Maleny. Once again, I changed my tickets to avoid seeing Anna. My daughter and I flew home in the morning.

A year later, on Christmas Day 2000, Mum rang me with some shocking news. She was hysterical and weeping as she told me that the police had found Anna crawling around the streets of Napier, New Zealand. Mum thought Anna was in England.

Homeless and penniless, Anna was admitted into the mental health ward of a hospital. A part of me felt vindicated. Decades of shame, for daring to suggest Anna needed help, needed to see a psychiatrist, began to lift. But we had no idea of the hell that lay ahead of us.

What had happened in that year after she had gone to New Zealand to scatter Dad's ashes? Anna owned several houses in London and a car. What happened to them and all her possessions? Mum mentioned once that she had sold everything and spent the money flying around the world, staying in expensive hotels and following the routes Dad took in the flying boats in the late 1930s, especially the Horseshoe Route, a route which circled the Indian Ocean in a semi-circle. It covered Cairo, Basra, Karachi and Singapore, with many stops in between before terminating in Australia. In an email to Susan Lea, Anna mentioned she once stayed at the Cataract Hotel, 'her favourite in all the world'. This is a five-star luxury resort hotel located on the banks of the River Nile in Aswan, Egypt; a week there today would cost about $6000.

By the 1990s, almost all psychiatric hospitals in New Zealand had closed. People with serious mental health problems like my sister were no longer confined to remote mental hospitals, they were in society's own backyard. It was difficult to get someone committed to hospital and if they were it was difficult to keep them there for long enough for treatment to be effective. Warwick Brunton writes in the *Te Ara Encyclopedia* that the transition to a system of community-based services in New Zealand was 'complex and messy', with the rapid growth of multiple agencies lacking coordination.

Patients, families of patients and carers were caught in the cracks, and there were harrowing and occasionally tragic tales of poor communication, missed opportunities, poor support, lack of continuity of care and unsuitable placements.[63]

Anna fell through the cracks. She was failed by the wreckage of deinstitutionalisation, which freed people from antiquated asylums, but all too often left them to fend for themselves without any support.

Over the next seven years she would be sectioned repeatedly into a facility for only a few hours or days and then released. Psychiatrists or CATT would say she presented to them as clear and articulate and they could only make a judgement about how she appeared at the time they interviewed her. A few said her problems were due to family conflict and dysfunction. Family members were never interviewed. As well as Mum and Robert, others called the crisis team numerous times over the years, including the police, neighbours, passers-by, but all to no avail.

Mum was the one most affected as Anna began to live with her most of the time. Even though she was tough – having put up with Dad for 50 years – sometimes she could not handle things. She would run away, go and stay in a motel up at Warkworth, hide from Anna. Although I wanted to help, Mum told me *not* to get involved, even though she often did involve me by ringing or writing letters.

Jay Neugeboren writes about his mentally ill brother in his book *Imagining Robert*. In this harrowing extract published in *The New York Times*, he describes the impact his brother's illness had on his mother:

Thirty years ago, my mother (a registered nurse), in her helplessness, was crying out, again and again – after virtually every hospital visit (and there were often five or six visits a week), 'Someday they'll discover it was all chemical – you'll see! Someday they'll discover it was all chemical.'

But eight years after Robert's first breakdown, when she was sixty-two years old, she left Robert in New York and moved to Florida. 'I've done all I can do,' she said. 'Let the state take over.

You be in charge from now on, Jay – I just can't handle it anymore. Nobody knows. Nobody can know what it's like to have a mentally ill child. Nobody! It's worse than death.' [64]

I don't know what it was like for Mum, it must have been sheer hell, but I didn't cope very well with Mum not coping and felt helpless. I took it out on Mum, writing her a letter in which I explain that I believed Anna was showing symptoms of bipolar disorder with her suicidal tendencies and mood swings, her spending sprees and outbursts of aggression.

I do not want to hear any more of Anna and her dramas. I'm tired of hearing excuses for her behaviour. I've heard them since I was a little girl. I've had a lifetime of people making excuses for the behaviour of bullies including Dad, Robert, Anna and men in my life. I have had enough ... Growing up in NZ, you, Dad and the Lovell family were so 'consumed' with Anna's problems and at times Robert's that I certainly got the message very early on that at least you don't have to worry about Mary. Dad probably wrestled with his own untreated mental demons all his life. What a tragic waste of human potential all around. I cannot help you anymore or listen to the ongoing dramas and crises. It is enough for me to manage my own life, my own problems. Please stand up for yourself and find a doctor who can give you the support you need.

This might sound as if I was being heartless, but I was struggling. At times it felt like life was too much for me. After Natalya had left home to go to university and I was no longer eligible for a sole parent pension, Centrelink suggested I go on an invalid pension due to the crippling migraines I was suffering. That way I could continue to work part-time when I was up to it. (Centrelink was different back then. The people I saw were kind and compassionate.) I was also hauling a suitcase full of trauma. Therapy had helped, for sure, but stuff always remains.

Mum replied: 'Thank you for your letter – understood! I am so sorry I couldn't do more to alleviate the misery. I apologise for errors and omissions.' She went on to say she was exhausted and still recovering after Anna's last visit but felt guilty for letting her go as she certainly was 'not fit and should be getting psychiatric treatment. One cannot make a 50-year-old take advice or see a psychiatrist.'

The more I read these letters now the angrier I get about New Zealand's mental health system and what they put Mum through for so many years, when she was trying to recover from being with Dad and have some peace in her last years. There was no system of services, no support services for parents with sick adult children who refuse treatment. While there obviously need to be rigorous checks and balances in place to ensure that involuntary hospitalisation is in the best interests of the person and society, you shouldn't have to wait for mentally ill people to deteriorate until they are dangerous.

Mum kept ringing me to offload. This is something I scribbled down on a bit of a paper after one of her rants:

Mum rings to give the latest instalment of 'Days of Anna's Life'. It is the second phone call today. I tell her that she has made a career out of worrying about Anna, but she says I'm getting hard, just like my brother. In the first phone call she said she thought Anna may have gone off to kill herself. Perhaps she drowned herself somewhere. She had walked out of Mum's small rental unit early in the morning before the sun came up. She had light clothes on. She disappeared without a word. Her car was sitting outside, broken down again.

Mum said my brother had said it would be a good thing if Anna did kill herself. I thought the same. It would be the end of our ongoing nightmare. No one will help. Not the mental health unit people, the police. No one. And especially not Anna. She is too clever for that. She is a liar and manipulator and so clever with words but the one thing she lacks that could solve the situation is insight. She has none. It is exhausting. My brain can't take any more and I'm the furthest away, sheltering in Queensland over the Tasman. For a very good reason.

There were also fines for dangerous driving as well as parking fines, thousands of dollars I was told, that Mum and Robert paid.

After Dad died, my brother and I were in frequent contact. We worked as a team looking after Mum and Aunt Ola, who'd both made me their power of attorney. I was in charge and did most of the work. I felt I was no longer the black sheep of the family, the outcast. I was a good organiser, efficient and reliable, just as I had been as a child. The good little girl, the helper, always ready to please. I made countless trips across the Tasman, even though Robert only lived about 40 kilometres from Mum and Ola. I'd sometimes stay at his farm if he was away, borrow a mountain bike and go cycling around some of trails he'd established on his property.

After Anna's assault on me at Helensville in 2005, I'd cut off from them all for a few months, as the psychiatrist had suggested, but was soon back helping Mum move into a rental unit. We gave up on Helensville. I found another place in Orewa, around the corner from her old unit and even closer to Aunt Ola. It was right next to the police station, which I thought would be handy for Mum as they knew about Anna's situation.

Over the next few years, I'd hear Mum and Ola talking about the incident at Helensville between themselves or to others: 'The way Anna attacked Mary that day', 'Mary did nothing wrong.' That was a new message for my brain. I'd never heard that before. It was *not* my fault.

On the first trip back after Anna attacked me, I collected my father's old leather suitcase, which Mum had said I could have. It was especially important to me now, as I was deep into my new project: a book on Dad's flying days. I was researching and collecting material, and any items connected to those days. Other family members were giving me stuff. For instance, Robert gave me the illuminated address presented to my grandfather in Tongue in 1908 for introducing motor transport to that remote part of north Scotland.[65] My cousin Rosemarie gave me the silver tea set which had been presented to our grandmother, Rebecca Garden, at the same time as the address. My cousin Derek, the son of Dad's sister, May, gave a pump he reckoned was used to pump up the tyres on *Kia Ora*, Dad's plane, and Derek's sister Jenny gave me a photo album that had belonged to my grandfather. Everyone was so excited that at last someone was going to tell Dad's amazing story.

I'd also been writing lots of feature articles on Dad's flying years, including stories of him being fined for giving joyrides on Sunday and being the first to land a plane on Stewarts Island. They were snapped up by magazines and newspapers, not only in New Zealand but also in Australia, Scotland, South Africa and even Florida. It seemed as though readers could not get enough of my odd, eccentric father, the unsung hero of aviation.

CHAPTER 12

Saving my Sister's Life

Occasionally Anna would find work such as cleaning or fruit picking. These jobs never lasted long, but they gave Mum a short reprieve. In 2006, Anna went up north to the Bay of Islands to try to find work there. I was in New Zealand helping Mum when I received a call from the owner of a backpacker hostel to come and get Anna as she clearly needed psychiatric treatment. He said she was putting the safety of visitors at risk. He gave me the phone numbers of other places where she had worked. All the stories were similar: leaving pots of food on the stove unattended, slamming doors and staring into space for long periods.

I did nothing. It would have been a waste of time and I would have been putting my safety at risk. Not only was my sister in denial – the lack of insight is itself a symptom of mental illness – but the mental health system had failed her so many times before; psychiatrists and mental health workers kept letting her down. They did not want to hear what we had to say, they were not concerned about the impact of Anna's illness on us. We were treated with disdain; they only wanted to hear my sister's version of events. In psychiatry you only get a 'version' of the person, based on what they say, but didn't they see all the red flags?

The nightmare began to end in January 2007 when Mum got bowel cancer and I flew over again to help. Anna moved out of Mum's unit and went to stay with Aunt Ola. Mum wanted me close by as she was frightened and not coping.

Mum's operation on her bowel was successful but it was decided she needed to be in a nursing home because she was beginning to show signs of dementia. All the stress from Anna probably contributed: research shows that 'stress could play a role in dementia development but is unlikely to be the only factor that causes the condition'.[66] After checking out all the options in the area, I found Milton Court, just around the corner from Ola's. It was a beautiful place, one street back from the beach, a restored character-filled house with courtyard gardens that had large established trees, and the staff seemed friendly and caring. I spent several days packing up Mum's lifetime of possessions, weeping most of the time. It was a truly harrowing time. At night I would have panic attacks, thinking Anna would turn up at the unit and attack or kill me.

When I visited Mum in the nursing home she would be wailing, wanting to go home to her own place, asking where all her things were, and why I had put her there. I had second thoughts. Maybe I should have sold up and moved to New Zealand and looked after Mum myself, and been close to Ola, too.

Having Anna staying with Ola, now legally blind and very deaf, was a disastrous decision. Ola could not cope and her health was deteriorating with Anna's erratic and sometimes frightening behaviour. After Ola told me Anna had asked her for $1000 so she could go back to England and that she was considering giving it to her as it was the only way to get her to leave, I decided to write Anna a letter. She had to pack up her things and leave ASAP, I wrote, or I would get the authorities involved. I explained that it was a total waste of time giving her money, because of her compulsive spending, and that this was a symptom of bipolar illness, which I believed she had. I pointed out that in recent months when she'd been doing some strawberry picking, she had spent money on Bibles, religious items, clothing, presents, expensive wool to make jumpers, numerous swimming costumes, etc. 'Yet you have not contributed anything towards living expenses at Ola's. Now you've resorted to asking Ola for money.' I told her this was unacceptable and elder abuse.

'A symptom of your illness is lying,' I wrote, and recounted how she had lied to the police and mental health team about her assault on me at Helensville. 'Goodness knows what you've told psychiatrists over the years. There is only ONE solution. You need to get treatment.' I explained that the side effects of medications for bipolar were minor compared to the damage done to herself and others without medication. I ended the letter with, 'We all love you, but will not tolerate your abuse anymore.'

I left the letter under the windscreen wiper of Mum's car, which we had let Anna use, along with some material I'd sourced on bipolar disorder. Later that day, Anna rang to say she had left Ola's and although she didn't agree with everything I wrote in the letter she agreed with some of the things. That sounded like a bit of a breakthrough.

A few weeks later, Ola woke up to find Anna standing at the end of her bed, all the lights in the house turned on. Ola was terrified and distressed. Although Anna no longer had her own key, she had managed to retrieve a Chubb key which was meant to be used for access only by emergency services. Two of my cousins then became involved and, along with Robert, we wrote a joint letter to the local mental health clinic that had seen Anna over the years; she even had a case manager there. We gave the clinic a list of conditions we thought Anna should follow, such as ringing Ola before visiting, and said that if Anna was unable to abide by these rules, we would have no option but to go to the police and take out a 'No Trespass' order. We hoped this letter would compel them to help her.

Although I thought Mum was now safe in her nursing home, Anna begged her for $650 for repairs to her car, to which she agreed, and I reluctantly deposited the money into Anna's account. Later, the police told me that Anna spent two nights wandering around the streets of Orewa as she had nowhere to sleep while the car was being fixed.

It got worse. I'd only just walked in the gate of the nursing home one day when the manager approached me to say Anna had been causing problems. She had been sneaking into the home and stealing food. My mother had also been woken up several times very early in the morning, with Anna leaning over the bed peering at her.

If you are homeless and mentally unwell and have no money you have no option but to steal. My head was in a spin by this latest development. Would this nightmare ever end? Homeless people can become so incapacitated by their mental illness they cannot recognise their own impairment or meet basic needs.

I walked around Orewa looking for Anna until I saw Mum's little old grey car parked near the beachfront. I crept up to the car as I didn't want her taking off if she saw me. Anna was sitting in the front seat, huddled up, reading some scrunched up pieces of paper – the stuff on bipolar disorder I'd left under the windscreen wipers. She looked unwell, had lost weight and was dishevelled. The car was crammed with stuff, mostly plastic bags of clothes, a dirty pillow and a large piece of pink insulation stuffed in the back seat, which presumably she slept on. My sister had become a bag lady.

My heart ached and I felt sick and unutterably sad. How had she become so broken? I knew I had to help her. That had been my job for as long as I could remember. When I tentatively knocked on the window she didn't lash out and seemed relieved to see me. We chatted for a while, and she said she hadn't eaten properly for weeks. I suspected from the way she smelled she hadn't bathed properly either. She said she wanted to go on medication as she was sure she had bipolar. She even agreed to go with me to Work and Income

(WINZ), the equivalent of Australia's Centrelink, to apply for a sickness benefit.

Anna rang the local mental health clinic and made an appointment to see a psychiatrist the next day. Surprisingly, she asked if I would be able to go with her, talk to them separately if I wanted to! When I agreed, she said, 'You are an absolute angel.'

I couldn't believe what was happening. It seemed to be a miracle. I arranged somewhere for her to stay that night, and gave her money for food and petrol, and we arranged to meet the next morning. She gave me a bag of dirty clothes to wash. Back at Aunt Ola's, I tipped the bag into the washtub. Several pairs of Anna's panties fell out. They were encrusted with faeces and stained with urine. Mum had complained about Anna's personal hygiene but I'd never believed her until then.

The next morning, as soon as I met up with Anna, my heart sank. Her mood had changed from the previous day, and she had an arrogant air about her. The lady we spoke to at WINZ was friendly and sympathetic, and pointed out that Anna had lodged several applications for benefits previously but cancelled them. She tried to persuade Anna to go through with it this time. Anna said she would have to think about it.

We then went to her appointment at the mental health clinic. After it was finished, Anna walked straight out the entrance door without even looking at me. The psychiatrist and Anna's case manager came out and when I approached them, they said they would not talk to me – on Anna's instructions. I was flabbergasted. I told them Anna was living in our mother's car, stealing food from the nursing home, had no money and refused to go on sickness benefits. They were dismissive of my concerns and said several times it was my sister's choice. They added that if there were issues in the community, then the community should report these things. I said I couldn't keep giving her money. They both just smiled at me and walked away.

I was fucking furious. I still am now, thinking about this. Wasn't I part of the community? Didn't they have a legal and ethical obligation to step in and help vulnerable people who couldn't act for themselves?

The psychiatrist had given Anna a prescription for Seroquel, a medication used to treat conditions such as schizophrenia and bipolar disorder. At least Anna had told them she thought she might be bipolar and agreed to take medication. That was a breakthrough. After procuring the medicine, I organised for her to stay in a cabin at a caravan park at Warkworth for a few days.

Still enraged at the way I'd been treated – and knowing the rest of the family had been treated like that for seven years – that night I googled for help. I wanted to lodge a complaint somehow. I stumbled across the site of the New Zealand Health & Disability Commission and found an online complaint form. I filled it out and hit 'send'. In the complaint I said I wanted an apology from the psychiatrist and case manager for the way they treated me and that in future my brother and I want to be able to provide relevant information to the team caring for my sister. 'We want to be heard and believed.'

I wrote that we could no longer afford to support Anna and added that we had already given her thousands of dollars over these past years. As Anna was now under the care of the mental health team and they clearly did not want us involved, they would have to look after her. She needed housing and care, as she had no money. She needed a stable environment and regular food. Was she to go back to living in her car and stealing food?

I went home to Australia for a few weeks, thinking I would never hear back from them. At the time I was doing postgraduate studies, which would eventually lead to a PhD in journalism, but I was beginning to cave in from all the stress and took leave for a semester.

On the next trip over to New Zealand, Natalya, who was now 24, came with me. She was easy company and wanted a holiday and to spend some time with her grandmother and Aunt Ola, whom she was very fond of. Same old routine. Fly to Auckland. Arrive early afternoon. Grab a cheap rental car, usually from Apex, head north towards the city, sometimes take a wrong turn and waste a while driving in circles, drive over the harbour bridge and then up the highway to Orewa, past North Shore Hospital, where I'd been spending quite a bit of time lately. I never felt excited, never felt nostalgic. New Zealand never felt like home. Going over the ditch was just something I had to do. My duty.

Before I left Australia, I was surprised to receive a call from the Health & Disability Commission. I was told I'd been assigned an advocate who would have a meeting with me the day after I arrived. Once in New Zealand I rang the advocate who suggested we meet at the hospital, where Mum was having a temporary ileostomy bag removed.

The advocate was warm and friendly and asked what outcome I wanted. For the first time it felt like I was being listened to and the family's concerns were acknowledged. Anna had another appointment at the mental health clinic and it was arranged that a new psychiatrist would see her and section her. However, she never turned up for the appointment. I'm not sure how this happened, but Anna somehow got wind that she might be sectioned and took off in Mum's car.

The new psychiatrist was worried and concerned for Anna's safety. Robert was too. I decided to be a detective and track Anna down. I've still got the small pieces of paper I scribbled on at that time. I searched all over Orewa, asking about her at various places. I discovered that the previous week she had worked cleaning at a local motel but was sacked after three days because of 'lack of hygiene'. They paid her $163. I popped into Pillows Backpackers, a local hostel where I knew Anna occasionally stayed. The owner said Anna had mentioned a few weeks ago she was thinking of going fruit picking.

I was able to form a timeline of her movements: around 7 am she was seen walking to Mum's (she was out of hospital by then and back at Milton Court), and then went to Ola's about 10 am. She told them both that they wouldn't see her for a very long time. I presume she then drove away from Orewa, as nobody had seen her since. I went to the police and filed a missing person's report and a detective was assigned.

For hours I sat on Aunt Ola's double bed, with its old-fashioned quilted cover with a pattern of small red, pink and orange roses, and went through the phone directory methodically, ringing orchards, backpackers and homestays on the landline phone on the bedside table. Eventually, I got lucky. The manager of Bunkdown Lodge, a backpacker hostel in Whangārei, about 130 kilometres north of Orewa, told me Anna had stayed there one night (using some of the money I'd given her, presumably) and had mentioned going to a homestay at Parua Bay, about 21 kilometres from Whangarei. The detective told me *I* should have been a detective. Robert did too.

Whangarei was in Northland, a different jurisdiction to Orewa with regards to mental health services. The psychiatrist told me the only option was for me to go up there, talk to Anna and try to persuade her to come back to the Auckland region. At first I said no, as I feared Anna would turn on me, plus I was exhausted from visiting Mum and organising things for Ola. Robert urged me to go; he was too busy with work, he said. Then I relented. Thankfully, Natalya said she would come with me to do the driving and be a support person.

We were surprised to see where Anna was staying. It was a beautiful white wooden house with sea views. We knocked at the door and the owner answered and showed us a side veranda where Anna was sitting at a table. She seemed surprised to see us. But she was friendly, asking, 'What are you doing here?' I said we were worried about her as she had missed her mental health appointment at the clinic. It was if a switch had been flicked. She went berserk. She stood up and started yelling. 'Fuck off', she screamed, 'fuck off you fucking cunts,' and lunged towards me.

We ran back to the car and drove away. I rang the local police and they said they would go out and see her. We were in shock and too shaken to drive all the way back to Orewa, so decided to break the trip and stay somewhere overnight. On the way, the police rang and said they had seen my sister, deduced that she clearly needed help and they had contacted CATT. Neither Natalya nor I slept well that night.

The next day, a woman from CATT rang to tell me they'd managed to have a long talk to Anna. 'She doesn't like you, does she!' she commented. She wanted me to know that the team did not believe Anna was in any danger, to herself or others. She was clear and *very* articulate. However, she had agreed to be driven down to Orewa.

I felt like punching her down the phone.

Luckily the psychiatrist assigned by the Health and Disability Commission had some common sense. Anna was to be sectioned for a lengthy period and at last receive the treatment she needed. The psychiatrist told me I'd saved Anna's life and Robert agreed. Who knows if this is true, but it was clear Anna had reached the stage where she was increasingly unable to care for herself.

In an email to her friend Susan Lea in 2017, Anna wrote that she once lived in her car for three months and it was hell. It was hell for us, too, especially for Mum and Ola.

New Zealand's 2018 Government Inquiry into Mental Health and Addiction found that a significant area of dissatisfaction for many families was their experience of marginalisation and frustration in trying to access services, and of frequent exclusion from communication.[67] This was often despite their day-to-day role in providing support and their understanding of their family member's needs and history. Their views were ignored, treated indifferently or given limited credence, which contributed to increased distress, anger and worry for their loved ones.

Problems of access, wait times and quality were reported all over the country. Gaps in services, limited therapies, a system that is hard to navigate, variable quality and shabby facilities added up to a gloomy picture of a system failing to meet the needs of many people.

A significant number of submissions from families told of being treated with contempt or indifference. They had been kept in the dark and excluded from treatment and discharge planning, based on misconceived privacy concerns, even though they were the ones there for the long haul. This was our story.

What really bothered me was that Anna had access to anything we wrote or said but we had no access to what she said or came up with. Soon after Anna was sectioned, a psychiatrist wrote to me and asked if I could give him my recollection of some of Anna's history. After providing a detailed account, he replied that this was 'most valuable information, and very personal' and he hoped it did not distress me writing it. He said he'd commit it to memory rather than include it in Anna's notes (which she might request at some stage). 'It naturally makes things more complicated! We have a series of "grand rounds" to discuss complex clients. I think I will convene an exceptional one to discuss your sister.'

Some of Mum's neighbours later told me they used to hear my sister shouting and screaming, slamming doors and smashing things and Mum weeping. On more than one occasion they had rung the police or CATT, to no avail. I was enraged to hear this. My mother had endured decades of emotional, physical and financial abuse from Dad and then she had to put up with the same from my sister. A repeat performance, just as Mum had feared.

At least Mum was now safe, and Aunt Ola too. Not me, though. Although Susan Lea later told me, 'It was really important you rescued Anna. Believe me, Anna deserved to be rescued,' after what she would do in the years to come I have sometimes thought it would have been better to have just let her go. Just disappear in Mum's little car, along with her batt of pink insulation stuffed in the back seat, mouldy pillow, plastic bags of dirty clothes shoved in the boot and dirty undies squeezed behind the seats. She could have died up in Northland somewhere: that would have saved me a lot of suffering.

CHAPTER 13

Temporary Truce

For about ten years after the intervention, I was on friendly terms with Anna, although the first few years were a bit rocky, as she harboured resentment about what I had done, having her sectioned. In one email she said, 'the official psychiatric view now is that I should never have been put into Taharoto' and she could sue over it with a good chance of winning. 'Needless to say, I have no intention of doing any such thing as suing because I am not that kind of person, as they knew when they told me.'

Robert was incredulous. 'Shit, I'm worried and amazed Anna thinks like that. She should be praising you for getting her out of her mess ... Shit, I can't believe Anna.' I was with him on this. We were the ones who felt like suing the New Zealand mental health system for their ineptitude, the hell they put us through for not intervening earlier.

For three years after the intervention Anna worked at odd jobs, including strawberry picking, and she returned to the UK several times. Robert and I were worried: she had no regular job, no permanent place to stay, and she told me before her last trip that there was nothing wrong with her and she didn't need medication.

Once she arrived in London, she had a hellish time. She worked for a while and then after 18 months of fruitless searching for another job, she considered coming back to Orewa, but only on the condition Robert gave her a loan for a car. He was reluctant, told her cars were 'bloody expensive' and that 'the cheap ones cost lots to run or will let you down'. He said he'd pay her airfare and some living costs until things worked out, and suggested income support from WINZ until she got a job. She was very disappointed, as a 'car was the key to the whole thing' and 'I can't go to WINZ if I know of a job I can get and do. It's too dishonest.'

I made it clear to her that if she returned, under no circumstances could she go back and live with Aunt Ola, who was now 96. I urged her to go back on medication: did she remember how good she felt while taking it, how well she functioned, and that she herself had said she feared becoming hypermanic again?

I reminded Robert that we should not forget how she had all those mental health professionals, including psychiatrists, wrapped around her fingers for years, as she knew all the lingo. 'It is more than likely that one loony psychiatrist has told her there's nothing wrong with her, and she should not have been sectioned. What a pity she didn't stay under the care of that psychiatrist who persuaded me to go to Whangarei.'

At one point it got too much for me. I was still looking out for Ola and organising things for her, mostly at a distance from Australia, even though she had other nieces and nephews. I told Robert I had blocked Anna's email address because of her bizarre and hysterical emails, in which she accused me of lying, being aggressive and over the top. I said they caused me so much distress and I needed to look after myself. 'I will not communicate with her while she is in denial of having a mental illness (and there's no shame in that) and while she has no remorse or insight into her past behaviour that caused so much havoc in our lives.'

Then Anna told Robert she had decided not to return to New Zealand, as 'we need to clear the air after wrangles with you and quite absurd wrangles with Mary', and added, 'It is a shame I will not see Mum and Aunt Ola again.' Robert said this was a pity but it was her decision and he hoped she was happy over there. 'I know it has always been your first-choice country.' I unblocked her email address and tried to placate her:

> I know you are angry at me for co-operating with the doctor who arranged your involuntary admission to hospital a few years ago. I regret having had to commit you, and I hope you will forgive me for the distress it caused you at the time. But it was done with the best of intentions because I care about you, and felt I had no other choice. At the time you were homeless, living in your car, had no job, and were not eating or sleeping properly. We were all very concerned about your welfare, including Robert and the doctor who persuaded me to go to Whangarei. If I was in a similar situation again, I would probably do the same thing but would handle things differently and be less fearful.

This was the response:

> I think one o0f the [problems with our communicaTION IS THAT YOU GET SOME WRONG STRANGE IDEAS. i HAVE neveR RESISTED THE MEDICATION and, as a reszult, have ALWAYAS been trusted with self mediaction while others who have been on medication longer than myself have been refused ... The problem with sectioning was that my case was not swerious enough for hospitalisation, given the brutality of it. They should have arranged commmumity care instead, wherer you still have a psichiatruist, social worker, OT, psychiatric nurse, psychotherapist, but you are in sheletered accommodation.

Anna returned to Orewa, did a few odd jobs while staying mostly at Pillows Backpackers, and then to the surprise of everyone, in March 2011, scored a job in Wellington working in the publishing division of the Ministry of Culture and Heritage. Her salary would be over $100,000 per year. We were incredulous. Mum and Ola were thrilled for her. Just days before Anna left to go to Wellington, Ola had a stroke. She died just two weeks later. Natalya flew over with me and we spent days sitting with Ola, lying on her bed next to her, massaging her feet. I was there early on the morning when she took her last breath, after I had whispered, 'You can go now.' And she did. She had almost turned 98 and I'd kept my promise to her of keeping her out of a nursing home.

Anna stayed in her new job for four years before being made redundant. 'It was fascinating to be up so close to bureaucracy. I couldn't really handle it very well,' she wrote to Susan Lea. In a later email she said the people in the public sector she worked in were 'cretins' and couldn't make things happen. While in Wellington, Anna occasionally flew up to see Mum and kept me posted on how she was, and let me know if there was anything Mum needed. I also arranged funds from Mum's account to be transferred to Anna, to help her buy a small house in Wellington.

Uncle Brian, Mum's brother, died in August 2012. In 2006, Aunt Alice and Uncle Brian bought a house in Nelson but kept their home in Westport where'd they brought up their six children (my only cousins on Mum's side). Nelson is at the top of the South Island on the eastern shores of Tasman Bay and is one of the sunniest places in New Zealand. It is about 220 kilometres from Westport, and they used to spend time in both places. Brian went into a rest home for his last few years and Alice emailed to say that he'd caught norovirus at the rest home, which he wasn't strong enough to fight: 'We are all pleased he will not have to endure any more of old age problems as he has been very miserable.'

Then, in October 2012, we received news that Mum was not well. Her doctor said she would not last the weekend. I flew over and Anna came up from Wellington. I stayed at a motel around the corner from the nursing home, Milton Court, right near the beach, so I could lie in bed and hear the gentle waves and breathe and smell the salt air.

Anna went back to her old haunt, Pillows Backpackers, down the northern end of Orewa. We took turns to sit with Mum. We never ate together but would text to say when we would be leaving Mum as we wanted someone with her most of the time.

This was the first time I had seen Anna since Whangarei, so I was a little on edge. I was nervous in much the same way I used to be around Dad when I visited him. The fear never went away, around either of them. However, we seemed to be getting on and I thought this might be the perfect time to clear things between us.

One morning, I took the plunge and suggested we go and get coffee. While we sat in the café having coffee and cake, and chatting about Mum, I brought up the incident at Helensville. I hoped she would be remorseful. Oftentimes, all victims want is a heartfelt genuine apology. But she laughed. 'Oh that! You traumatised me; you humiliated me in front of Mum and Aunt Ola.' I felt crushed. I didn't say anything. There was no point.

Why did Anna have no insight into her abuse of me? She did towards others. In a letter to Mum from Scotland in 1999, she regrets things she's said: 'I was sorry about some of the things I had said to you (about both of you).' And she admitted to Susan Lea that her letters were insane and revolting. Why did she have a brick wall as far as I was concerned?

Mum held on for two more weeks. She knew she was dying but would not let go, even though we all had said goodbye. Was she waiting for someone else? Possibly her son, Michael, whom we did not know about then but soon would. The doctor was astonished. At one stage he shook his head and said, 'What a tough old bird.' Even in those last years, when you think you could at last let go of things, not once did Mum mention that she had another son.

When Mum could no longer speak, I asked her if she wanted some brandy. She nodded furiously. She'd always loved a brandy at the end of each day, and during the Anna troubles would sometimes have one earlier. I took off to the shop and bought a bottle, and back at Milton Court one of the staff gave me a syringe so I could squirt quite a few shots of brandy into Mum's mouth. Her eyes twinkled and her face lit up as if in ecstasy. I've got photos to prove it. Anna and I drank some too.

She was 95. The five years at Milton Court had been happy ones for her, perhaps her happiest for many years. Now they were all gone: Ola, Brian and Mum, within 18 months of each other. Aunt Margaret had died in 1986.

When I got back to Australia, I sent an email to Anna. 'Thanks for last week, feeling sad that Mum has gone but she really did have a 'good' death. Xxx' She replied, 'I feel a lot better about her death because I spent that time with her. She deserved to have us hanging round like that. Send me your address so I can send you your jumper (soon).' Anna had been knitting me a jumper – she had always liked knitting.

When I told a second cousin about Mum's death he said, 'They don't make Westcoasters like that anymore. Really loved your mum's wit and sense of humour. When she and Ola were in form, they made a formidable pair. I miss that and often think of them both.'

I missed them both deeply for years. I sometimes had to stop my car to weep when memories came floating past.

During the years of looking after Mum and Ola, I was still working for our family bicycle business and had unexpectedly gone back to university. In 2007, I had enrolled at the University of the Sunshine Coast to do a single course on editing, as I thought it would help with my freelance writing. To my surprise, I obtained a High Distinction and the lecturer said I should aim for a Masters. I'd never considered that, but my ego got the better of me and I kept going. Over the next few years, I completed a postgraduate certificate and diploma in journalism. I did far more work than was needed, as I was driven to get high marks.

I wasn't particularly enthusiastic about academia, finding some of it excruciatingly boring, but a part of me was determined to finish.

Having given up on a Masters degree in 1972 I felt I'd failed. It may sound strange, but I also wanted to prove my brain was not too damaged from everything I'd been through, especially in India. Anna was very supportive, as she often said doing her PhD was one of the highlights of her life. She told me it was good I was doing well in my courses. She said she never told Mum and Dad how well she was doing at MIT. 'When I finally finished my PhD and told them they said, "Oh yes, we expected you to." No joy there.'

Neither Mum nor Dad encouraged us to go to university and they never seemed enthusiastic if we received high marks. Mum showed no interest at all in my return to university. Instead of doing a Masters, I was propelled into a PhD in journalism and won a scholarship. At the time Anna wrote: 'Good news about the PhD. It's a long haul, isn't it.'

I'd given up on the idea of writing a book on Dad, although I'd still write the occasional article or receive an email from someone who'd give me some information about Dad's flying days, which I'd share with Anna. She was thrilled to receive these. 'What bliss,' she once said.

While in Wellington, Anna wrote her second book, *The Roles of Organisation Development*, which was published in 2015 by Gower Publishing.[68] Lotte Bailyn from the Sloan School of Management in the United States, called my sister 'a gifted OD consultant' and said the book was 'full of keen psychological insights'. Susan Lea congratulated her on the book and warned her about 'zombies'. Ordinary people, like me, I presume. Susan wrote that zombies are a huge problem. 'So out to lunch. Cannot compute, track or engage in critical thinking of any kind. It's all been planned and continues to be generated moment by moment from tv to idiot teaching, to relations solely with one's cell phone. People! 99% couldn't read your book, to be honest.'

My sister replied: 'I hope you are wrong about the 99%! Actually, I handed copies out to a whole lot of people on the Church group I was in for a course and only three of them can read it. That is where the zombies start from.'

In 2013, I completed my PhD; it took less than three years. My thesis was titled 'Blogging in the mainstream: Australian journalist-blogs and public deliberation'. It was hugely stressful. Cycling saved me. Most mornings I'd jump on my bike just as the sun was rising and go for a ride to destress my brain and relax.

In early 2006, I'd moved back down to the Sunshine Coast hinterland to be closer to my son and be nearer to Brisbane Airport, as I was making so many trips over to New Zealand to be with Aunt Ola and Mum. It was flat in the Bundaberg Region, with no hills. Now I was back among the lushness, hills and rainforest trails, with the majestic Glasshouse Mountains nearby and steep hills to pedal up and down.

I was glad when the PhD was finished and a part of me regretted the years I had spent back at university. Most of the courses were as boring and as useless as those I'd done at Waikato University in the 1960s. Nothing much came out of a PhD except the realisation that if I could write a 60,000-word thesis, then I damn well could finish the book on Dad.

Susan told Anna she was excited about my book project about our father, 'the unknown Charles Lindberg', and said she was glad she got to meet him. 'Your dad deserves as much fame as Lindy got.' She added, 'Mary looks quite a bit like your mother, at least based on my memories of your mother.'

At the end of 2015, Anna moved to Waiwera, six kilometres north of Orewa, to be closer to Robert. She bought an apartment overlooking the Waiwera estuary. The Waiwera Thermal Hot Pools, first established in 1848, were a favourite haunt of mine during all the years I flew over the ditch to help Mum and Ola. I'd try to go every day, swim laps, and soak in one of the hotter pools.

Although Anna set up a website advertising 'bespoke organisational consulting services', I don't think she ever got a contract. However, she soon got a part-time job working at Piri Pono, an innovative peer-led, acute residential mental health facility in Silverdale, only about 10 kilometres from where Anna lived. 'Piri pono' is a Māori term meaning to be loyal, faithful and devoted. This facility established in 2013 provides a community-based alternative to hospital admission for people experiencing acute mental health conditions. They are able to stay ten days, and are called guests, not patients or clients. Such a place could have been ideal for Anna during those difficult years before we resorted to having her sectioned in 2007. A core element of Piri Pono's therapeutic approach is to employ support staff and registered nurses who have lived experience of mental health conditions.[69]

In 2016, she told Susan the job suited her somehow, even though she sometimes worked long hours and night shifts. The latter she hated, as there was a lot of cleaning and 'trying to rescue people who can't sleep'. When she got home, she slept for three hours, then got up for three hours and then slept again. 'Am still a bit addled even after that.' She mentioned that they 'have tonnes of suicidal and self-harming people'.

In an email in June 2017, Robert told me she has settled into her new home and has just had another book published, *Organizational Change in Practice: The Eight Deadly Sins preventing effective change*.[70] He said she got $5 per book sold. She wrote it during night shifts. I asked him what the book was about, adding, 'Hope it's more readable than the last one!', referring to her first book, *Reading the Mind of the Organisation*. Robert said it was along the same lines but had only glimpsed it.

Aunt Ola gave me her signed copy of *Reading the Mind of the Organisation*. I don't think anyone in the family read it. Mum and Ola rolled their eyes and were dismissive about it. Over the years, I've wanted to burn it many times, but it's still here. I glanced at it occasionally but found it impossible to read not only because I had no interest in the subject but also because anything associated with my sister stung me.

Dr Jean Bartunek of Boston College reviewed *Organizational Change in Practice* for the journal *Organisational Studies*.

> The author definitely has an axe to grind against large consulting firms and is upfront about it. There are political purposes, in a sense, to denigrate such firms and approaches to consulting often practised by them. The writing is full of evocative language. Reading the book was quite refreshing, from an academic perspective. If I belonged to one of the large consulting firms, the reading would not be quite so refreshing ...
>
> I learned from Garden's language and imagery about the morality of organisational change. There is something important in her use of the term 'deadly sins' to describe what consultants often do. Deadly sins are transgressions that are fatal to spiritual progress ... the fact that there are eight deadly sins of organisational change is a very strong claim about the immorality of many organisational consultants and about how destructive their work is for clients ...[71]

Deadly sins? She must be a Christian and believe in the Bible, like Anna, like Dad!

Dad also had an axe to grind against an organisation – TEAL. He used to wave his fist and say, 'those bastards up there'. Anna is her father's daughter in more ways than one: the chip on the shoulder, conservative Christianity, holding things inside, being loose with the truth and exaggerating.

Over the next few years, Anna wrote three more books, all on her field of interest, the psychology of business and organisations. The first was *Burnout: The effect of Jungian Type*, published in 2018.[72] The next that same year was *How to Resolve Conflict in Organizations: The power of people models and procedure.*[73] *Burnout and the Mobilisation of Energy* was published in 2021.[74]

I've always pooh-poohed these books as they looked very uninteresting to me, but considering just years before she was living in a car and stealing food from the Milton Court nursing home, it was quite an achievement. How did she write so quickly?

Unlike her other books, which were all published by reputable publishers, her book *Burnout and the Mobilisation of Energy* was published by vanity publisher, Austin Macauley. (Vanity publishing is where authors pay for their books to be published.) On their website they proclaim 'Annamaria Garden's Book Gets a Noteworthy Review by NZ Booklovers',[75] but the review is by Chris Reed of Austin Macauley Publishers.

In 2021, a revealing interview[76] was featured in the local paper *Hibiscus Matters* on Anna's book *Burnout and the Mobilisation of Energy*. Anna said that the book came from 40 years of her own experience of burnout, together with her PhD experience, consulting work and clinical interviews in London and the United States. She explained, 'After my career, I wanted to do something completely different. It's fabulous. We work with a wide range of people, some of whom need a great deal of care.'

Forty years of her own experience of burnout? I think that's a typo, unless Anna was exaggerating: she spent 20 years in the UK and the US. At the time the article was published I only glanced at it and thought *what an imposter*. When I read it now, I see an aspect of Anna I never knew. She did have a compassionate and caring side and enjoyed helping people in real need. After her own struggles, she would have felt a real kinship with the people there. Dad also had a caring side. Here is something I wrote about him in that regard in *Sundowner of the Skies*:

> But there was something I admired about him – he had a strong sense of injustice which he must have inherited from Rebecca [his mother]. For example, there was a man and his overweight son who lived down the road in a shed on an overgrown property. They were shunned by the neighbourhood who thought they were weird or mad, and they smelt terribly. But Dad used to take them things such as clothing and food, and sometimes he'd take

me with him. We would ride our bikes to school but the boy, who we would call 'fatso', used to walk. My father was the only person in Ōtūmoetai who would pick him up to give him a lift, but he'd leave the windows of the car down for hours afterwards to let the smell out. He never seemed to care what people thought of him.

An old school friend of Robert's emailed me after reading my book. He said he was sorry to hear my home life wasn't a happy one. He remembered this family living in the shed and said the boy, whose name was Vernon, was very bright at school. 'He'd wander around with a shot gun he had made, or more perhaps like an old-style musket,' he said, which was powered by 'a Triple Happy firecracker that when exploded would shoot out a bunch of nails and paper he had forced down the barrel'. He went on to explain that none of them thought this gun would work but Vernon shot a bird one day from quite a distance and killed it. They certainly respected him after that.

I think Dad would have been really proud of Anna for the work she did at Piri Pono, much prouder than of her success in the worlds of academia and business consulting, where she earned a lot of money and accolades. However, Anna never mentioned in this interview, or any other, that she herself needed a great deal of care and spent time in a mental health facility. She could not write anything for many years. She did not mention that for almost 20 years she had no career, no regular job, and for about seven years lived mostly off Mum until Mum was in such dire straits that we had to sell her unit and move her into a rental property. She kept this part of her life hidden. When Dad became a famous pioneer aviator, he also kept large bits of his life hidden. He never told the press his parents were separated (the shame!) or that his father was violent and died of chronic alcoholism.

Those years were happy ones for Anna. Robert said she was 'really pleasant to catch up with and discuss politics or whatever'. She wrote to her friend that she loved solitude, and she needed 'masses of alone time, masses of music, the sea and a spiritual life'. She admitted she needed exercise and was trying to work out what else she needed. 'Ultimately, I don't think I will be bipolar if I work out my set of needs.' I discovered her music tastes: classical music, including Beethoven, Bach and Mozart; Leonard Cohen, Bob Dylan, Joan Baez, Emmy Lou Harris, the Travelling Wilburys and Tom Petty. She often listened to Christian radio and Christian music on YouTube.

Unlike Mum and me, Anna did not read widely. In all the email exchanges with Susan Lea there is no mention of any books except the Bible and *Talking with Angels* by Gitta Mallasz, which Anna had sent Susan. This is a story of four young Hungarians during World War II who claimed they were channelling messages from the angels. Susan and Anna would recommend articles to each other by conspiracy theorists, such as Jon Rappoport, who denies climate change, germs and the efficacy of vaccines.

Mum and I were avid readers and read a wide range of fiction and non-fiction books, and kept up with new releases. We would share reviews of books published in newspapers and magazines. Reading had been Mum's escape from Dad. When I was a child, she seemed to be different from other mothers in that she would send away for magazines such as *The Economist* and *The New Yorker*, and had no time for *Women's Weekly* and such that Aunt Ola would buy.

Anna and Susan often chatted about politics in New Zealand, the UK, America and Turkey. Anna was a supporter of Brexit: she believed 'leaving the EU would be good for the UK financially and in terms of the spirit of the country. The real problem is the aristocracy including the wealthy royals and the "City" (which runs the UK).' She said she watched the Brexit news daily and found it fascinating after living in the UK for 20 years.

Although Robert reckoned Anna hated Donald Trump, for a few years she supported him. In 2015 she told Susan she was fascinated by him. 'He is a bit of a na-na but I hope he does well and changes the conversation. I am always looking for a radical to change the terms of political debate and get some solutions moving.' A year later she wrote that his detractors 'hardly ever have the facts straight'. Hilary Clinton, she believed 'would be HOPELESS' at managing the global issues. In September 2016, she hoped he'd win the election. 'The news on the radio said that Trump is beating Hilary in the polls. How exciting. Is it true?'

When Susan Lea first contacted me in 2015, I told her I was trying to make space in my life to write Dad's story, to which she replied, 'You are quite a journalist, and with your insights you are perfect for writing Oscar's story,' repeating her view that, 'he is the Charles Lindberg we never heard about'. In July 2016, Susan asked Anna, 'Did Mary ever write that book on your dad? Needs to be done. Great story', to which Anna replied, 'She has all the raw materials for it but I doubt if she would hand them over. I'd do it if I could.'

By September 2017, I was on the final leg of *Sundowner of the Skies*. It was being edited before being submitted to publishers. I'd decided to go to Tauranga for Christmas and asked Anna if she would like to come too; we could spend time with our cousin Margaret MacColl and her daughter Gillian; Alistair Barclay, the son of our old family doctor; and Alys Ingrid Wicksteed, the daughter of Mary Revfeim, who'd been Mum's close friend. It would be my first visit to Tauranga since 1976, when I'd popped down to see Mum and Dad after I'd flown back from India, and before I became a Rajneesh sannyasin. Anna was thrilled at the prospect. A few days later I freaked out: what was I thinking? I couldn't spend time with Anna. I told her I'd changed my mind and I wanted to go by myself. I explained that I'd been rereading letters: Mum's letters to me and Margareta about her 'struggles/despair/stress' about Anna, as well as her own letters to Mum, and the one she wrote to me about after reading *The Serpent Rising*. I even attached that awful letter. I told her it all made for depressing reading and I needed time to process it. There had never been any resolution and I didn't feel I could play happy families at this time.

She replied, 'That's just fine. Glad you are so clear. See you sometime.'

I felt overwhelmed with guilt while writing this chapter. For ten years Anna and I had been on friendly terms, although I had put aside my anxiety, ignored it, to broker a temporary truce with her. I ask myself if our final falling out was my fault. Did I sabotage things with that email? Rattled by my guilt, I reach out to author Katrina Casey, who has also suffered family and violence and estrangement. She grew up in New Zealand and escaped to Australia. She tells me trauma is 'a tricky beast. It warps how we think about everything.' She urges me to have deep compassion for myself.

From my correspondence, I see that I tried to explain to Robert why I have changed my mind about spending time with Anna again:

> I do not feel like having contact with her. She has no insight into her abuse and the way she treated Mum and me. You were never attacked or assaulted by her. We were. I was stabbed at 15 and ended up in Auckland Hospital. And she attacked me at Helensville when I was with Mum and Aunt Ola. The Orewa Police said then I should have nothing to do with her.
>
> After reading her letters to me and Mum and going over the history for the book I made the decision that for my own mental health to cease contact. The psychologist I am seeing thinks it is a good idea. Other mental health people over the years have also advised this but I had lapses and became civil only to help Mum and Ola. I have had an anxiety disorder and PTSD much of my life as a direct result of her verbal and physical abuse. I can't keep making excuses because of her mental illness.

His reply was friendly but largely unsympathetic. He said she has 'certainly changed a lot in the last few years, and accepts her issues, and discusses them, plus keeps on medication'.

What was driving my decision, I now know, was a normal reaction to trauma. I went into flight mode, because of Anna's prior violence towards me. The emotion of fear serves as a safeguard and a warning: I had a deep fear Anna could kill me. While there is little evidence to show that people with mental illness in general are more likely to perpetrate violence compared with the general population, higher rates of violence have been identified among people with particular types of severe mental illness, namely schizophrenia and bipolar disorder, although this is lessened or eliminated with proper treatment and if they are on medication. Those with schizophrenia and bipolar disorder who are unmedicated are much more likely to lash out and commit violence.[77]

Some even kill those close to them, such as Michael Laudor, who killed his pregnant girlfriend in 1988. Jonathan Rosen, a close friend of Laudor's since childhood, writes in his heart-wrenching memoir *The Best Minds* that Laudor was spared prison thanks to the legal finding that he acted under delusional thinking, but this was not sufficient to medicate him beforehand.[78] Laudor remains in the Mid-Hudson Forensic Psychiatric Centre in New Hampton, New York.

While writing this book, I received the horrifying news that a friend of mine had been brutally stabbed to death in his home near Maleny by someone he knew, someone who suffered a mental illness.[79] I was shocked to the core; it confirmed for me that some people with untreated psychosis can kill.

The thought of going down to Tauranga with my sister terrified me. You might think I was heartless and neurotic, but maybe you don't understand the chill of fear – the impact of assaults and the compounding effect on the brain. I needed to set some boundaries, to protect myself from potential injury. Unlike when she cut herself off from me in 1980 for no apparent reason, at least I gave Anna my reasons.

That was the last time I had contact with Anna for three years. During that time our half-brother died.

CHAPTER 14

My Lost Half-Brother

On 31 December 2012, two months after Mum died, I discovered I had another brother. Michael James McLennan. Mum had lived and died with this secret.

A second cousin called Jeanette, whom I'd had very little to do with over the years, rang me and said she had some news and hoped I was sitting down. The news was a bombshell: before she met Dad, Mum had given birth to a son and placed him for adoption. I burst into tears. I don't recall much about the rest of the conversation, except that she said something about Michael being very well known in New Zealand as he'd been a famous footballer.

It didn't make sense. How could Mum not have told me? After Dad died, we had become very close, especially when I was researching *Sundowner of the Skies*. I'd often ring her several times a week to tell her about something I'd discovered about Dad. I'd also shared so much about my personal life with her. I was a mother too, and she knew I'd had two abortions.

Jeanette had already told Robert, so I rang Anna. Anna emailed me a few hours after our conversation to say that it felt like an explosion in her life. That's exactly what it felt like for me, too.

I was the first of us three siblings to talk to Michael. Although still reeling with shock, I rang him the next day, even though it was New Year's Day. It was a very long phone call, maybe a few hours long, although I spoke mostly to his wife, Martha. She was clearly the dominant partner, as whenever Michael spoke I could hear her interrupting him in the background. I can't remember what we all talked about. I was very emotional and often wept.

Over the next few days, there was a flurry of emails from another second cousin called Rhonda (who seemed to know much of the history) and from Martha. Bits of the puzzle began to fall into place, although a few pieces remain unclear as several people changed their stories over time. (While writing this book, I didn't feel like contacting them again in order to clarify things. The reasons for my reluctance are made clear later.)

Although Michael waited until after Mum died to contact with us, Martha first made contact with Mum 17 years earlier. SEVENTEEN YEARS.

In 1996, Martha began searching for Michael's birth mother and got in touch with the Salvation Army Family Tracing Service, who were able to provide Mum's maiden name: Lovell. I'm not sure now how Martha found out Mum's married name, but she then managed to track down Mum and Dad's address, perhaps from electoral rolls. Presumably she found their phone number by looking up the White Pages residential phone directory that was delivered yearly to each household. She then rang Mum out of the blue (Dad could have answered!). Such a direct approach was against the advice of the Salvation Army, who'd recommended that their organisation initiate contact.

Reunions can be difficult and complicated. Ideally, contact should take place *after* an adoption counsellor has gauged the mother's wishes or vice versa, usually by letter. Both the child and the birth mother need to decide on reunion. Mum was given no such choice.

Not surprisingly, Mum was mortified. She was not friendly at all. Mum's anger was usually held inside but I can imagine her high-pitched nervous voice saying she did *not* want to meet Michael, or talk to him. She told Martha not to ring again and that she'd contact her in future. She begged Martha not to tell us children. She was worried about what we would think of her. Martha agreed to keep it a secret from us.

(Martha did not have to go along with Mum's wishes. She could have said she was going to tell us, perhaps said something along the lines: 'Helen, I know you are fearful of their reaction but I think they have a right to know about their brother. Times have changed. They most likely would be very understanding and compassionate.')

I can't imagine how distressing Mum's reaction and rejection was for Michael, he'd have been utterly devastated. But it was clear Mum had tried to forget all about him, repress all memories of him, to pretend he didn't exist. Shut the door on that past. Suddenly he re-entered her life, at a time when Dad wasn't well. To have this secret dug up unexpectedly, when she was barely coping with Dad, would've been too much for her. From the 1970s, Dad became increasingly obsessed by his physical health and saw almost every ear and nose surgeon in the North Island. His fixation with surgery led one doctor to write: 'The man might be a potential "Munchhausen".'

Michael was born in Auckland on 26 January 1944 at the Catholic Church's St Vincent's Home of Compassion, a place for unmarried women to have their babies. Adoption was often seen as the only option due to the stigma associated with being an unmarried parent and the lack of financial support available. Martha rang the Catholic Family and Community Services hoping to obtain more information regarding Michael's birth and adoption. Subsequently, in a letter dated 30 January 1997, they wrote to Michael explaining that his wife had been in touch (why didn't Michael ring them?) and that they had searched all their files but the information they had was limited 'only by the social climate of the times' and would not add much to what he already knew. This letter stated that his birth mother was Helen Varie Aroha Lovell and her parents were Henry and Ivy Lovell of Westport. Mum's address was listed as c/- Hobson Street Hospital, Wellington:

> The records mention that she was recommended to the Home of Compassion by a Sister Elizabeth, with no indication of who Sister Elizabeth was, and it was recommended that Helen be instructed in Religion and that she made her First Communion on 10 February 1944. Helen was admitted to the Home of Compassion in Auckland on 12 December 1943 and was discharged from there on 10 February 1944 ... There is absolutely no reference to your birth father as is most often the case during that period.

I'm not sure what Mum was 'instructed in', but presumably she was told she had sinned – sex outside marriage was regarded as unacceptable – and should seek forgiveness.

Between World War II and 1975, approximately 35 per cent of women who became pregnant out of wedlock spent time in an institution to conceal their pregnancies, as Mum did. This invisibility continued afterwards. Case studies show that mothers kept the secret, often not sharing it with friends, subsequent husbands or children.[80] This secrecy and silence would have been hellish for the mothers. Mum would have been throttled by shame.

The number of 'illegitimate' births – those outside marriage – almost doubled in New Zealand between 1939 and 1944, and the number of adoptions and abortions also increased.[81] This rise was partly due to the influx of American servicemen.

Michael's birth father was John Hughes Riley. John had enlisted in the American Army on 26 February 1942 when he was 34 years of age.[82] During World War II, about 20,000 American servicemen came to Wellington to rest or prepare for the war in the Pacific. At the time, Mum was a nurse at the Hobson Street Hospital in Wellington and was one of the many women these servicemen swept off their feet, with their good manners and gifts of nylon stockings, chocolates and flowers. The Americans were more outgoing and demonstrative than New Zealand men, who resented 'the Yankee boys running off with our women' and muttered that they were 'bedroom commandos'. Although dances were organised at the American camps or in service clubs, a favourite haunt was the Majestic Cabaret, where they would foxtrot, jitterbug or jive as a band played the 'Chattanooga Choo-choo'.[83]

I wonder how long Mum and John knew each other and what they felt about each other. I'd like to think they had lots of fun together and had lots of great passionate sex, as Mum sure missed out in that department with Dad. By the time Mum discovered she was pregnant, John had already left Wellington to fight in the Pacific. She told Martha that John died in the war, and so never knew she was pregnant (did she write to him, I wonder?) but when Martha tracked down John's family (after she first contacted Mum), she discovered it had actually been one of his brothers who was killed in the war. John had died on 17 April 1976. Sadly, his American siblings did not want to meet Michael. Another rejection.

According to Martha, the only people who knew about the pregnancy were a friend of Mum's and Aunt Ola's called Carlton Johnson (we knew her as Carl) and a doctor at Wellington Hospital, who was a friend of Mum's family. Carl was named on the baptism certificate as the godmother. She evidently checked in on Michael and the adoptive parents every month for two years (by then Mum had met Dad) and gave Mum photos. I wonder where she hid these and what became of them. I'm not sure how Martha found out these details and I didn't think to ask her at the time. Perhaps Michael's adoptive parents told her.

The baptism certificate also revealed that Mum named her son John Patrick Lovell: John after his father, presumably. I later discovered Mum had been engaged to someone with the first name Patrick, who'd gone to fight in North Africa in 1943. Mum broke off the engagement when she found out she was pregnant. (No one could shed any light on this Patrick fellow or what his surname was.) I don't know why his adoptive parents changed his name to Michael James.

According to Martha, over several years Mum rang Martha about ten times and also sent two letters. Martha read out these letters to me. I was mortified at the contents. It was like a person I'd never known had written these letters. They were cold and nasty. Mum said that having Michael had 'destroyed her life'.

Martha recalled that in one phone call Mum remarked how *lucky* Michael was that he was a single child, while she had been saddled with three. Martha had stood up for Michael and retorted, 'He didn't ask to be born, Helen.' Mum was told that Michael had had a very happy childhood, with loving adoptive parents. Rather than feel relieved for him, Mum might have resented the fact that he fared better than us, and that his parents had a happy marriage (or so she was told), unlike the miserable marriage she had with Dad.

Mum would ring when Michael was at work, but one day he answered the phone (Martha later told me this was something he seldom did) and Mum told him who she was. I'm now kicking myself for not asking Michael what this was like for him and what they talked about. Was she friendly?

At that time, Michael was a famous rugby league footballer who played for the New Zealand national team, and from 1990 he became a leading coach and mentor. He coached the Tongan team in the 1995 World Cup and was the technical advisor to the South Africa team at the 2000 World Cup. Mum loathed 'footy', as she called it, but I wonder if after hearing the news of her son she paid more attention to sports news on television.

Mum also told Martha about some of the challenges she'd faced over the years with Anna and her mental illness. When I told her of the hell Mum went through after Anna turned up in 2000, Martha said she would've been able to help at that time. I doubted this. I sent her several letters written in 2007, including the one my cousin sent to the mental health unit and the letter with the family history I'd given to Anna's psychiatrist, after Anna had been sectioned. It was a nightmare, I said; she could not have helped.

Anna met up with Martha and Michael on the 2 January 2013, the day after I first rang Michael. She had been on holiday up in the Bay of Islands and drove down and spent about six hours with them at their home in Manly. Anna reported back: 'They are really nice people, exceptionally so. He doesn't talk much – Martha does all the talking and interrupts him. He looks just like Mum. I found her letters distressing. You can sense her terror behind all the other emotions.' She said Michael had been an only child and had always wanted a sister. Now he had two.

On that same day Robert made a brief phone call to Michael and Martha and said he was going away on a holiday and would be in touch when he returned.

After Mum moved to Orewa in 1999, she did not contact Martha again. Coincidentally, Martha and Michael lived at Manly, only about 12 kilometres away from Orewa, and knew where Mum lived. Over the years, respecting Mum's wishes, Martha did not contact any members of our direct family, including my aunts and first cousins. But other people came to know about Michael, that he was Mum's secret son.

In 2004, Martha phoned the Coromandel Museum enquiring about the Campbell and Hannaford families, on Mum's side of the family. The curator gave her a phone number of Rhonda, my second cousin, as he knew she was interested in genealogy and was researching our family history. Martha rang Rhonda and – at last, after so much rejection – Michael was welcomed with open arms by someone in the family.

Mum's mother, Ivy Campbell, was born in Coromandel, a coastal town on the Coromandel Peninsula, about 170 kilometres southeast of Auckland. The peninsula is one of the most beautiful places in New Zealand, fringed with white beaches and flanked by steep rainforest-clad mountains. In 1837, William Moores, my great-great-grandfather, bought 400 acres at Industry Bay (now Hannaford's Bay), Coromandel, from the Māori. That land has been transferred from generation to generation, with 25 acres still remaining in the possession of the Hannaford family. Ivy's sister, Olive, married Frederick Hannaford in 1923 and they stayed in Coromandel for the rest of their lives. Ivy, my grandmother, moved far away to Westport in the South Island after her marriage to Henry Lovell.

Rhonda sent me photos of Martha and Michael having lunch with seven members of the Hannaford family at their holiday home in Hannaford's Bay. She said he was a lovely man and was sure we'd all click into place very quickly.

I felt betrayed. Rhonda said she had been sworn to secrecy: 'It was always paramount in Michael's mind to respect Helen's wishes and her right to privacy.' I felt annoyed hearing this, and replied, 'I wish someone had told me; I don't believe in secrets and Michael had a right to meet us. I so much want to talk to Mum about it all, but she's not here.' Again, as with Martha, Rhonda did not have to agree to keeping this secret. She could have said, 'Sorry, but I believe Robert, Anna and Mary should hear about their brother.' I'm pretty sure that is what I would do in a similar situation. Apart from Rhonda, one other cousin was told early on because Michael had coached her sons. I wonder if these cousins shared this 'secret' with those close to them, their husbands at least?

I loathe secrecy. I believe that keeping family secrets is harmful. I would have liked to have known about Michael at the time Martha tracked down Mum. Who knows, it might have been healing for Mum: she would have seen we were not ashamed of her in the slightest. I would've been relieved as the adoption would've shed a light on her never-ending sadness. Although they thought they were doing the 'right' thing (and perhaps felt a bit self-righteous doing so), I believe what they did was wrong. All they did was enable Mum's guilt and shame, and they left Anna, Robert and me with a gap of 17 years, during which time we could have had Michael in our lives.

The secrecy didn't bother Anna or Robert at all.

I was gobsmacked when Rhonda told me that Michael and Martha had attended Aunt Ola's funeral in April 2011. 'It nearly broke my heart to see Michael pacing up and down at the end of driveway when we were all outside with the hearse.' (Mum was there, holding onto a walking frame. She was teary, and was comforted by Natalya and me.)

Rhonda said Michael and Martha went to the local restaurant where some of us had a get-together. (I wonder who told them where we were going? One of our second cousins?) I vaguely remember a couple sitting on bar stools looking over at us, listening to us. I'd put together a display of photos on a large laminated board, and we reminisced about our favourite loving aunt who was so devoted to her nieces and nephews, and to my children. Martha later told me that before the funeral they went to a second-hand shop and bought clothes so they could dress up in disguise.

During those first few weeks after discovering I had another brother, I found myself crying for long periods of time. I even burst into tears when I was in public, once with a group of cycling friends before we set out on a bike ride. I'd never experienced grief like this before.

For many years, I could not understand why the news of Michael shook me up so much, but now I realise I was crying for my mother. For what she had suffered. Her miserable years with Dad, threaded with harshness and cruelty, at the same time trying to help Anna, as she grappled with a mental illness that would torment her much of her life. And now this other trauma – the loss of Michael, a grief that we were all born into. How on earth did Mum cope with *all* of that. No wonder she had no space for me.

I met up with Michael a few months later. In April 2013, we arranged to spend a week in Nelson so that Margareta and Maurice, Aunt Alice and a few of my cousins could also meet him. Margareta had been flabbergasted when I'd rung to tell her about Michael. I was excited and secretly hoped Michael would be a better brother than Robert had been. Perhaps he'd show more interest in my children, become more involved, and I'd become part of his family. Michael had one child, a son called Brian, who had three children – a son aged 13 and twins aged 11. When I'd told my son, Eamon, about Michael, he just said, 'Wow! You mean I've got a real uncle at last?'

It was not the happy reunion I'd hoped for. In fact, it was a disaster and nothing like the reunions we see on television. Martha decided to stay at the same motel I'd booked at, and they arrived in the morning. It was a long day of travel for me: a commute to the airport, and then a flight to Christchurch and another flight to Nelson. I left home at 5 am and arrived about 10:30 pm. I'd made it clear that I would not be able to see them until the next morning. I don't travel well, and often get headaches which can develop into migraines. No sooner had I entered my room and put my suitcase on the bed then was there a knock on the door. Martha and Michael!

The week was challenging for me. For much of the time, I didn't feel well. Perhaps it was not a good time as I was still in deep grief over Mum's death and missing her terribly. As she'd done with Anna, Martha did most of the talking and I ended up asking to spend some time alone with Michael. It was a very strained conversation. Michael told me he had not wanted to contact Mum and that the Salvation Army had advised them that they should both get counselling but there was no way they would have, he said, as they did not believe in that sort of stuff. I felt very rattled to hear all of this.

People have high expectations of reunions, but the experience is not always positive. Just because someone is a relative does not mean they will like each other. Although related, they are intimate strangers. Michael and I had no shared history and little in common. Like Mum, I had no interest in football. Michael was also beginning to suffer from dementia, no doubt caused in part by head injuries from football. I felt I'd lost my brother before I'd even met him.

At the end of my week in Nelson, Aunt Alice[84] and I both agreed that Martha should not have contacted Mum. Alice had been close to Mum. We reflected on how deeply retraumatising it would have been for Mum, the way contact was made. Plus, it was also terrible timing, as Mum was entangled with Dad's ongoing health dramas.

Whereas previously I'd felt sympathy for Michael, about the way he'd been rejected, now my sympathy swung towards Mum. I felt angry that Martha had rung her with no consideration of what Mum could've been going through. I did not share these feelings with them, but before I flew back to Australia I told them I needed time to process things. I couldn't help but think that if they'd taken the advice of the Salvation Army back in 1996, there may well have been a very different outcome. Perhaps if Mum had been contacted *after* Dad died, things could have been different. Or even if Michael had sent Mum a hand-written letter, to test the waters so to speak.

Anna, however, remained on friendly terms and connected with Michael and Martha in a way I wasn't able to. Two years after meeting Michael, Anna left Wellington and moved up to Waiwera, which is six kilometres north of Orewa and only about 25 kilometres away from Manly, where the McLennans lived.

Now that both Mum and Aunt Ola had died, there was no reason for me to keep flying over to Auckland. I was back to being the black sheep of my New Zealand family, but busy and happy with work and my own family in Australia. Natalya had her first child in 2015, so now I had a new life as a grandmother. I was determined to be as supportive as possible, which Mum could not be for me when I had my first child – she'd been caught up with Dad and Anna's problems. I was also busy working on *Sundowner of the Skies* and as I described earlier, in 2017 I decided to cut all contact with Anna. I seldom received any news about Michael or Anna, except occasional snippets from Robert during his once-a-year phone call on Christmas Day. He'd tell me Anna was stable and Michael's dementia was worsening.

On Wednesday, 16 October 2019, six months after *Sundowner of the Skies* had been published, Robert rang me from Auckland Airport (he was on the way to Canberra for a cycling event) to tell me Michael had gone missing. By now Michael had advanced dementia and had escaped from the rest home Milton Court, Orewa, where he'd been staying temporarily until his own home was made more secure. (Milton Court was where Mum spent her last years, and coincidentally Michael had even been staying in the same room where Mum spent her last days.) I said I wanted to go over, but Robert said not to. There were already many people looking for him and search and rescue crews were conducting searches with help from helicopters.

Michael was last seen on Hibiscus Coast Highway in the late afternoon. The police would later release CCTV footage: the grainy images showing him leaning forward slightly as he walked quickly northwards along a stretch of the Hibiscus Coast Highway near Hatfields Beach. I'd walked or driven up that road many times when visiting Mum and Aunt Ola.

The police thought it was possible he may have been given a lift in a car by someone. I did not believe that. I told Robert I had a hunch he was near Hatfields Beach. Over the next few days, I put numerous posts on social media, or commented on others' posts, and suggested that the searchers and police look in the bush near Hatfields Beach. A journalist from *The New Zealand Herald* saw one of my posts and rang me. I blurted out that I couldn't really say anything because Michael's wife would not want me to mention that I was his half-sister. My rebuff is odd, as I'd already declared this fact on social media. I now regret not saying anything to the journalist.

On Saturday, I told Robert I still felt like flying over and joining in the search. I mentioned that that morning I'd been signing my books at Rosetta Books in Maleny and someone from Auckland had bought my book and said he knew about Michael being missing. It was all over the news in New Zealand.

Robert replied: 'It's now sounding pretty bad as there have been so many searchers and they're finding nothing. I can imagine hundreds of old league mates and friends and people he coached, plus neighbours and relatives have been helping. I would not go.'

That afternoon I sat on my couch for hours zooming in on Google Maps to the bush area near Hatfields Beach. I just knew he was there. I read a story which supported my theory. The body of a dementia patient was found after 40 days and she was only a few hundred metres away in the bush. They'd used tracker dogs and helicopters and searched for weeks.

On Tuesday at 7.12 am, I sent Robert an email. I again said I wished I'd gone over to look for him. 'I never thought he'd been given a lift. That made no sense. He is more likely to be somewhere near Hatfields Beach where he was last seen. People are sometimes found in places previously searched. Can't see it being a good outcome.'

His body was found in dense bush at Hatfields Beach that night.[85] Police dogs had begun barking at a fence. The area had been searched several times. Later it was revealed that Michael had climbed the hill overlooking Hatfields Beach, scaled a fence and then went down through thick scrub and bush. He'd fallen over, most likely in the dark. He had puncture wounds from spikes from palm fronds and had broken his nose.

Robert said I should have been a detective. I said it was so strange that I'd had such a strong conviction of where Michael was, as 'I don't really believe in that psychic/spiritual stuff'. I told Robert that both Natalya and I felt devastated about Michael. He said he was surprised we would be so distressed by his death.

Neither Robert nor I attended Michael's funeral, but Anna did. It was reported that 'hundreds gathered to say their final goodbyes to the rugby league icon'. He was remembered as a good bloke, cheeky and determined.[86] I later watched a video of the funeral. In the speeches there was mention of his birth father, John Hughes

Riley, but no mention of Mum, his birth mother: Helen Varie Aroha Garden (née Lovell).

I'd originally included a section on Michael and his adoption in a draft of *Sundowner of the Skies* and emailed Martha in December 2017 to confirm some details. I included this note, to which she did not respond:

> I am sorry things did not work out better for us all in Nelson. It was a very stressful time for me with my university studies, and I was exhausted from spending so many years looking after Ola and mum, and managing their affairs. It would have been wiser if I had come over to Auckland and just met up for a few hours.

Martha was not happy about me writing anything about Michael. 'Michael would like to respect his mother's wishes and keep her secret. If you do go ahead, please use only M & M, not our full names.' I was dumbfounded. Mum was dead! I pointed out that Mum's 'secret' was no longer a secret as many members on both sides of the family knew about him and his name was already on the MyHeritage site. The section on Michael never ended up in the final version of *Sundowner of the Skies*, although I included his name in the family tree at the front of the book.

Michael is now dead too. I am *not* keeping him a secret.

CHAPTER 15

The Mad Gardens

I'd always been a bit envious of the Coromandel mob: they seemed close and often had family reunions and get-togethers. No sign of fractures on that branch, or none that I knew of. But after the secrecy and games played around Michael, I began to think they were just as odd as most families, although perhaps not as odd as the Gardens.

Mad has many meanings. It can mean mentally ill or insane, intensely angry, or carried away by enthusiasm. The word was chucked around a lot in my birth family. Mum always called us the 'Mad Gardens'. She often said Dad's mother, Rebecca, was mad. She'd call her 'stark raving mad' and 'a lying toad' and said it was her fault that Dad turned out the way he did.

Aunt Ola met Rebecca twice and also thought she was barmy. 'I'll always connect her with Marmite. Brown bread, chives and Marmite. That's all she knew about. She came out to visit me twice, and that was all she'd have. I passed her cake once and she thrust it back, saying 'muck'. She was full of him, your father. Religious crank. Over brainy but odd, definitely odd.'

Rebecca's husband, Robert, also thought she was mad. After Rebecca had run away from Robert, she petitioned the Scottish

Supreme Civil Court in 1910 for custody of the children and maintenance. In response Robert said the marriage had never been happy due to Rebecca's 'excitable and emotional temperament, hasty temper, extreme and intolerant views on temperance, and her jealousy and suspicion'. He claimed she was 'mentally abnormal in sexual matters', possessed of a hysterical temperament and morbid imagination, and constantly concocting false stories about him being immoral and a drunkard.

The words Robert used to describe Rebecca – hysterical, excitable, emotional, liar – are all words a few men have used to describe me. I don't believe Rebecca was lying. I think it is more likely she was reacting to his violence and drunkenness.

Towards the end of the abusive one-year relationship I had after my marriage ended, my ex-partner rang my doctor and said I'd been behaving strangely, adding that he thought I was psychotic. When my doctor rang me, he was surprised to find me well and said I sounded fine. I shared a little of what had been going on, including the bruises and choking, and he suggested we see a psychologist. My partner agreed to go as he thought we were getting help for me.

After we'd each told the psychologist our stories of what had been happening, and I even dared to say my partner had been pinching and twisting my nipples and called me a baby when I cried out in pain, she said to him, 'I think you need help: you have a sadistic streak and need long-term counselling.' Suddenly it was as if a light had been switched on. I was relieved; he could get therapy and we could stay together. Funnily enough, hearing that he had a sadist streak didn't worry me. But that night was our last. He moved out the next day. Blamed me. Said I was a nutter. Accused me of brainwashing the psychologist.

I was very emotional and disturbed during those last few months with him. I realise now that my behaviour, like Rebecca's, was in reaction to his cruelty. I was mentally distressed and having a normal reaction to abuse.

'Mad' can also mean reckless or foolish. Mum had every reason to think we were all mad in that sense. In a letter to Margareta in 1974, she wrote, 'I can't cope with this mad family. At least I am light-hearted about my madness, whereas the rest are so earnest.' The sale of their latest property had fallen though and she admitted to a 'little bit of behind-the-scenes scheming', as she simply could not 'face the thought of packing, moving out in a fortnight with Oscar resting most of the day, not fit enough to do anything'.

When I was in India, Mum was worried about Anna. She wrote to Margareta that she'd been to Auckland twice to shift Anna's belongings because an ex-boyfriend had been stalking her. (I knew nothing about this.) A court case was coming up in a week, and then Anna is off to Australia: 'I think she is too dim and naive to be let loose in Sydney, but perhaps it is time for her to break away and find herself. Anna just seems to eat and eat when she has problems. She will bust if doesn't learn to cope some other way.'

My father was also impatient and impetuous. When I give talks on my father's life and *Sundowner of the Skies*, someone invariably asks the question: 'Do you think your father suffered a mental illness?' This always surprises me, because in these talks I focus on his epic flight and aviation adventures, with only a brief mention of his flaws as a father and a husband.

His epic flight from London to Australia in 1930 in an open cockpit Gipsy Moth was pretty manic. He'd kept the flight a secret (just like my sister kept her many projects a secret) as he did not want to be talked out of going. After he'd left, Reginald Bunning, his flying instructor, said he was foolhardy and didn't have a hope in Hades. On the first day, after nine and a half hours flying, my father reached Munich, and even he began to question whether the whole thing was such a good idea: 'Whatever am I doing? I must be mad.'

On arrival at Wyndham in Australia, Dad was determined to take the shortest route to Sydney over the Great Sandy Desert to Alice Springs even though aviation experts said it would be wiser and safer to fly down the west coast to Perth. Dad ignored them. Stanley Brown, a pilot from Western Australian Airways, accompanied Dad on the first leg to Halls Creek. In various interviews, Dad said Brown told him he was 'stark staring mad', or perhaps those were Dad's own words to describe himself, for he was lucky to survive that 12-hour trip, flying much of the way through a red dust storm, with water out of reach as he'd put the half a dozen beer bottles full of water in the front cockpit, in case he had a forced landing.

Madness can lead to great things and achievements. Recent research indicates a link between bipolar and creativity, not only in artistic accomplishment but entrepreneurship. Marina Jones in her essay on Sir Isaac Newton[87] explores his manic depression, or bipolar disorder as it is now called, an illness he suffered from most of his life. His mania led to 'intense periods of productivity, faith in one's own talent, and the need to prove oneself right'. But as she points out, regardless of the inspirations one gets when manic, or how extraordinary the achievements are as a result of it, bipolar can cause immense pain and torment and tremendous pain for those connected to the sufferer. Newton had a violent temper and often struck out in rage and would punch his sister.

Before my sister was diagnosed and treated, she engaged in risky behaviour, including spending sprees, binge eating, destroying property and physical violence. According to Mum, in 1999 Anna sold her house in London and her car and spent all the proceeds flying around the world. And then turned up in Napier, homeless and penniless.

In *Sundowner of the Skies*, I explored the possibility that Dad may have suffered from a mental illness and mentioned Anna's diagnosis.

I also believe that underlying his behaviour was a mental illness. Did he have Asperger's? There were his social and communication difficulties: his failure to develop friendships, his awkwardness, his long-winded rants about his medical ailments or reminiscing about his flying days, his insensitivity and disregard to others' feelings and his aversion to crowds and large gatherings. There was also his acute sensitivity to noise and his need for routines. His lunch had to be on the dot of 12.

Or was his incessant need to move house, his impulsiveness and restlessness, symptomatic of manic depression or bipolar disorder, as it is now known? He was a problem gambler, and evidence suggests that those who suffer bipolar disorder often have a gambling addiction. Also, my sister, Anna, suffered from bipolar disorder, although she wasn't diagnosed and treated until after Dad died.

Author and historian Ross Fitzgerald reviewed *Sundowner of the Skies* for *The Weekend Australian*[88] and said I dealt 'sensitively with Oscar Garden's mental illness, his gambling on horse racing, his insomnia, extreme restlessness'. My brother was angry about this review: 'This is really false about Dad. He did not physically abuse. Why say these things? Do you think being dramatic will add to the story?'

I'd just returned from New Zealand, where I'd found promoting a book exhilarating but at the same time stressful. Robert's email felt like a punch in the gut at a time when I was trying to keep things together. I was pretty pissed off with him. I told him I had not written the review. I reminded him that I did not write that our father was mentally ill, but that he probably suffered from an undiagnosed mental illness. I had his medical records, which show he suffered depression for years. 'Antidepressants didn't help which is why he more likely suffered bipolar as antidepressants make bipolar people agitated – hence his incessant need to move.'

In response to his denial that Dad had been physically abusive I wrote,

What crap, Robert. He was damaged like many men of that generation. Old school friends I met up with said their fathers were cruel bastards. Dad was physically abusive. He was violent to Mum. She had half her thyroid removed because of Dad choking her.

Robert replied:

> You have overreacted on this. I am proud of your book, and it is on the bench for any visitors to see, and most people want to hear about it. I know Dad was brought up in an era of abuse, but I tend to ignore all that, as I don't believe it had much effect on me.

It was Robert who had overreacted. His response was gaslighting, which means to undermine another person's reality by denying their feelings. Instead of apologising, he blamed me. Although people have very different reactions to the same kinds of challenges, it is difficult to believe that Dad's abuse didn't have much effect on him, on some level.

Far more than any other type of illness, mental illness is stigmatised. The National Study of Mental Health and Wellbeing,[89] conducted in 2021, found that an estimated 21 per cent of Australians aged 16 to 85 experienced a mental disorder that significantly interfered with their life in the previous 12 months, and 44 per cent reported having experienced a mental disorder during their lifetime. This included anxiety disorders, affective disorders, psychotic disorders and substance use disorders.

Everyone is a bit mad, everyone at some time in their life will be negatively affected by their mental health. When we were growing up, people with mental illness were shamed. Robert may have thought I was discrediting and shaming Dad, not only because I suggested Dad may have had had a mental illness but also because I revealed his violent streak. He was uncomfortable about me writing about Dad's flaws. Before I sent Robert the manuscript of my book, I warned him that he might not be happy about some of it as it was the warts-and-all account Mum wanted. His response was that it all happened a long time ago and he hoped 'the warts and all are not too dramatic!!' (Note, manuscript means the typed document, the final version of a book before it is submitted to publishers. It is not the rough draft of a book, which may go through various revisions.)

The feedback from readers of my book proved Robert wrong; his fears were unwarranted. They responded positively to warts and all. Readers like the truth. I'd get comments, even from elderly retired pilots, such as, 'You have done your dad proud'; 'Love your honesty coming from your own experience with Oscar'; 'You have done justice to the forgotten aviator Oscar'; 'We now know of him & his achievements warts & all as you say'; 'It is a very honest book, which is refreshing in this day and age of airbrushing anything inconvenient'.

All the Gardens are mad in various ways, including Mum – she was mad to stay with Dad. But madness, however it is defined, is no excuse for abuse and violence. Many people with bipolar disorder or schizophrenia are not violent. Dad's likely mental illness does not excuse the damage wrought on us. Anna's mental illness does not excuse her abuse of me or Mum and others.

Mum trained as a nurse and worked for some years in Wellington, but after the birth of Michael she got a job at Auckland's Carrington Mental Hospital, originally called the Whau Lunatic Asylum. Dad met Mum in August 1945, and he'd drive out to the hospital in Mount Albert to see Mum on her breaks. Sometimes coming back from Sydney in one of the flying boats Dad would fly in low over the mental hospital and nurses would run out and wave to him, jump up and down.

Mum and Dad would sit in the car and listen to the screaming of patients in Ward 3. 'There was only straw in that room,' Mum told me. 'They couldn't put anything else because they would destroy it, tear it apart or try and hang themselves.' Before psychotropic drugs were developed, the treatment in such places included straitjackets, electric shock treatments and lobotomies. It was relatively easy for a family member to have someone admitted and often difficult to leave. It was one of their biggest fears that Anna would end up in such a place.

CHAPTER 16

To Cut or Not to Cut

When I was writing my book on Dad, I was indecisive about mentioning Anna's mental illness. I thought it would be useful to include it as I explored the possibility Dad might also have suffered from bipolar. Also, her story had a miraculous outcome and would be inspirational to others. After reading an early draft, an editor provided this feedback:

> I think everything in the book is relevant and has been handled in a balanced way. But of course, in the interest of maintaining healthy relationships with other family members who have contributed, it would be courteous to allow them to read the book before you send it off to a publisher. I would hope they could accept that you have backed up your statements with solid research and you haven't really pushed one point of view or another. At the end of the day, the story is about Oscar, his challenges and how his ancestors' behaviour has impacted the following generations.

Some writers decide to share their manuscript with subjects before it is published to give them a chance to provide feedback. But many writers choose not to as they don't want anyone telling them what should or should not be included. They figure that if any family member disagrees with it, they can write their own book, which is what members of the Turcotte family did after they claimed there were fabrications in Augusten Burroughs's best-selling memoir *Running with Scissors*.[90]

Publisher and editor Jane Friedman suggests letting 'one trusted reader, preferably someone who knows all the characters in real life, comb through the manuscript first, imagining what others will think'.[91] So I sent mine to Robert (who passed it on to Anna), Margareta and Maurice, and my Garden cousins, Gillian MacColl and Rosemarie Toynbee.

Not one of them came back and said that is not correct, that did not happen. Not one of them challenged my portrayal of Dad, or pointed out that something I'd written was incorrect or exaggerated. This is highly unusual. Family members often have different versions of the past. Memory is a slippery beast after all, but in our case we seemed to be all on the same page.

Margareta and Maurice made no comment about the section on Anna. When I asked my cousin Rosemarie whether I should leave out Anna's illness, she replied, 'Oh no, leave Anna in. Makes an amazing story and it's very current today. It's the full deal. It gives a very good account of many years gone by.'

Robert had nothing negative to say, except he thought there was too much on Anna. 'It was fascinating reading and what an effort to get all that history. How many thousands of hours did you take? Bet you never kept count as it was ongoing for so long.' A few days later he emailed to say he'd caught up with Anna, and she is 'quite hurt by the stuff you wrote about her'. He said they wanted the section about her removed, as 'it is not necessary for the overall story'.

I replied that it was part of the story and asked whether Anna felt bad about the way she had treated me and Mum. Ignoring my question, he urged me to 'really minimise what you say about Anna but mention the remarkable recovery she has had to the stage where she had a job paying 100k plus per year, and now owns her own house.'

Anna only owned her own house because I transferred funds to her before Mum died, even though the agreement in Mum's will was we manage and control Anna's share of our inheritance so she would not fritter it away.

A few weeks later Robert emailed to suggest I focus only on Dad's flying. 'There is too much family stuff, and not a great enough proportion about Dad, the famous aviator. If I was keen on the flying story, I would want 90 per cent plus on the flying.'

My book found a home in early December 2018. It was accepted by two publishers, but I chose New Holland as they have offices in both Sydney and Auckland, which suited my book as it bridges both countries. It was a quick birth: *Sundowner of the Skies* was released in May 2019, which was remarkable, considering most books can take a year or two from the time of acceptance to being launched.

A compelling endorsement by Trent Dalton, which encapsulated the heart of the *Sundowner of the Skies*, ended up as the blurb on the back cover. Describing the book as a 'rattling, searing soulful story', Dalton wrote in part, 'Author Mary Garden travels back through the turbulence of her own startling family history to find her father, Oscar Garden, a legend of long-distance aviation who soared through any sky but crash-landed the one-way journey of his life on earth.'

Although I'd written two chapters at the end of the book on Dad's post-aviation life, initially the publisher's editor wanted me to only have one chapter, cutting back on the family dynamics and issues. I disagreed, arguing that if some of this material was retained the book would appeal to a wider audience, not only those interested in aviation. I pointed out that several reviews of a recently released book, *Charles Ulm: The untold story of one of Australia's greatest aviation pioneers*, were critical because of what was left out. 'Searle's biography does not say much about Ulm's personal life.'[92] 'There is so much more to tell. Where is the sense of who Charles Ulm was, as a person?'[93]

A compromise was reached and I kept two chapters, albeit shortened. In the final version, about 10,000 words were cut, and there were only three paragraphs on Anna, in which I said, 'her recovery has been nothing short of miraculous'.

After my book came out, several readers told me they skipped the aviation stuff because they found it boring and went to the end, which they found more interesting. Margareta wrote, 'I stopped about half-way through the flying history and concentrated on the relationship/family stuff. I really enjoyed the family parts – I think found fascinating might be a better term.'

In fact, it was the family dynamics that appealed to the judges of the NSW Premier's Awards and one of them would later tell me, 'I admired the way you went above and beyond the typical (aviation) biography and painted a rounded, though difficult figure, of your father.' Reviewers also highlighted the family issues. Denise Newton wrote:

> [T]he most engrossing aspect of the story is the family history behind it. Oscar came from a wealthy Scottish merchant family, but family disputes and factions resulted in a troubled, restless, loner of a man who ended up suffering from mental ill-health and was unable to find any happiness in life ... It's a poignant story of an emotionally frozen parent and a young adult trying to emerge from beneath his influence.[94]

I got in touch with Anna's friend Susan Lea to tell her the good news about my book and mentioned that Robert and Anna were not happy about me sharing some of the Garden secrets but at least they had not challenged my recollection of our childhood. She replied that it didn't matter what they thought:

> They'll be super happy later, and this is YOUR story. Neither of them has managed to give your father the kudos he deserves for his flying accomplishments. Your mother was a darling, and I know Anna would respect her opinion on these points about what to include in the book.

Researching and working on *Sundowner of the Skies* brought me closer to my Garden cousins, a few of whom I'd had little contact with over the years. I also became good friends with Alys Wicksteed. They all enjoyed the book.

Alys wrote, 'Congratulations! WOW. Sat in bed most of today and read the BOOK. It made me sad and happy. Great Girl Mary. You have done the Ultimate.' She said she was so proud of me and thought my mother would be beaming with joy and pride. Rosemarie said it was 'incredible', very thought-provoking. There was so much she didn't know and she felt I treated everyone 'kindly and fairly'. She thanked me for my years of research and 'hard work for us all' and felt it would be a huge success. 'Puts this huge jigsaw of the Garden family puzzle together.' My cousin Gillian said, 'You've done the most amazing job with the book fantastic research and very well written – you just want to keep reading and not put it down, and unbelievable effort to get to this point.' Margareta enjoyed it 'hugely' and thanked me. Maurice's feedback was extensive but here is an extract:

> I've just finished *Sundowner* and found it enjoyable in every way. Beautifully told, Mary, and bravely too. The width of your research is astonishing, you've found everything. Readers after an aviation story will be more than satisfied, it's a gap filled in, and fits Oscar into his proper place as one of the great pioneers. But then the other side, I hardly know what to say. He's a sort of archetype of the damaged man (broken family, Calvinist indoctrination), and one who inflicts damage. So, congratulations on a great piece of writing. (How the hell did you survive?)

How the hell *did* I survive? Not just my childhood, but survive what happened in India and the nightmare years in Maleny in the 1990s. I forwarded Maurice's feedback to Robert, who said, 'What a superb recommendation from an expert in this business. As he says, the research has been phenomenal. Fantastic.' He also sent me the feedback from one of his friends in response to a double-page spread article on my book published in *The New Zealand Herald* in July

2019.[95] This included a lengthy excerpt from *Sundowner of the Skies* from the chapter on Dad's 1930 epic flight, as well as photographs. His friend wrote, 'It was a superb article. Wow. Brilliant work on your sister's part. That is just sooo good to have all that history recorded and published before its lost. She clearly has put her heart and soul into it and what an amazing story.'

CHAPTER 17

Te riri Pākehā:
The White Man's Anger

Despite my troubled childhood, I'd long clung to the myth of 'beautiful Tauranga'. I'd often told people how lucky I was to have grown up there, its physical loveliness and beauty a stark contrast to the coldness and cruelty of what went on at home. At least I had that. That was some comfort.

This myth was upended about a year after *Sundowner of the Skies* was published. In my book I described Tauranga as beautiful and wrote of the 'idyllic playground' we had at our back door. I now realise the land is only beautiful on the surface, just as my father could be charming on the surface to outsiders. To my horror, I discovered I had actually grown up on stolen land.

Although we learnt a little Māori history at school, we were never given the full story. We did not learn about the New Zealand Wars (1845–1872) in which several thousand people died, most of them Māori. Some call these wars Te riri Pākehā, meaning 'the white man's anger' – the white men, after all, were the invaders, greedy for land. These wars led to the *New Zealand Settlements Act 1863*, which authorised land confiscations, raupatu, as 'punishment' for tribes who'd fought against the Crown. Five large chunks of Māori land – about 3.4 million acres – were confiscated. Land was also taken from tribes who'd been allies. According to Vincent O'Malley, a Pākehā historian, raupatu has meant 'generations of Māori were condemned to lives of landlessness and poverty'.[96]

One of the chunks of confiscated land was Tauranga. Some of it was subsequently returned, including a 109-acre block that had been the site of Ōtūmoetai Pā, once a large fortified village where different kin groups lived, but was eventually sold to Robert and Sarah Matheson. Over the years, sections were sold off, leaving a farm called Fairview, which was two kilometres away from our house at Levers Crescent. I cycled past this farm hundreds of times as a child, ignorant of its historical significance.

Wi Te Tau Huata, who'd been a chaplain in the Māori Battalion, called Tauranga 'he whenua pōuri', which means a dark country. 'The land is still wracked with grief because of what was done there. The field is now covered in soft grass, and the past has been furrowed deep in the land with each new planting. But the histories remain.'[97] Tauranga is streaked with violence, just as my father was.

How ironic that Tauranga was the place Dad stayed the longest on his restless journey through life. It is scarred, just like his childhood home. He grew up in the far north of Scotland, an area ravaged during the Sutherland Clearances, the forced and brutal evictions of small crofters by the Duke and Duchess of Sutherland between 1806 and 1820. Houses were destroyed or burnt, people starved or froze to death. It has been said that the Highland Clearances left scars on the psyche of Highlanders for generations to come. Did Dad carry those generational scars, as well as all the others he collected?

New Zealand has a shorter human history than most countries. The Māori were the first inhabitants, settling in the North Island in the mid-thirteenth century, and the first European settlers did not arrive until the 1840s. As is typical of colonial societies, they were intolerant towards the indigenous people, subjecting them to racism and discrimination.

As well as growing up on stolen land, I also grew up in the shadow of racism. After *Sundowner of the Skies* was published, I discovered that Ōtūmoetai Primary School was one of the few schools in New Zealand to be segregated. In 1939 the Department of Education gave permission to remove Māori children from the school after they received a petition from Pākehā parents concerned their children's health was threatened because 'native' children came to school wet and often had colds. Forty-two Māori children were moved to Bethlehem Native School, leaving 35 children of European descent on the roll. On 30 October 2020, Zara McIndoe, the principal of Ōtūmoetai Primary at the time, made a formal public apology for the removal of Māori children from the school.[98]

I reckon my father would have been furious if he'd known about this discrimination. He would have sold up and moved elsewhere, enrolled us at another school. Although he could be harsh and controlling, he had his good points. He loathed racial prejudice. He would boast about being flung into jail for a night in Johannesburg in late 1931 because he was 'drinking with some natives at a party'.

The 1950s and 1960s in New Zealand are often recalled as a 'golden age'. It wasn't for many of us. New Zealand was a conservative, repressive society, and I believe many of us children were damaged and scarred by authoritarian fathers and uptight, sad mothers. I believe we were further damaged by not being around Māori children, learning from their culture and their connection to the land.

In August 2021, I flew over to Tauranga for a second launch of *Sundowner of the Skies*. I was yet to learn of the dark history of my hometown; if I'd known about it I would have included it in the book. Tauranga was now a city, almost unrecognisable. None of the original buildings at my old school remained, and the paddocks behind had disappeared, gobbled up by houses and roads. The swimming pool and clump of old trees nearby were still there, and so was the sports field, although the long line of fir trees had gone. Our house and glasshouse near the school had gone, as were our next house and the hut at the end of the peninsula. The house which had been next door to us, was still there, as well as the row of silver birch trees up the driveway. (The property was called 'White Ladies'.)

I found a way down to the beach. It was a grey overcast day. The shoreline was deep mud. I sank up to my knees and had to struggle to extricate myself. It had changed from the 1950s, the continued land clearing no doubt added to its silt and mud. I thought I might spend some time down on the beach, bask in nostalgia, but I couldn't get away fast enough.

I spent a morning signing books and chatting to people at the local bookstore, Books A Plenty. The book was selling well, the owner said. A few old classmates turned up and we went to lunch afterwards. They told me there were plenty of men like my father, some worse, their abuse hidden behind closed doors, and none of us knew what was going on. That was news to me and reassuring. I'd always felt an outsider, ashamed of my father and his anger.

After the book launch at Classic Flyers Aviation Museum, we wandered across to Tauranga Airport for an unveiling of a portrait of my father. Some months earlier, Alys Wicksteed had given a copy of my book to renowned Māori artist Graham Hoete (Mr G), who is of Ngai Te Rangi and Ngāti Ranginui descent, and told him, 'You must do a portrait of Oscar.' And so, he did.

I couldn't understand why Robert didn't come down for this special occasion – it was only a two-hour drive – but I'd find out a year later.

Mr G opened the ceremony with a mihi, a ceremonial Māori greeting, and explained the meaning behind the portrait. On one side of the frame was Mauao (Mount Maunganui), the mountain at the entrance to Tauranga Harbour; Edinburgh Castle was on the other side. While preparing for his solo flight from London to Australia, my father flew cross-country flights to improve his navigation and flying skills and on one occasion ran into thick haze and almost hit the side of the castle. His clan tartan was also painted on the frame. Mr G said he wanted his portrait to educate people, so my father could be remembered. In an article on the event for *Sunlive*, he told reporter Kate Wells:

> My priority was presenting the portrait to Mary, Oscar's daughter, in a nice, respectful and intimate fashion. I wanted to make sure Oscar had a strong connection to Tauranga Moana. He was an aviation legend. He brought this second-hand Gipsy Moth plane, flew it all the way from England to Australia, the plane was called *Kia Ora*, he had a Kiwi battler mentality. He went out and gave it a go and did it on a shoestring budget, and he was a humble man who didn't like to talk about himself.[99]

Tauranga Mayor Greg Brownless, Alys and I gave speeches. I said my father would be chuffed as he had a huge chip on his shoulder about being forgotten and overlooked. There was a deeply moving blessing by members of the Ngai Te Rangi iwi. I wept as I listened to their beautiful chanting; in some strange way it felt healing and that, in spite of everything, forgiveness was possible.

My father now sits in the Departure Lounge watching people come and go, no longer the forgotten aviator. I don't know if either my brother or sister ever went down to Tauranga to see this mural. Alongside it, on the floor, is a glass display. Inside is a copy of my book, with an information sheet on my father the Tauranga City Council asked me to write.

PART 2

the reckoning

CHAPTER 18

Have You Seen *Stuff*?

I had just finished cycling with my friend, Debbie. We've been cycling together for years, and although we'd sometimes go out with local groups, we preferred just going out together, or with her partner, John, who sometimes tagged along.

We had just finished our favourite route on the Sunshine Coast hinterland, about a 30-kilometre ride. The first stretch across Bald Knob Road has for most of the way stunning views of the rugged volcanic peaks of the Glasshouse Mountains, which are spiritually significant to the area's traditional Aboriginal owners, the Gubbi Gubbi people. I always felt uplifted by the sight of the mountains. On a visit some years ago, Robert, who has travelled widely, said this was the most beautiful view he'd ever seen.

Pedalling along, I would feel myself begin to relax as my feet turned rhythmically. Reaching the end of the road we would turn left and then fly down the mountain, with the occasional whoop of delight. I'd often think of Dad, in his open cockpit Gipsy Moth, high above the earth, the rush of wind against him.

Cycling calms my restless mind. It's the ideal meditation for someone like me. Debbie and I would chat a lot on the long climbs.

I would talk about my writing, the lows and highs. Not that she would fully understand, but she was a keen reader so that counts.

The previous month, *Sundowner of the Skies* had been shortlisted for the NSW Premier's History Award 2020.[100] I was on top of the world. Apart from the birth of my two children, this was the best thing that had ever happened to me.

My bike was in the back of the car; helmet, shoes, gloves stowed away. I wiped the sweat off my face and checked my phone. There was an email from one of my Garden cousins to say she thought an online article on *Stuff* 'would be of interest'. I clicked on the link and it took me to an excerpt from a book: *Oscar Garden: A Tale of One Man's Love of Flying*.[101] The author, Dr Annamaria Garden. Anna!

I felt like I had been punched in the head and was suddenly disoriented and dizzy, as if I was going to pass out. I could not believe what I was reading. The excerpt was the story of Dad's 1930 epic solo flight from England to Australia. I'd had numerous articles published in magazines and newspapers detailing his epic flight and a detailed retelling was in *Sundowner of the Skies*. The flight is the focus of the very first article I wrote about my father: 'Sundowner of the Skies: Mary Garden takes flight with her father', published in 2005 on the centrefold pages of the *Australian Financial Review* (*AFR*).[102]

Why didn't the editors of *Stuff* check? Didn't anyone use Google? If they had, my article in *AFR* article would have come up straight away. The *Stuff* extract had exactly the same details. My father keeping his plan a secret. Half a dozen sandwiches on his lap. His only spare equipment a propeller, two valves and two valve springs. His hazardous 18-day flight across mountains, deserts, rivers, and finally across the Timor Sea to land unexpectedly at the tiny town of Wyndham, in the far north of Western Australia. The first to land there, as other aviators all made landfall at Darwin.

It was as if I was reading something I'd already written. My throat felt tight. I managed to say to Debbie, 'What the hell. I can't believe this.'

Some months later Debbie and I were reflecting on this time, those seconds when my whole world tilted, and she recalled glancing over to see me standing there, frozen, looking at my phone as if I'd just learnt that someone close had died.

I got in my car and drove home.

On the way, I rang the cousin who'd sent me the email. I couldn't get much sense from her. She was not shocked or upset for me and didn't think it was anything out of the ordinary. She was going out to buy a copy. I felt let down by her. Where was the sympathy? She had been very helpful while I was working on my own book and when it was published had said, 'I enjoyed reading your book and I'm amazed at all the research you've done.'

My heart was now racing so quickly I thought I was having a heart attack. When I reached home, I didn't bother taking off my sweaty lycra. I collapsed on my lounge and began to ring people. Ivy, my little toy cavoodle, plonked herself on my lap, and occasionally gazed at me with her large dark eyes.

I rang my daughter, Natalya, who was working in the family violence sector. She was incredulous. 'What the hell? Looks like an extension of her abuse of you. You need to see your psychologist as soon as you can.'

I rang Margareta. She told me she went into town to buy a copy as soon as she'd read the *Stuff* article. She thought the book very odd. 'It has just short pieces of text and she doesn't mention me at all, and hardly anything on you. There's very little on your family life.' I grimaced when she told me their local bookseller had my book and Anna's book sitting next to each other.

Maurice was listening on the other phone. He sounded annoyed. 'I won't look at it. I've read the only book I need to read on Oscar. And that is your book.'

I rang my son, Eamon. He was shocked but laughed. 'This just proves the whole point of your book. The weird, crazy Gardens.'

I left a message with my psychologist that I needed an appointment. It was urgent.

Throughout my ringing, the thought persisted: *Haven't I had enough abuse from Anna by now. Why has she done this? To try to humiliate me in public? This is too much. I don't deserve this. And what if her book wins an award, sells more copies than mine?* The idea was mortifying.

On Thursday I was heading down to Glen Innes in New South Wales for their second High Country Writers' Festival. I was to be a guest speaker. The region had been in lockdown because of Covid-19 and the border had just opened. I had been looking forward to a holiday and being in my happy place, among writers and booklovers. How on earth was I going to cope with the long drive, then speaking at the festival, smiling and pretending everything was fine? Perhaps I should cancel. I was in no state to go anywhere.

I broke a 5 mg tablet of Valium in half, swallowed a piece, then emailed my brother, forwarding our cousin's email. I was too distraught to ring him. He'd had no contact with this cousin since he left home. Nor had my sister. They'd not kept in touch with any of our five Garden cousins (Rosemarie, Roger and Margaret, Jenny and Derek) or our half-sister Margareta and her husband Maurice Gee. Not that there was any enmity; I think they just couldn't be bothered.

Robert had been very enthusiastic when he received a copy of my book in late May 2019: 'Brilliant. It really is amazing and thank goodness you got your book published. I'm very proud of you. You look great in the photo, also.' Now, just 16 months after the publication of my book, Anna's book had popped up out of nowhere it seemed.

I wrote to Robert: 'This is very bizarre. You made no mention of this. She has just rewritten, paraphrased what I wrote. From the excerpt it looks like plagiarism. And a hagiography. WHY??' At the end I added, 'PS I never call myself Dr. It should be used only by those employed in academia.'

I don't know why I assumed her book was a hagiography, perhaps because the *Stuff* extract ended with this: 'Notice his [Dad's] positive interpretation of what had happened to him. With this attitude, he couldn't lose.' Dad had been knocked to the ground by the propellor of his Gipsy Moth on his first stop at Munich. The police told him he should not continue that day but he persuaded them he was alright and took off for Salzburg, Austria.

When I finally found the courage to read my sister's book, which wouldn't be for some months, I noticed an occasional mention of our father's 'positivity', 'his optimistic nature', how much he 'loved' this or that. In his early days of flying, he may have been optimistic (determined would be a better word), but he became a negative and bitter person. I thought everyone who knew him agreed on that.

I didn't have to wait long – perhaps minutes – for a reply from Robert. He said he had asked Anna quite a few times when she would tell me about what she was doing, but she wanted to wait until it was published: 'She got me to swear I wouldn't tell you.' He said he hadn't seen the book yet but was getting a copy that week.

I fired off a long rant to my brother. This is a bit of what I said:

This will play out very badly for Anna. You have to wonder what her motive is, piggybacking my book. All my research. Looks like JEALOUSY. That is how it will look to others. She has always been jealous of me, even as a little girl, and that was what led to her ongoing attacks and abuse. Didn't she think of the consequences?

Why didn't you try to talk her out of it? Journalists will ask her why she wrote it when my book was published last year ... What is she going to say?? Of course, they will contact me as it is a good news story. All her abuse will come out. Why would Anna want all that in the open?

His reply was friendly but brief. He said I'd need to read it as from what he knew there were quite a lot of differences. 'She did not want to bring up family issues like you did but concentrate on the flying. She has done a lot of research herself.'

I took umbrage at 'family issues' and in my reply reminded him that *Sundowner of the Skies* was shortlisted for a top book award *because* it included the personal story, and that when I gave talks people wanted to hear about our family life, not Dad's flying. I told him I'd be taking legal action as Anna has plagiarised some of my writing and used the material I'd donated to Auckland's Museum of Transport and Technology (MOTAT) in January 2018.

At this stage I was only assuming Anna had plagiarised me. It certainly looked like it from the *Stuff* excerpt, not that I could bring myself to read it again.

Robert replied: 'I think you should not consider legal action. The only winners are lawyers.'

I don't know what I was expecting from my brother. But it was not this. I could not think clearly. I kept on at him, reverting to capitals, desperate to convey how upset I was: 'WHY?? A BOOK OF SPITE, REVENGE? I expect a journalist will contact me. There will be an article headline: "Estranged sister writes another book about their father's flying career within a year!!"' and I was going to tell any journalist the truth – the long history of her abuse since childhood. I made it clear that I would never read Anna's book, nor any articles published about it, and it would be best if we had no more contact. I asked him not to email or ring me.

He replied straight away. 'You don't realise how stable, and changed she is now, and you dwell far too much on the past.' This really annoyed me. I fired back: 'Her book proves she is not. You have no understanding of this stuff at all. You have never dealt with your past, only buried it. You need to go and talk to someone about this.' I suggested that he see a psychologist to try to get some clarity about all this and his part in it. The press may see it as sibling rivalry, but it was not. It was an extension of her abuse. I told him he was enabling her.

As if my brother would see a psychologist. He had told me he didn't believe in looking back, 'wallowing in the past' as he described it. Looking back on the emails I shot off to my brother that first day

I sound hysterical and half-throttled. I signed off all my emails to him with just M; he put Cheers. Robert's emails were short, mine were long and wordy as usual.

I've always been garrulous, talking and writing. Once, when Mum went up for a parent meeting at my primary school, my teacher, Mr Jopson, just opened and shut his hand repeatedly to mimic me talking. That year – my last year at primary school – I spent a lot of time sitting out in the corridor at an empty desk doing nothing. They would not even let you read a book, write in a notebook or draw.

I'd been diagnosed with PTSD after my sister attacked me in Helensville, not to mention all the times when we were growing up, as well as from my time in India and my past abusive relationships. I am what they call a chronic trauma survivor. This book was compounding it, adding to the cluster. My poor brain.

According to Dr Benjamin Todd Thatcher, a specialist in forensic psychiatry, trauma affects the brain, effectively rewiring it. He explains that neuropathologists have seen overlapping effects of physical and emotional trauma upon the brain. 'Traumas like physical and emotional trauma often lead to PTSD which can typically be a lifelong problem for most people, resulting in severe brain damage. Those who suffer from emotional trauma on the brain will often exhibit more fear of traumatic stressors than others.'[103]

There is some evidence that trauma alters people's genes, that the experience of trauma – or more accurately the effect of that experience – is 'passed' from one generation to the next. Perhaps a propensity towards intimate partner violence, parent–child abuse and sibling abuse is 'transmitted' from one generation to the next.

None of it made any sense. My sister had never written about our father's flying achievements, except for a brief mention of TEAL in her book *Reading the Mind of the Organisation*.[104] A book she had dedicated to our father. She'd had academic articles published in the 1980s and '90s, and her other books published since 2015 were on organisational change and development in business.

It got worse. As well as the excerpt, I found *Stuff* had published an article by Kelly Dennett titled, '"I think he'd be very proud of Air NZ": Daughter's book about flight pioneer father Oscar Garden'.[105] Dad proud of Air New Zealand! I don't think so. He'd shake his fist in the air whenever TEAL or Air New Zealand was mentioned. 'Those bastards up there,' he used to say. Dennett, who'd interviewed my sister, makes no mention of my book, widely publicised in New Zealand the previous year.

In fury, I spat out some tweets on Twitter, tagging *Stuff* and Dennett, who replied that it was 'just a family matter'. I screenshot her tweet and texted it to Natalya, who replied. 'A "family matter". Yep, just like family violence is a family matter. It's obvious that if they did their research they would see this story had already been published! You should write an article about how your sister stole your story.' She suggested I take advantage of Anna's book and promote mine as the 'true story'. 'You do realise, you can *now* write all about Anna and what she did to you.'

Like a troll I prowled social media sites, found the publisher's Facebook page, and spat out some comments on a few posts that were promoting my sister's book and the cover. I ended up deleting them a few days later. Natalya, who'd been very close to my mother, was angry too, and posted on Facebook:

Some of you know about the book my mother wrote about her father Oscar Garden and his understated contribution to aviation along with his complex behaviours. My grandma wanted it to be 'warts and all' so that's what Mum gave her. After all that my grandma sustained in a long marriage riddled with violence perpetrated by him, she deserved an account which included the stuff most biographies leave out.

And some of you have heard about my aunt, who has recently written a book about my grandfather Oscar, which looks like it has plagiarised Mum's work, and is her attempt to rewrite Mum's story of their father. You might say after almost a decade of advocating for Mum to write her book and supporting her through the process, I'm pretty pissed off with my aunt and really disappointed with her behaviour. Family politics is personal and ALSO political – as it impacts us all. Time to air out the dirty laundry.

The next day, while taking Ivy for a long walk down Mountain View Road, which is my favourite route near my house as it looks out over the glorious Glass House Mountains, I rang my New Zealand publisher. He was shocked and said it was the first he'd heard about my sister's book. He'd arrange for a copy straight away and would get back to me.

I went down the mountain to Maroochydore to see my psychologist. Like Natalya, she said Anna's book was an extension of her past abuse of me. She told me not to blame myself or beat myself up, an old pattern of mine, and suggested journaling could be helpful. That night I decided to write an article about my sister's abuse and her book. I'd stand up for myself, set the record straight. Perhaps that would help my traumatised brain.

I was expecting one of the numerous New Zealand journalists who had interviewed me about *Sundowner* or written a feature article or review about it, to contact me and ask why there was another book about my father out so soon after mine. But there was deathly silence. To my dismay almost all the media coverage of my sister's book treated it like it was the first book on Oscar Garden. This really stuck in my craw.

Thankfully, supportive emails flew in. One was from an old friend from Papakura High School:

Can you sue for plagiarism? It's weird but maybe she's short of money and hopes to make some. Nothing we can do about our dysfunctional family members. I have a batty sister my brother and I have nothing to do with. Toxic as but having no contact is way less stressful. You wrote a great book, you're so talented. Breathe in, breathe out and move on.

Another was from an aviation buff I'd met on a research tour of New Zealand in 2007:

> I was up in Wellington over the weekend and while we were in a bookshop, I was shocked to find another book on Oscar. Reading the Author's Note, it seems she didn't accept the story you told so had to put her own spin on it. I had a quick read and wasn't impressed. It is NOTHING compared to your well-researched work. It seems to skip over each part of his life — no substance at all and nothing to add to the story. Apart from the obvious and understandable anger you must feel, you have nothing to worry about from this lightweight effort. I wonder if Mary Egan [publisher] knew of your book.

I got this response from a leading bookstore:

> When I saw your sister's book coming through, I must say I thought it a little odd, following on from your one so soon. There hasn't been the same interest and we have told customers about your one at the same time! We have sold 5 of her title to 56 of *Sundowner*.

This was the worst, from Dave Homewood, host of *Wings Over New Zealand Aviation Forum*, who had promoted *Sundowner of the Skies* when it was released:

> I assume that was you this morning on RNZ [Radio New Zealand) under a new name? Your book has been reprinted with a new title?

I cringed. How embarrassing. The Mad Gardens. That's what Mum used to call us. She'd be turning over in her grave to hear about Anna's book. Dad would too. Maybe they've heard about it wherever they are.

CHAPTER 19

We Act for Your Siblings

For a year after Anna's book was published, I felt unhinged. I was enraged at her for doing such a thing. All I could think of was exposing her, revealing the full story, the history of her abuse behind her decision to write it. I fantasised that her book would be pulped and taken off bookshelves. I did not want it sitting next to mine. What I probably really needed to do was cry or weep or howl, but I could not summon any tears. Rage instead extinguished all other emotion.

I also felt betrayed by Robert for both supporting Anna's book and keeping it a secret. Previously he'd said he was so proud of me when my book was published and appreciated the help I'd given over the years. 'You did an amazing job with Mum and Ola, and I won't forget that. I really do appreciate how you got everything moving when Anna was ill. Thank you so much for getting her out of her mental troubles.'

He had never objected to my portrayal of Dad when he read the draft manuscript; he had never said, 'Dad was not like that'; he had only wanted me to cut down on the stuff on Anna, which I had, drastically.

I felt such a deep sense of betrayal. How would I ever recover?

On returning from the writer's festival at Glen Innes, although I'd told my brother I wanted nothing more to do with him, I emailed him. I wanted to get some information for the article I was writing about Anna and her treachery so I was friendly and contained my rage, well aware I was being manipulative. I even signed off with a cheesy 'Cheers', whereas all previous emails since I heard about Anna's book simply ended M.

I asked him, 'Do you know why Anna wrote the book? And why did she want to keep it a secret? Could you send me a copy of the Author's Note?'

He replied later that day to say he didn't know why, but it wasn't to spite me. 'She did it pretty quickly, after your book came out, and I suspect she wanted to put a different perspective on it keeping away from family issues, as she didn't like that. She was quite pleased with the shortish time it took her.'

Shortish time? I began working on *Sundowner of the Skies* in 2005, and spent years contacting people, researching archives and collecting material, just for Anna to piggyback all the information I'd collected!

He said he had begun reading her book and it was different to mine and he'd be interested to see what I thought of it. He added that Anna had not wanted me know what she was doing in case I tried to stop it being published.

I reminded Robert that I would never read Anna's book, but Margareta had bought a copy and said the layout was very strange and she was hardly mentioned. I also said my publisher thought it was 'commercial suicide' publishing it so soon after mine. He replied, 'Margareta saying she's hardly mentioned!! Nor are we, and anyway, it's not about us, it's about Dad.' He said he didn't know about the economics but pointed out Anna's book was released a year after mine. He thought I should read it, to see what she has researched that was different.

I wondered if he was hoping Anna's would sell more copies than mine? Later that day he sent me screenshots of the Anna's Author's Note. This is part of it:

> I read my sister's biography. This was good, but it was her version, not my own. I needed to write my own. I wanted to tell a story that gave a complete picture of my father's life showing what an extraordinary man he was. Having had a good relationship with him, I feel I am in a good position to write his story. It took me only eight months to write the basics. I got up at 4 a.m. to do it. It was a thrill to piece together all the newspaper clippings. If Dad had seen them all he would have had a chuckle. He had had a few hidden in his suitcase, but there were numerous one she missed. My brother, Rob, supported me totally in this.

The first thing I thought when I saw she took only eight months 'to write the basics', was that she was mad in the sense of not being well. Perhaps she'd been going through a manic episode: the upward swing of her bipolar illness, with heightened energy and creativity. Had she stopped taking her medication and that allowed her to work around the clock on a wave of mania?

I bristled to read 'My brother, Rob, supported me totally in this' and that hers was a 'complete picture'. Anna was casting doubt on the veracity of my account and implying I had had a bad relationship with Dad!

Rage shot through me. She knew nothing about my relationship with Dad. We had never been together with Dad or talked about him since we were teenagers. I don't know why it bothered me so much that my sister implied she'd had a better relationship with Dad. Was it the child in me, feeling rejected and dismissed by Dad? Or was it to get back at me after I'd told her that even though I wasn't religious a few years before he died Dad had given me one of his most precious possessions, his mother's Bible. I think she'd have felt pretty pissed off about this, since she was the religious one of us three. His mother, Rebecca, had written in it extensively, her curly writing travelling up and down the edges of the pages. My cousin Jenny, who lived in Christchurch, recalls our grandmother sitting and reading it every day and making notes in it.

I have to admit that a very small part of me felt pleased for her when I read that she'd found it thrilling to piece together all the newspaper clippings. When I began researching Dad's life I felt as if I'd entered Aladdin's Cave and discovered gems from my father's flying days, as well as the treasure trove of his own family history. I was pleased at the thought that my sister got to feel that same thrill.

The next morning, I heard back from my publisher.[106] He said he had obtained a copy of Anna's book. 'To be totally and brutally honest, it was a sad and poor display of writing. I'm glad she didn't plagiarise you, as it would be a negative reflection of your unique writing skills.' He said it wasn't selling well and he wasn't aware of any bookstores in New Zealand actively working it. 'Relax Mary – not worth losing sleep over. If there was even the slightest hint of "skulduggery", we would unleash Armageddon on her. Not to be.'

I was disappointed. I had hoped Anna had plagiarised me so the book could be removed and pulped. But I was relieved to hear that her writing was so bad! I could have left it there, just accepted it, got on with my life, as my brother urged. But there is a part of me, like Dad, that is infuriated by injustice, and this part wanted to fight against this wrong, keep at it like a terrier. Later that day I came across an interview on NZ Booklovers, an online hub for books, in which Anna had said she disagreed so strongly with my rendition of her (note the *her*) father that 'I put pen to paper and wrote furiously putting together my tale on Dad. When my brother read it, he said, "You and my sister had two different fathers." He agreed with my version as being a closer picture of Dad.'[107]

I felt devastated. My brother had just told me he had only started reading her book. And as I would later discover (when I finally found the courage to buy a copy), the little she wrote about Oscar as a father was towards the end of the book. So how could he have agreed with her version? Booklovers provide authors with a standard list of questions to answer about their book before they feature it, so it is likely she completed it before Robert even began reading her book!

What makes Anna's comments so unfair and hurtful is that my book entailed years of research and was not just my view of Dad but numerous recollections of others. I interviewed many people, including Mum, my aunt, friends, my half-sister, and some of the pilots who Dad had trained. Was she infuriated by their recollections, too? What about Mum saying, 'He was a bastard of a father and a bastard of a husband'? And there was also this comment from Mary Ewart, one of Mum's friends, 'It used to make me absolutely furious to hear the men, typical of men, you know, go on and on about your father's flying achievements when he used to treat your mother and you children so abominably. I admired his tenacity but didn't like the way he treated your mother or you children.'

Another friend, Tiki Burley, remembered my father as being a recluse who, in his later years, locked himself in his bedroom when they visited, and only came out to walk down to the TAB. She said they were aware of his gambling problem and my mother always making excuses for him. In her view, 'He probably should never have been a father.'

My sister interviewed no one. All the relevant people were dead by the time she decided to write 'her version'. Now she was saying my book was in effect a lie, that my portrayal was not a true picture. I felt like I'd again been stabbed in the back.

I got stuck into my article, compelled to reply to what I felt was Anna's attack, and to stand up for myself. I wrote about Anna's book, the shock of it all, and included the story of her assaulting me at Helensville in 2005, and the impact of that assault. I called my article 'The Hagiography: Why my sister's book feels like a stab in the back.'

Blinded with rage, I emailed it to my brother, presuming he'd forward it to Anna. I told him it was being published (that was a lie) and urged him to see a psychologist who would help him understand what was really going on. I explained that my view of Dad was also Anna's, as I had some of her letters to Mum to prove it.

Naively, I expected them both to realise Anna's book had been a mistake and they would feel remorseful and apologise to me. One of my flaws is that I expect people will see things the same way as me. Robert and Anna had never apologised in the past or shown me any sympathy (with the exception of the one time when Robert did express concern for me after I was attacked at Helensville). So I don't know why I expected them to do so now.

I was surprised to get a short reply from Anna. 'I didn't write my book to spite you at all. My views on Dad are very different to yours and have been for some time.' So, she changed her mind? Where once she thought he was harsh and caused damage, and had actually written those words to Mum, now she didn't?

I was shaken by the response from Robert. He said my article was 'a load of rubbish' and that he never found Dad as harsh as I found him and I have always exaggerated things, such as Anna's abuse. He said I was trying to push my perceptions and ideas of how his life was supposed to have played out. 'I know what I remember and feel and this is personal to me. You have no idea of my personal experiences.'

Always exaggerated Anna's abuse? I'm too sensitive and too emotional? Most of his email made no sense.

I thought that would be the last I would hear from either of them. A few days later I was lying back on my couch after a bike ride with Debbie and her partner John – this time we had cycled a route from Mapleton, down the steep Phillips Road, across to Palmwoods for coffee, and then the slow grind up the steep hill to Montville, a hill we call The Windy. I was still in my sweaty lycra posting photos of Debbie and me on social media when I received an email from a lawyer. This is an extract:

> We act for your siblings Robert and Annamaria Garden.
>   Our clients are very distressed by the tone and content of your article, the way in which you portray them personally, the things

you have said about them and the things you claim they have said and done. They are also very upset at the lens through which you view the Garden family history as it does not reconcile with their own lived experience.

We are instructed many of your claims are either exaggerated or simply untrue ...

I was warned that I was on notice, and that proceedings would be commenced against me for defamation, not only if I published the article but if I made any comments about Anna or her book on social media, as a guest speaker or presenter at any event. 'As a precaution, we are writing to a number of publishers and news outlets to warn against publication of your article or they too will be joined as defendants to our client's claim.'

My brother was the last person in the world I'd expect to threaten me legally.

I'd never been threatened with defamation in my life. I burst into tears. None of this made any sense. Mum would be horrified, I thought. Dad, too. I reckon he'd be furious at both of them. He hated injustice. He would belt them both if he was here, even Anna. They knew I was telling the truth.

I felt as though I'd been punched in the stomach. Legal threats have a chilling effect. This wasn't about reputation or defamation, but power and control. Threatening me with defamation for writing about abuse is using the legal system to abuse me further; they were using the law as a weapon to attempt to silence me. Journalist Michael Burge said that the fact they could threaten me writing about their 'secretive extra Oscar Garden book felt so abusive'.

I presumed my brother was behind this, although I'd never seen this side of him. I knew this would be the end of my relationship with him, that there would be no coming back from this. I felt devastated. Although we only had a superficial relationship, he had been in my life since I was born and now I was estranged from him as well as my sister.

The thing that puzzled me was that there was little mention of Robert in the article except a few extracts from his emails and this paragraph:

> If Dad's abuse didn't affect him, that is great. Some children are more resilient than others. However, people who suffer trauma can consciously try to suppress their recollection of painful events and overtime the forgetting becomes automatic.

After ringing my daughter, Debbie and my cousin Gillian to offload on them, I went to Google and found Brian Martin, Emeritus Professor of Social Sciences at the University of Wollongong. He'd written extensively on defamation. I emailed him and attached my article. I was surprised to hear back from him the next morning, as it was a Sunday. It was a lengthy email, so this is a short excerpt:

> Your article is a sad story beautifully and sensitively told. What to do depends a lot on your goals, so here I'll give you some options. There's no need for you to see a lawyer at this stage. You don't need to reply to the lawyer letter. Anna and Robert aim to deter you from saying anything in public that reflects badly on them.
>
> Option 1. Do not seek publication of the article. That will be the end of the matter.
>
> Option 2. Write back to the lawyer asking for any statements you've made that are false and defamatory. If you receive some feedback, you can then judge whether to change the text or provide supporting information. Then you could send the lawyer a revised version of the article.
>
> Option 3. Find a publisher for the article. Most editors are wary about potential legal action, so if they know about the legal threat, many of them would back off. Following lawyer letters like the one you received, very few writs are ever issued. After writs, very few cases ever get to court. They are settled.
>
> Option 4. You can publish the article yourself, on a blog or website.
>
> In short, don't worry about being sued. Think strategically about what you want to achieve and proceed with caution. I'm happy to discuss these and other matters any time.

I was relieved to read this, and felt deep gratitude for his generosity. I was even more determined to try to get my article published. It was important for my mental health to speak out, and I also thought there would be public interest in shining a light on sibling abuse.

In *How Many More Women?* Jennifer Robinson and Keina Yoshida examine the laws around the world that silence women in cases involving sexual and gender-based violence. They write that 'women who remain silent out of fear of facing those [legal] consequences also suffer adverse physical and mental consequences because they must endure their pain in shame and isolation.'[108] (Although they use women here, they also acknowledge that abuse is suffered by people of all genders.)

I decided to contact my siblings' solicitor directly. In the email I requested that she ask her clients for a list of any statement in the article which is 'exaggerated or untrue'. I pointed out Anna was alleging I was lying about our father, even though there was a large amount of documentation to support the fact that he had a violent streak. I signed off 'Regards, Dr Mary Garden'. I am not a fan of titles, but I considered this was a good time to use it, to give me more credibility.

The next day the solicitor replied that she had had a family emergency overnight and would not be able to respond to the issues I raised for a day or two. She needed to wait and hope for things to improve at the hospital.

I sent her my condolences and added, 'I have been through those emergencies with my mother and aunt. I was always the one to be called upon. I flew over the ditch and back many times.' She thanked me for my 'kind words', and said they were hoping for better news that day.

That is the last I ever heard from the siblings' solicitor.

CHAPTER 20

I'll Bags It

I ignored the legal threat. I kept sharing my story on social media and talking about my sister's book and her betrayal in radio interviews and at book events.

When I was down at the High Country Writers Festival at Glen Innes, just days after my sister's book was published, I'd also spoken about it. In a session on memoir, moderated by journalist Amanda Woods, I was joined by author Mary Moody. Amanda, author of *Adventures All Around*, one of Australia's best travel blogs, had read some of my rants on social media and asked beforehand if she could bring up my sister's book and I agreed.

It was a healing session for me. The audience was sympathetic; I vaguely remember saying I felt like flying over to Auckland and strangling my sister, which made everyone laugh. I decried her book, said it was just a hagiography, and mentioned that I'd left out a lot of material from an earlier draft, including things that happened after Dad died as well as Anna's violence. Interestingly, a few in the audience who'd read *Sundowner of the Skies* said they felt like I'd left things out in my book, that there were things missing, that they would have liked more. You can't win.

The festival took place at the luxurious Shearers Lodgings of the historic Waterloo Station, circa 1908, which looks down Matheson Valley with the Waterloo Range in the background. Sprawling rolling green. That night, we were sitting on couches in front of a fire before dinner and someone asked what 'hagiography' meant. Mary Moody gave a long explanation – something along the lines of a biography that treats the subject in a flattering light, with excessive or undue admiration – and we all laughed and chatted about my sister's book, how bizarre it all was. I couldn't think of a better tonic after the shock just six days earlier.

After I returned home, I decided to seek advice via the Arts Law Centre as to whether my article, now retitled 'The Hagiography', was actually defamatory. The barrister I was assigned said he enjoyed reading it. He explained that there was 'the common law defence of qualified privilege on the basis of reply to an attack' and to make sure I mentioned in my article that it was 'a reply to an attack', namely Anna's book. The defence is that if your character or conduct is attacked, 'you are entitled to respond to that attack. While responding to that attack, any defamatory statements you make will be privileged – and you will not be liable for them'.[109]

He suggested, however, that I leave out any mention of my sister's mental illness as this was an invasion of privacy. People were often concerned about defamation, he explained, but invasion of privacy was a bigger legal risk. I'd never considered this. I'd included some details of her illness in my book and felt chastened to hear this.

I reworked 'The Hagiography' and submitted it to various magazines and online sites in New Zealand, Australia and even the United States. Most did not reply, others said it was not for them. A few were sympathetic, which kept me going. One said, 'I'm sorry that you've had to go through what sounds like a complex and frustrating, hurtful experience. Unfortunately, we are going to say no to publishing this piece. Good luck finding elsewhere to publish.'

I was determined. I was not going to give up. I still had not got up the courage to buy a copy of my sister's book and was relying on her Author's Note, her comments on NZ Booklovers, and emails from both her and Robert, for my article. I also dipped into several radio interviews and was surprised to hear Anna parroting some of Trent Dalton's endorsement for *Sundowner of the Skies*; for example, 'crashlanding his life on earth' and 'a rattling, searing soulful story'. I felt creeped out. It was as if she was trying to take over my life.

About a month after receiving the legal threat, I was out cycling and once more began to fume about all the work I'd done for my book and the thousands of hours researching, writing and interviewing people. And how unfair it was that Anna had largely based her book on the back of my work and the documents I'd found and gifted to the MOTAT. I had this bizarre idea that if I sent Anna a list of all the people I'd interviewed and some of the transcripts, including Mum's, she might change her mind and realise she had made a mistake writing her book. She might even withdraw it. Again, this was rather naive of me! I'm shaking my head at me back then; it shows that I was still traumatised, unable to think clearly.

At the end of the ride, I didn't wait around for coffee with my friends but chucked my bike in the back of the car and took off. As soon as I got home, I wrote a list of people I'd interviewed. I emailed the list to my sister, attaching some transcripts of interviews, including one with Mum, and said rather sarcastically that I had wanted to write a *complete* portrait of Dad. I asked if she wanted the rest of my research material and my photo collection, as I had no more need for any of it. I felt I'd had enough of Oscar Garden and wanted to get rid of him out of my life, along with the misery he'd brought me.

In her reply she thanked me for my generous offer, but added that one of the reasons she wrote her version was, 'I considered everything you wrote about me was wrong starting with my date of birth, year of completing my PhD, my diagnosis, yelling at Mum and so on. It all went public.'

There was no mention in my book of the year she completed her PhD – that was only in the original manuscript – but to my horror I discovered I'd gotten her birth date wrong in the final version. It was a year out: 1953 instead of 1952.

To appease her, I explained that no one had made any comment about what I'd included about her, but as my book was going into a reprint I would replace her name with 'a family member'. She was happy with this and added, 'Most of the people where I work just about had a heart attack reading my name in your book. We work in a mental health facility so focus on the rights and wellbeing of our clients.' This is what the barrister had warned about my article.

I was also surprised to hear I had her diagnosis wrong. Wasn't it bipolar? She replied: 'My diagnosis comes from the discharge notice from Taharoto Mental Health Unit and what was given verbally when I was there. It is schizoaffective with bipolar type plus PTSD. This means it is primarily schizophrenia. However, most of my treatment focused on bipolar.'

Schizophrenia. Mum's worst nightmare. Janet Frame called it 'a disease without hope'.[110] On hearing this, my heart hurt. I wept. I thought how she must have struggled and suffered throughout her life and probably did still. I decided to break my silence with my brother and emailed him about Anna's diagnosis. It was the first he had heard of it, even though he lived nearby, looked out for her and helped her from time to time. One of the main symptoms of schizophrenia is distorted, fractured memory. Perhaps she was unable to tell the truth because of her illness? Perhaps the illness and the medication she had taken for it over the years had led to cognitive deficits and memory loss? It was a lightbulb moment in my life to hear this. Everything started to make sense.

Why, then, I ask myself now, was I still hellbent on getting justice and revenge, knowing about my sister's illness. Was I a monster too?

I told her I'd already removed any mention of her mental illness in my article and had included the anecdote of me breaking my leg and Dad not taking me to a doctor and a bit on his coercive control with money. She replied, 'That sounds all good. I think it is better to not focus on my illness.' I concluded from this that she was happy for me to publish the article.

It felt like a breakthrough. Afterwards, I fantasised about flying over to Auckland and driving down to Tauranga together. We would explore Ōtūmoetai, go down to the beach, visit the site where the historical Ōtūmoetai Pa had once been, check out Ōtūmoetai Primary School, and I'd show her the portrait of Dad at Tauranga Airport. We would catch up with our cousin Gillian MacColl and her daughter, and Alistair Barclay, the son of our family doctor. I felt a warmth towards my sister, and all the love I had for her long ago return. All I'd ever wanted was to have a close loving relationship with her.

After a day, though, the wave of sympathy passed. *Fuck her.* It wasn't love. It was the rescuer in me, the part of me that causes many of my problems. The part that feels sorry for her, wants to help her. Later, I regretted not asking her if those people at her work made any comment about her behaviour, her treatment of me and our mother that I'd briefly mentioned in my book. Weren't they shocked? Perhaps she denied it all. Told them I was a liar.

As mentioned, Mum gave me Dad's old, scuffed leather suitcase, which had a few faded stickers on it, including one of the Eiffel Tower. I don't know how old this suitcase is. Dad had visited France in 1935. Mum reckoned that's where he learnt to gamble, in Monte Carlo. There is no casino grander than the Casino de Monte Carlo in Monaco on the French Riviera. Built in the 1850s, the ornate gambling house has been featured in many James Bond movies. There was also a fading sticker which had a blonde lady in a 1940s bikini, her hands on the side of a wooden surfboard, upright against her back. The words Wentworth Hotel were across the top of the sticker;

Sydney, Australia, along the bottom. Wentworth Hotel was where the TEAL pilots stayed overnight after flying the Awarua or Aotearoa flying boats across the Tasman Sea from Auckland to Sydney, a flight that could take up to 11 hours.

Or is it even older? Could it have been stashed in the front cockpit of his Gipsy Moth plane when he made his foolhardy flight from England to Australia in 1930, with only 39 flying hours under his belt? I pored over all my old photos looking for a picture of a suitcase. I could only find one. Dad is standing in front of his plane, hat in one hand, cigarette in another, talking to another pilot. There is a suitcase resting on the grass touching his left knee, but it looks bigger and more battered than the one that ended up under his bed.

I had considered gifting Dad's suitcase to MOTAT in 2019, along with the other things I'd given them, but I changed my mind at the last minute. Now I didn't want the suitcase. I'd give the bloody thing to Anna. I stuffed it with folders of some of the research material I'd promised her. I even chucked in a bag containing some brass buttons from his TEAL uniforms. I was going to exorcise Oscar Garden from my life. I'd promised Natalya I'd leave the suitcase to her when I died, but I didn't give much thought to this. I just wanted it out of Australia.

Anna received my gift ten days later. 'Suitcase is wonderful. Love all the stuff. The folders are magnificent. Love them. Rob has been over and ploughed through them.'

That suitcase was very precious to me. Dad used it in the 1930s when flying for United Airways and in the 1940s while flying for TEAL. It had travelled with him on the flying boats as he amassed about 10,000 flying hours. *Why on earth did I give it to her?* I thought soon afterwards. Also, I'd promised it to Natalya. *Why was I so reckless and impulsive?*

I emailed Robert and pointed out he had misread my last email, and that I'd said 'my view of Dad is also Anna's', not that he and I had the same view. I also pointed out I'd never mentioned his personal experiences, only my own. I explained that after feedback from Anna I had made some changes to the article and she had said it was fine to get it published. Also, it had been checked by a barrister. My brother replied, 'I think I did misread your email. I'm really glad you have removed those references and been so communicative with Anna. Cheers Rob.'

Did he issue that legal threat in part because he misread my email? We were back to playing happy families, although I no longer trusted him.

I felt worse after reconnecting with my sister and brother. Being cut off from them felt much better than being civil on top of so much damage and betrayal.

Never have I spent so long working on an article. Sometimes I can whip up an article in no time and find a home for it quickly, even the same day; other times, I write something I think is terrific and send it off and get no reply. This is usually because it is half-baked and pretty crappy. And there are times when a good piece never finds a home, for a range of reasons.

I ended up dividing the article into two: the first one, 'Siblings at Loggerheads', focused on the Helensville story, with a brief mention of our books; the other, 'The Hagiography', was the story of my sister's book and mine, the betrayal of it all, and how hers was just a hagiography. I asked a friend who had been a journalist for a national newspaper for help. After she'd read 'The Hagiography' she said she thought it needed 'a bit less of the argy bargy between the siblings' without detracting from the drama and suggested some edits.

The new version worked. Within hours, two news sites were interested. The books editor of *Oasis*, an award-winning New Zealand online website, was the first. 'Families, eh? Far out.' She said she was sure it had been incredibly stressful for me but I'd written a very measured piece and she would love to publish it. 'Can I please bags it?' she asked, before adding that they may need to give Anna right of reply.

She also asked to see 'Siblings at Loggerheads'. She wanted to publish that too, and said her editor was impressed with both pieces.

The New Zealand Herald was also interested. The journalist said they would do a news story on it but also run my piece below that. They, too, would want Anna's right of reply.

The right of reply is a highly disputed area of media law. Some see it as an alternative to expensive defamations lawsuits; others see it as interference with editorial independence.

Regardless, my journalist friend advised, 'I don't see any value in being involved in a news story pitting the two of you against each other. The article stands on its own so give it to a publication that will run as is. Your sister is gaslighting you with her book.'

I asked journalist Michael Burge for his view:

> We in the media have gotten a bit too carried away with including 'right of reply' in every article. It's risk-averse behaviour guided by a readership that demands just about everything gets 'both sided', particularly in politics. It's also a tempting timesaver in an overworked, understaffed media landscape. But the job of editing requires being judicious, not to umpire between the most obvious players.

After many emails going back and forth, the editor said that while 'it's beautifully done and a heck of a story', they would not proceed without Anna's right of reply.

These email exchanges were happening when Auckland was in the middle of an extended lockdown because of the pandemic. (Queensland was lucky in this respect: we only had several short lockdowns, unlike the lengthy lockdowns that Victoria, New South Wales or New Zealand experienced.) The editor later explained to me that she had been a journalist for 18 years and 'had never experienced anything like the stress and precarity of that time'. Contributors were suddenly working from home – she was trying to work with two small children and no childcare.

Also, various mastheads had been closed down. Bauer Media, who published some of New Zealand's best-known magazines, including *The Listener, North & South* and *NZ Woman's Weekly*, had shut down, with 237 staff made redundant.[111]

'It was not a time to take potentially expensive and time-consuming legal risks for stories that were anything other than compellingly in the broad public interest', the editor said.

Reluctantly I sent a copy of 'The Hagiography' to Anna, pointed out there was no mention of her mental illness, and asked if she'd like to give feedback which the editor may publish at the end. She replied, 'I think it is insulting. It is pretty insulting to me. I certainly never said I was happy with your article without reference to mental illness.' (Looking back now, I think Anna had been referring to my book and not my article, when she said, 'That sounds all good. I think it is better to not focus on my illness', even though I was talking about the article and how I'd removed any mention of her mental illness.)

I had a panic attack. My heart started beating rapidly, I became short of breath, there was pressure building in my brain and all I wanted to do was find a way to escape this awful familiar feeling. Dealing with my sister was doing my head in. I knew it was not good for my mental health to be in touch with her.

CHAPTER 21

Smash Hit

At the end of that turbulent month, I received a copy of my sister's book, just over three months since it had been released. I'd decided, after all, to get a copy and ordered one from a New Zealand bookshop.

It was mid-summer. Summer stretches in Queensland, with months of hot humid days, and rain can bucket down for days on end. Up on the mountain I often woke to thick fog enveloping my house. The fruit trees in my backyard were heavy with ripe fruit – mangos, papaya, guava, grapes. My free-range chooks scuttled under my veranda to escape the heat or the rain. I didn't need air-conditioning in my rammed earth house.

I read *A Tale of One Man's Love of Flying* in one day. It was not as long as mine, perhaps half the length. The book was well-produced: a hardback, a glorious cover – it was much nicer looking than mine, although Robert had said he was just warming to it – and used good quality paper. It was what you would call a coffee-table book and would have been costly to print.

I was angry the moment I opened it. It was nothing like I had expected. I thought it would be completely different to mine. However, it was obvious to me she had piggybacked my book, using the same layout, the same anecdotes, the same photos, even including letters and documents I'd sourced.

She had reproduced scores of items from the collection I'd gifted MOTAT, including photos, logbook extracts, letters, extracts from passports, and navigator and pilot licences. Nowhere in her book did she acknowledge my contribution.

In early January 2018, MOTAT received two large boxes of materials I had posted to them. The museum is only 45 kilometres from where Anna lived. The credit line for the Oscar Garden Collection is: 'Mary Garden. 1875–2005. COL-2018-2. Walsh Memorial Library, The Museum of Transport and Technology (MOTAT).'[112]

I wonder what went through my sister's mind during the hours she spent at MOTAT's Walsh Memorial Library, rummaging through items I'd spent 15 years collecting. She would have seen my writing, my notes. Did she feel guilty? A sense of unease about what she was doing? She later told me she found the materials very useful: 'I could have used more!!' On realising what Anna had done, I wished I'd donated my collection to a museum in Australia, which I did consider.

I was also annoyed to see that in her book she used many of the same stories: Dad landing unexpectedly at Wyndham and his stay at the Blazing Stump Hotel; a piece that reports the launch of the wireless telephone service from New Zealand to Australia and the television conversation between Dad and Charles Kingsford Smith; and the *Sun* piece dated 5 November 1930 in which Dad is first called 'Sundowner of the Skies': 'Oscar Garden, the casual flier, blew into Wyndham yesterday evening, after his last hop on the flight from England. Kingsford-Smith has dubbed himself a Vagabond of the Air. Garden, then, is the Sundowner of the Skies.'[113]

But what really disturbed me were the scores of errors throughout. I was livid. Historical biographies require extensive research using a wide range of sources and typically take years to write. Facts need to be cross-checked for accuracy: you don't just rely on newspapers or books, as my sister did. Many of the newspaper articles reporting on Dad's 1930 flight had errors in them as he did not tell the truth. He did not want people to know his parents had separated, for example, so he lied about when he emigrated to New Zealand and said he went there in 1915 instead of 1921.

Most of the figures in Anna's book were out by a mile, and numerous dates and ages were wrong. For example, she stated that our grandfather built the only big shop in Tongue, 'in six days sometime around 1902'. It wasn't our grandfather but our great-grandfather, Robert Garden Sr, who built the shop – in the early 1890s – and it is unlikely it was built in six days. His son, Robert Garden Jr, my grandfather, moved to Tongue in 1897 to manage the shop. Another error: Dad's older brother Bertie was not 12 years old when he died, he was eight.

Towards the end of her book is a photo captioned 'Oscar and Helen Garden at a family wedding ... circa late 1940s'. This is a decade out. The wedding was of Robin Barclay (Dad's cousin) to Patricia MacKenzie, which took place in Tauranga in January 1957. I was only six years old, but I remember how beautiful Mum looked in a gorgeous black-and-white lace dress with a floral pattern and an elegant black swooped-brim hat.

Now that I had a copy in my hands, I could not understand how it had been accepted for publication. She wrote in the Author's Note:

It took me only eight months to write the basics ... When I had finished the basic draft, I sent it off to several publishers, all of whom rejected it. I figured it still needed some work so I sent it off to two manuscript assessors. Their feedback sorted out the book and I sent it off to literary agents and publishers. This time I got a more positive response especially from the delightful team of publishers (Mary Egan and Sophie Egan-Reid) who cared about the book. Without them you would not have had this book. And so, this is the book I wrote.

A manuscript assessor considers or appraises the worth of a manuscript to assess its potential for publication. They examine things such as the structure, content and style, and their feedback may include legal issues to be aware of, such as defamation or copyright. Did they consider these issues? I wondered if the assessors knew about my book.

Robert had mentioned that Anna paid for her book to be published and so I found the courage to email Mary Egan Publishing and ask if they could confirm this. I also attached my article 'The Hagiography', and said it was going to be published. I received this reply from Sophia Egan-Reid. (She did not mention my article.)

> Hi Mary
>
> I can confirm that Annamaria self-published this title. She accepts full responsibility for the content of the publication. She specifically indemnifies Mary Egan Publishing against any action by other parties relating to the content or presentation including but not limited to libel, slander or breach of copyright.
>
> Kind regards
>
> Sophia

A recent trend among traditional publishers is to also offer self-publishing services. Coincidentally, I found an article published in 2016 by *Stuff* about this trend. Written by journalist Eleanor Black, the article warns authors about scam publishers and recommends that they use reputable publishers such as Mary Egan Publishing, a firm described as doing 'commercial projects and high-end self-publishing'. Reportedly, scam publishers had been charging authors large amounts of money – between $5000 and $15,000 – and all they received was an ebook and a few 'poorly edited print copies of their manuscript'. According to Black, Mary Egan told her that $15,000 should cover all costs associated with making a book, including design, editing, proofreading, printing and ebook production and delivery. For that price, depending on the number of pages in their book, the author should receive about 1000 copies, although Egan said 'she rarely recommends such a large print run'.[114]

The website of Mary Egan Publishing lists the various services they provide, with approximate costs for each. For example, cover design $1400–$2500; copyediting $60–$80 an hour, and proofreading $40–$60 an hour. 'We guide out authors through editing, proofreading, design and printing to market and sales (and everything in between).'[115]

It appears that an author can choose what services they want. As mentioned, *A Tale of One Man's Love of Flying* is a beautifully produced book – the cover is gorgeous – but I wonder if Anna availed herself of their editing and proofreading services?

I was especially upset to read what Anna wrote about the scattering of Dad's ashes in Mechanics Bay, where he used to land the flying boats. 'My sister Mary wouldn't come as it meant flying over from Australia.' This reads as if I could not bother going over, whereas she flew all the way from England. In fact, I had gone over with Natalya, but I had an anxiety attack about seeing Anna and we flew back the next day.

Bizarrely, there is only a short section of about 1500 words at the end of the book describing Dad's life after he left TEAL: Oscar the father, the tomato grower, the retiree. In contrast, my book devoted two chapters to Oscar after he left flying: 10,433 words to be exact. You would think if my sister was furious with my depiction of our father, she would have spent more time defending him. She paints a picture of a happy childhood, where, she says, we had quite a free rein. 'All in all, Dad managed to make ends meet. We always had great houses to live in. My favourite property had three acres of land to play in including the sea at the end of the section. We shrieked and hollered and occasionally got told off by one of our parents.'

She makes no mention of the hut with its smelly dunny, nor of Dad's gambling addiction and that our maternal grandfather contributed towards our expenses. Although she says Dad was strict and could be quick-tempered and critical, she leaves out his miserliness and his violence towards Mum. I rolled my eyes when I read Dad was 'occasionally moving house'. That's an understatement.

Even more bizarrely, the rest of her book, which describes Oscar the pilot and his flying achievements, portrays an Oscar that is no different to mine.

What was completely mystifying was that none of the reviews I'd read had been negative or critical, and I could only find two that mentioned both our books. Jim Sullivan's review in the *Otago Daily Times* concluded that each book enhanced the other, 'perhaps with some extra insight here, or more information there, and, taken together, they provide the aviation buff and history reader with pretty well all we need to know about this remarkable man.' He recommended reading them both 'for a chance to examine just how two sisters might view the same subject. A rare opportunity.'[116]

In *Aviation News*, Garth Cameron wrote that both books are 'well-researched and written' and complement each other, although mine includes a detailed account of family life. 'Some people want their heroes to be perfect, but I do not. Oscar's life story is more interesting knowing he was not perfect.'[117]

My sister even mentions *the* suitcase in her book.

> My first memory of his [Dad's] connection with flying was when he hastily cut out a picture from a newspaper, and then it disappeared. Mum found it later, when he was out of the house, under his bed, in a suitcase, where he kept all his important things. It was a picture of a landplane TEAL had just bought.[118]

That's the suitcase I'd sent to her just weeks before. Just thinking about it gave me an ache in my heart. If I'd read her book first, I would never have parted with this treasure. I'd promised Natalya she could have the suitcase when I died, so I don't know what I was thinking. I wanted it back.

I'd hoped to find large chunks cut and pasted from my book, but my publisher was right, 'it was not to be'. Although there were bits and pieces, the odd sentence copied here and there, there was nothing substantial – however, it was clear she had piggybacked on my book. In many respects the books were similar.

My sister had got away with everything her whole life. She'd never been held to account for any of her attacks on me. I decided she was not going to get away with it this time, even if she has a mental illness. On Monday, I rang a solicitor in Sydney, a widely respected intellectual property lawyer, who asked me to send him both books.

A week later I heard back from him. He explained that my sister would have infringed my copyright if she had reproduced 'a substantial part' of my book. What amounted to 'a substantial part' is not just a matter of quantity – how much has been reproduced – but also quality – which bits she's reproduced. His advice was that it would be possible to make out a case that *A Tale of One Man's Love of Flying* infringed my copyright, but success was by no means assured.

Plagiarism and copyright infringement are often confused, although they may overlap. The biggest difference is that copyright infringement is illegal, while plagiarism is not, although it is an ethical violation. If someone uses your work without your permission, adapts or copies it, this is copyright infringement. Plagiarism refers to using – stealing – someone else's work without providing attribution.

The solicitor had drawn up a table of comparisons, examples of phrases that were the same or the use of the same source, which came to several pages, although he didn't go through the whole book. The more prudent approach, he suggested, might be to use the infringement argument to deflect any defamation claim my sister may bring against me with the article I wanted published, or any others.

I emailed my brother to let him know that I'd at last read Anna's book and that expert legal opinion was that there could be a case of copyright infringement. I told him it was a real shame he had encouraged her and suggested they pull the book and get it pulped. I told him her book had been hugely traumatic for me. 'No doubt you will say, like you always do, that I exaggerate. Like Anna's abuse and attacks, even though you were not even there.'

He replied, 'Why don't you just accept what has happened, and move on, and save yourself lots of money? I find it hard to believe it has been hugely traumatic. Anna funded her book herself, but any litigation that arises, I will fund.'

I was furious. For the first time in my life, I stood up to him. I told him he had always been a bystander. I reminded him that Anna's abuse of Mum and Aunt Ola only stopped with my intervention. 'How dare you. How fucking *dare* you tell me I always exaggerate Anna's abuse when you were not fucking there. How fucking *dare* you tell me that I am not experiencing what I am experiencing.'

I don't regret saying this. I'd had enough of the way he treated me, and not only through this book saga. There are times when rage is justified. 'Wrathful compassion' the Buddhists call it, although they may not endorse the use of 'fuck'. Some years ago, I interviewed a visiting Tibetan lama at the Chenrezig Institute in Eudlo, 23 kilometres from Maleny. We were discussing 'clear' anger versus wrathful compassion and he said it was good to sometimes to get angry with people who mistreat you, to stand up to them, if it was safe to do so.

As for Robert saying he found it hard to believe Anna's book *was* traumatic, that was not how most other people saw it. At one point I went to see my doctor as I couldn't cope with the stress and the freezing sensations in my brain. He referred me to Dr Todd Cash, one of the leading psychiatrists on the Sunshine Coast. I only saw Dr Cash once. He was incredulous to hear the bizarre story of Anna's book and said it would have been a major trauma for me, on top of other traumas I have experienced. He advised me to keep seeing my psychologist.

I shared the legal opinion with the literary editor of *Oasis*. She was still keen to publish my piece, or an updated version if I wanted to add something about the possible case for copyright infringement. Then the following day they got cold feet and said they were going to pass. They were concerned about the legal ramifications, as well as the vulnerability of Anna and me. She explained that she did not have the capacity to read both books and carefully go through all the claims and counterclaims. She suggested approaching Steve Braunias at *Newsroom* and gave me a general email address.

That is all I wanted – someone to read both books carefully. I had no space to think of the impact on Anna. But I wondered: if she was male, a perpetrator of intimate partner abuse, would they have been worried? Why was sibling abuse any different?

I sent 'The Hagiography' to Steve Braunias and got no reply.

Reading over all my emails during this time when I was determined to find a home for my ever-changing article, or for a journalist to write a story about the obvious injustice, it is clear I was not well. I was traumatised from my sister's book and the untruths she was saying in interviews and the lack of support from the media. No journalist contacted me. No one from *Stuff*. No one from *RNZ*. No one from *Newsroom*. Not one of the journalists who'd reviewed Anna's book or interviewed her contacted me. No one from anywhere.

I wonder if any of them received that warning from my siblings' solicitor, who said they were writing to news outlets to warn them against publication of my article or they too will be subject to a claim of defamation? Or was that just a bluff?

Journalist Michael Burge remarked:

> Since the books are about an historical figure it was imperative that someone in the media questioned why a second book was published so soon after yours, without your knowledge, using your research. If there were contested facts about Oscar Garden, then they should have been publicly debated, not buried in a sibling rivalry confection.

I was also in the grips of my past, my childhood, and the impact of all the blows in my life, the imprints of trauma bubbling up. For months rage surged through me, kept me alive, kept me from sinking into depression. I was angered by the injustice of it all. It felt like a repeat of my childhood, no one helping me when I was bullied and attacked. No one standing up for me when I was older, all the things she did to me as a teenager and even later in life. People putting it down to sibling rivalry, conflict between sisters, saying they will get over it, sort it out. Parents. Neighbours. Teachers. Aunts. Police. Nurses. Doctors. Psychiatrists.

One day, while standing in my backyard, I felt an overwhelming surge of frustration and screamed out: 'IT IS NOT FUCKING SIBLING RIVALRY, YOU FUCKING MORONS.' I wonder if anyone walking around one of the paths that meander throughout the Mary Cairncross Rainforest Reserve, which borders the back of my property, heard me.

Luckily, I was getting support from a few close friends and other family members. Debbie and her partner John, a retired pilot, were huge supporters. They'd both had very rough childhoods. Debbie was only six when her mother gassed herself in an oven. John had a violent father and has long been estranged from his sister, who has mental health issues and a history of violence. I felt an affinity with both of them and felt safe sharing the seemingly never-ending episodes of this Garden saga.

My cousin Rosemarie was incredulous about Anna's book, and wrote, 'Ahhh families, drive you nuts. It must hurt a lot. Big disappointment.' Gillian asked, 'How could she have written a book so quickly without the intensive research done by you over many years, and at great cost to get the facts and information correct?' That was a good question.

A long-lost cousin also tracked me down. The owner of the Maleny Bookshop rang me and said my cousin Derek had rung from Christchurch and left his phone number. Derek did not use the internet or email but saw somewhere that I lived in Maleny so rang the international directory and asked for the phone number of any bookshop in Maleny.

It was wonderful to chat with Derek. For many years he lived on Waiheke Island off Auckland, but we had lost touch. Due to poor health, he said, he moved to Christchurch to be closer to his sister, Jenny. He had seen Anna's book and bought a copy. He already had a copy of mine. He said he'd been worried about me and wondered how I was coping, as to him it was obvious Anna had copied my book. 'It is clear that your sister took your book and rewrote it poorly.'

An author friend, who is estranged from her sisters, commiserated. She's been to hell and back over the years. 'The venom of siblings is far more devastating than anything I have ever experienced in my life. I'm trying very hard not to let it damage my heart too much. A difficult task.'

I was also seeing my psychologist regularly, cycling and going for walks as much as I could to calm my mind. I practised a walking meditation I'd learnt in Pune, India, in 1978 at a Zen Meditation Retreat. Sometimes I'd chant silently single-syllabled three-word mantras such as 'Calm the Mind', or if I was especially agitated, 'Fuck you Bitch'.

It is a miracle I did not have a complete breakdown. Luckily, I worked from home, remotely, and seldom needed to go down to our warehouse at Yandina, a 40-minute drive away. The work – mainly accounting and secretarial stuff – was flexible; I could complete it when I felt like it. My son was the manager of the rapidly growing business, wholesaling bicycle parts, but understood that I was going through a hard time. I'd sometimes switch off my phone for hours at a time. I was lucky to be able to do this.

I feel a deep sadness thinking about this time. I feel bad about myself and the way I behaved. I feel sorry for this bruised and battered Mary, fighting to be heard. Should I have given up? Despite my unstable state of mind, I was more concerned about the effect on my mental health if I did *not* have my say. I felt publicly humiliated by my sister's book but I was not going to hide away in shame and isolation. Susan Lea later explained that Anna's attachment to the church, may have caused her to feel righteous in lashing out. She thought it was important for me to clarify things so readers were better informed and could fully understand. Michael Burge also encouraged me to keep going, to keep trying to get my side of the story of what had happened out there, as it bought my reputation as an author into question.

Even though somewhere deep down I knew I was making a fool of myself and behaving erratically, I kept going. In that I was like my father. People had thought he was mad, too, when he flew from England to Australia in his second-hand Gipsy Moth. He did not give up. It was a miracle his little plane did not break down on his 19-day flight. He was determined to survive. Luck was on his shoulder. Luck was on mine too.

I continued to email the odd journalist and news site to let them know about my sister's book and the alleged copyright infringement, hoping someone would do a story. Finally, *Stuff* decided to do a feature for their *Sunday Star Times*. A journalist interviewed Margareta and me, photos were selected, and it was earmarked for publication on Easter Sunday.

In the meantime, I'd made a few changes to 'The Hagiography' as I now had my sister's book and could quote her. I changed the title to 'Why My Sister's Book is a Stab in the Back'.

Scrolling through my Twitter feed one day, I saw a tweet by Steve Braunias, a New Zealand author. I thought he sounded interesting and then went down a rabbit hole exploring Steve's world, finding him to be witty, hilarious, cutting and controversial. I'd completely forgotten that the editor of *Oasis* had recommended him to me some months previously and given me a general newsroom email address, to which no one replied. I located Steve's personal email address and emailed him. Hours later he replied:

> What a bizarre story! I love it. Bits of it are confusing – I'm not sure about some very basic things – like, where did your family grow up? Was your dad a Kiwi? And, what did he do, exactly, that makes him some kind of admired aviator? It's like you assume things like that are already known but I am in the dark! ... Anyway, these things are easily fixed – just a few additions here and there – plus I might have to take out the bits at the end about your sister being violent. The bigger portrait, with its psychological depth, is fascinating – this is a terrific yarn. I'd be very happy to publish it at *Newsroom* – thank you for sending it my way.

Two articles, both on leading New Zealand news sites and due to appear around the same time. My head was spinning. *The stars were aligned*, I thought.

However, at the last minute, *Stuff* pulled their story. I was given different reasons. One reason was concerns over how provable a plagiarism accusation could be; another was that it was a normal part of the story selection process, which sounded a bit odd after all the work that had gone into it. A part of me was relieved as the journalist told me my sister had also been interviewed, and I did not want to read anything she said, as to date she'd not been truthful in her interviews or, at the best, loose with the truth.

The next day 'Why my sister's book is a stab in the back' was published on *Newsroom's ReadingRoom*. I was ecstatic. A number of owners of bookshops emailed me to say they'd read my piece. One said it was mindboggling, another that they were astonished that this could have happened. I sent the article to Darrell Innes, my old flame from the 1960s, and his response was: 'You poor soul. This revelation from your sister's pen is staggering, unbelievable in fact.'

Steve Braunias told me the article was 'a smash hit, and very widely read'. It is featured on the website as 'The Best of the Year'.[119]

CHAPTER 22

Another Betrayal

You'd think that now I had my article published in *Newsroom* and it had been a smash hit, I'd be satisfied. But several months later, I was still hellbent on exposing my sister's treachery and ignoring the possible consequences especially on my mental health, let alone the impact on my sister.

I contacted the literary editor of *The Australian* to see if she would like me to write something on my sister's book. She said she had read my *Newsroom* article, had thought it was a fascinating story and was planning to ask me to write something. She suggested writing a piece explaining where Anna and I grew up, our age difference, when we became estranged, how I came to know about her book and what I thought of the whole thing. They would not include anything on sibling abuse, she said, because of the risk of defamation, which 'has become a monstrous thing'.

Defamation *has* become a monstrous thing. Perhaps that's why my articles on my sister were like darts disappearing into the dark. I presume that's why Steve Braunias said, 'I might have to take out the bits at the end about your sister being violent.' That's why the magazine *Oasis* got cold feet. That's why *Stuff* pulled that piece, with concerns about 'how provable a plagiarism accusation' was, although to accuse someone of plagiarism is not defamatory if it actually happened.

Defamation writs are on the rise in Australia. Daniel Joyce, a senior lecturer in law at UNSW, Sydney, argues that defamation laws in Australia continue to burden our freedom of expression. (Note, the law of defamation is Australia is similar to that in New Zealand.) He says that defamation law is notorious for its complexity, for the risks associated with litigation and for the burden it places upon freedom of expression. 'This burden – sometimes referred to as a "chilling effect" when media freedom is at stake – is a prime example of how freedom of expression is limited by our laws.'[120]

Women are fighting back. Jennifer Robinson and Keina Yoshida in their book *How Many More Women* write that women are using the law to countersue men 'for defamation for accusing them of lying for speaking the truth about their experience of violence'. They are pushing back to defend themselves. Some women have gone further and countersued for the assault itself, to hold men to account.

The editor asked whether I thought Anna would talk to her about why she wrote her book. I replied that it was probably not a good idea to contact Anna but it was up to her. I gave her Anna's email address. Now I'm wondering why I didn't point out that Anna had already written why she wrote her book – her reasons are spelt out clearly in her Author's Note.

A few weeks later the editor got in touch to let me know Anna had sent a copy of her book and had answered some questions, 'like you, she's happy that readers get to choose!!' I'd never said that. She said she had mentioned to Anna the great sibling rivalries – 'Lily and Doris Brett; David Sedaris and his sister; Knaussguard and his whole family!!' – and Anna had said she was happy enough to be in that company.

I hadn't heard of David Sedaris's sibling rivalry so googled him and discovered the story of his troubled sister Tiffany, who suffered from bipolar and later ended up killing herself. David sent her a draft of a book he'd written and she replied that he'd captured her perfectly. However, when the book came out, in an interview to the *Boston Globe*, she said he'd invaded her privacy and ruined her life.[121] A few parallels there with my story of me: my sister also had bipolar and had told me I was the reason her life was such a torment.

Why didn't I ask the editor what she was going to do with the information she got from Anna? I naively thought she would write a short piece defending my book. A month later she told me publication would be that coming weekend: 'Your story on top, and Annamaria's below. The two covers, and a picture of your dad. It looks lovely. And intriguing!'

Anna's below! *What the hell*. I had a panic attack. I shot back an email pointing out that my article stood alone, it was my response to her book, and asked if she would reconsider including Anna's. It was too late; it was at the printers. The editor tried to reassure me, saying Anna's article was not unkind and she just wanted to tell her own version of the story, that it would have looked strange if only mine was published.

The stories were published on 10 July 2021 and titled 'Daddy Dearest: Sisters in Full-Flight Book Battle'.[122] It pitted the two of us against each other. In an introduction to the stories, the editor wrote:

> Oscar Garden ... has clearly left his mark on each of his daughters, because both have now written separate books about him.
>
> Journalist and author Mary Garden was first to put pen to paper ... Sixteen months later, Mary discovered that her sister, Annamaria Garden, from whom she is estranged, was about to publish her own book about their father. Which makes for a delicate situation. Sibling rivalry is hardly new: you've got William and Harry; the brothers Gallagher; the Boleyn sisters; Cain and Abel, not to mention Lily Brett and her sister, Doris, who wrote very different books about their parents, prompting Lily to issue a statement saying: 'There are some things not worth replying to. My sister's book is one of them.'

This was not sibling rivalry! I'd mentioned Anna's abuse to the editor. I felt shattered to read what Anna wrote:

> Mary's book infuriated me. I felt that another version of Dad needed to be written. He was dead. He couldn't respond or defend himself. He had an esteemed reputation in flying. This had to be respected ...
>
> My relationship with my father was good. I had one argument with him my entire life. He never abused me, wasn't physically violent with me. He was quite a hard man, but I did not want him held up for disdain. That is why I wrote the book.

If Anna had read *Sundowner of the Skies* (or however much she'd actually read) without her veil of hate and envy, she would have seen that I did not hold Dad up for disdain at all. No reader has thought that. I wrote about Dad with love and deep compassion. I mention in my Author's Note how 'history, going back, can be a healing process. Digging up his past and going on this journey helped me, and my mother, understand in part why he became who he was.' Did she read that?

She was in effect accusing me of being a liar, lying about our father's violent streak. What about Mum and Alys Wicksteed and others who knew Dad and how he treated us? Were they all lying? I'm mystified as to why she mentioned he wasn't violent to her, when I said the same in my book, that she had been mollycoddled. And why didn't she mention that Dad hit Robert, me and Mum? Why try to make out Dad was someone other than he was?

Anna was in fact not being truthful. In July 1999, in a letter to Mum, she describes Dad as an angry and bitter man, who caused damage.

> I thought recently about you and Dad and empathised a great deal with what you went though. I felt some of your despair and distress when we were small children, and the horror you lived through. It was a devastating experience. I still love Dad very much but in recent months felt some of the horror and damage from

him. Dad always got angry instead of whatever other real emotion he was feeling. Everything came channelled out of him in either anger or bitterness.

Anna also brought Robert into it: 'When my brother read my version, he commented that "you two had different fathers".' Again, she did not elaborate. She did not include anything I'd overlooked. She simply left out things: Dad's miserliness, his violent streak, his bitterness, the way he treated Mum. She writes in this article that the two books are 'very different'. That's the problem. They are not. Hers is the same as mine, with holes in it, things left out.

She also wrote, 'My brother Rob sent Mary's manuscript to me. I was a short way into it when I decided to write my own.' Surely this is a lie? In her Author's Note and in the *Booklovers* interview (and perhaps elsewhere) she said she began writing her book *after* reading *Sundowner of the Skies*. Robert also clearly said she began writing her book soon after reading mine.

She added, 'I know Mary thinks I copied some of her book, but if that's true, how come they are so different? I didn't copy one letter, one word, or one sentence of Mary's book.' Even if she didn't 'copy' one word, wouldn't my words be rattling around in her head? She'd have remembered the layout, and things I'd included. At the best, there was some 'cryptomnesia'– the unconscious, unintentional appropriation of my work.

I told the editor how upset I was. She was kind and tried to reassure me. 'You come out of it as the first writer, the historian, the one who got shortlisted for the prize, and your sister came along with her version, which she has a perfect right to do.'

I know, now, how victims of domestic violence or rape feel when their perpetrators are interviewed in the media and deny any abuse and accuse their victims of lying. It is retraumatising. In hindsight, I should never have approached this editor, or I should have clarified how the story would be presented when she got back to me to say she had heard from Anna. I could have pulled my story then. I had only myself to blame.

Although I received reassuring emails and messages from friends – including one who said I sounded credible and my sister unhinged – I'm sure some readers thought I was lying, and that Anna's article cast doubt on the veracity of my account. What about those who didn't know me? What about those two ex-lovers who'd be laughing with glee, no doubt thinking: there's proof Mary is a liar.[123] I felt like suing my sister for defamation.

I received this email from Michael Hart, a retired pilot who I'd communicated with while researching my book:

> I read the articles by you and your sister in *The Australian*. I must say I'm surprised but not surprised. Many parallels with my own family and siblings so it jumped out at me. I'm estranged from my siblings. My father was a violent man, who drank a lot and gambled obsessively to the point of ruination. A man you could never talk to or live with. I left as soon as I was able. The bizarre thing is my sisters have a different perspective. The death of my mother was the cathartic event that caused me to cease any discourse or contact with them. Anyway, I am sure your memories are authentic, I think the eldest is older in many ways and tends to bear the brunt of family dramas more – so we remember things more acutely and in more detail. I thought your book was a great read and it has a special place in my library.

This article was the worst thing Anna had written. I felt stabbed in my brain. My attempt for justice, for the truth, had backfired. Was the problem me? I seemed to be attracting trauma into my life: first the legal threat, then all the rejections from journalists, and now this. Maybe my brother was right. I should've just accepted my sister's book and moved on with my life. I felt utter despair. I hated myself.

It was July, mid-winter. Winters are mild in South-East Queensland and I seldom need to light the wood fire, but for days I curled up on the rug in front of the fire, sometimes in a foetal position. Ivy would sometimes come and lick my face and nestle into me. I'd walk her around the block very early in the morning so I didn't run into any humans and be forced to smile or chat. I feared meeting someone who had read *that* wretched article.

I reached out to a friend who was a journalist, told her I needed help. I was going to see my psychologist but needed something more. Earlier in the year I'd laughed when she'd mentioned she had seen a psychic, but I now felt so desperate I'd do anything.

It was a half-hour phone consultation costing $50. When I rang, I only gave this woman my first name. She got many things right. A son who I worked with and who was very successful; a daughter who I was very close to and who had two daughters herself; she mentioned my ex-husband, said not very flattering things about him which I won't repeat here; and mentioned my sister's book. How did she know about it? She said my sister had made a laughing stock of herself writing that book (*had she?*), she was a psychopath and would commit suicide within a year (*was it ethical for her to say such a thing?*). And I should write a book about it all as soon as possible. (*As if.*)

I dismissed most of her reading. It was over the top. What my sister did was monstrous, but I believe we all have a psychopath and a saint inside us, we have the potential to be both. To tell you the truth, the thought that my sister might die soon was comforting, although I'd have preferred some healing, a resolution.

Towards the end of her memoir *Fractured*, Katrina Casey mentions a visit to a psychic to get in touch with a dead relative. At the time I thought it was brave of her to include this, she would open herself up to ridicule, and I'd never admit to such a thing. But here I am ...

CHAPTER 23

Mum to the Rescue

Throughout the saga of my sister's book, Katrina Casey was following the story on Twitter and occasionally responding to my tweets. She, too, had grown up in a dysfunctional family in New Zealand and sought safety in Australia. She told me, 'It certainly sounds like you've been thought the mill with your sister. I'm happy to support a fellow Kiwi on this side of the ditch, especially as we're both writers.' When I heard that her memoir was about to be released, I tweeted I couldn't wait to read it. The publisher read this tweet and sent me an advance copy. Twitter can be a cesspool but also the source of amazing things.

Trigger warnings, a recent phenomenon, are a way of letting people know the content they're about to consume may contain details that could cause a person to recall a traumatic experience. Triggers can also be opportunities to confront or process issues. There's a trigger warning in the front pages of Katrina's book about issues of self-harm and suicide. These didn't apply to me, but I was triggered by something else.

Katrina describes the way she was drawn in as her mother's confidante. There was favouritism in her family too, and periods of estrangement between herself and her younger sister, Rachelle. As the elder sister Katrina felt an urge to protect and shield Rachelle, who'd been diagnosed with various disorders, including schizoid affective disorder. Hers was a 'strange case' they were told, much the same as we had been told about Anna: a 'very difficult case'. I messaged Katrina: 'OMG too many parallels. I'm weeping.'

I was triggered by the lack of empathy of Katrina's mother. I began to think of my own mother and lost it. Rage swelled up in me. How could she not have shown any sympathy for me? How come she never felt sorry for me? What was with her pathetic response 'I apologise for errors and omissions', after I'd shared with her how difficult my life was?

Fuck her. Fuck the, 'We don't have to worry about Mary bullshit.' Why the fuck wasn't she worried about me? What the fuck was wrong with her? Was she that repressed? I helped her so much after Dad died. Why did I even bother?

I thought of my book *The Serpent Rising*, how she'd not made one comment about the coerced abortion when I was six months pregnant from the 'celibate' yoga guru, Swami Balyogi Premvarni. Not once had she said, 'I'm so sorry for what you went though.' I almost died in a dingy hospital in Old Delhi. I could have died months later when Premvarni and a female disciple bashed me and banged my head up and down on the concrete floor in his ashram in the jungle in the Himalayas. As if that wasn't enough, my mother knew my children and I had been though some nightmare years in Maleny, when we were subjected to even more violence. Not one ounce of sympathy from my mother, not *one fucking ounce*.

In her award-winning memoir *The Mirror Book*, New Zealand writer Charlotte Grimshaw wrote about 'being assaulted and beaten up, about seeing a violent death, about loneliness and distress'.[124] When she pointed this out to her mother, she made no comment; her only response was one of disdain. Charlotte was born in 1966, so 17 years younger than me; a generation separated us and our mums, but the same lack of empathy was evident.

I've mentioned the loopy letters I wrote to Mum from India. They clearly show I was under a spell, caught up in something dangerous, trapped in a cult. In the letters Mum wrote back, she'd mentioned the weather, Dad's health problems or moving house.

Anna was the same. She'd had no sympathy for what I'd been through. Nor any remorse for her assaults. Were they both psychopaths? Robert too, who said I exaggerated Anna's abuse. *Fuck him as well!* Was my whole birth family a bunch of fucking psychopaths? How could they not empathise for me?

If Mum had stood up to Anna when she was a child, if she had taken Anna to see a psychiatrist, if she herself had got some help, if she had left Dad – then my life would have been different. I wouldn't have gone to India, fallen in love with abusive men, been abused by my sister. And my sister would not have written this fucking book.

I began howling and screaming at the top of my voice. I shouted out to the sky, to wherever Mum was, even if she was nowhere. I kept on all day and into the next. Hours of crying, wailing, screaming.

Luckily, I had no neighbours nearby. I was surrounded by trees and bush and noisy birdlife. The rainforest on much of my one-acre block and the park reaching over my back boundary were teaming with birds and wildlife. In the mornings, especially, there was an almost deafening cacophony of birdsong, a chorus of loud whip cracks from whipbirds, whistles from golden whistlers, robins and pittas, *whu-whoo* and *wolluck-woo* sounds from fruit doves, the strange cat-like *heer aar* of the cat bird, to name a few. Plus, there were sounds from crickets and frogs. I lived in the perfect place to have a good catharsis.

I screamed out to the universe, to my mother, to hear me. I gave her 24 hours to send me a sign that she'd heard me, that, for the first time in her life she cared, that she felt sorry, had some sympathy for me. Twenty-four hours.

'IT IS ALL YOUR FUCKING FAULT THAT MY LIFE IS COMPLETELY FUCKED.'

My rational brain does not believe in prayer, or calling out to the universe, so calling out to a dead person was a very strange thing for me to do.

However, I knew that howling and screaming can be good for you. Despite the Elisabeth Kübler-Ross workshops I'd done years before, I still tend to push my feelings down, put on a happy face and go out into the world. You have to in order to survive. Since I learnt about my sister's book, I'd been pushing my grief down, only allowing myself to feel anger. I needed anger, I figured, to get justice. Now other emotions were surging out. But I knew I was not having a breakdown or losing my mind. I was saving it.

Slowly I began to feel lighter. The storm passed and I woke to a new day. Early in the morning, my son rang to see if I wanted to go for a bike ride. I chucked on my cycling gear, put my bike in the back of my car and headed over to Yandina. On the way I said to my dead mum, 'I gave you 24 hours, so not long to go.' I laughed at myself.

It was a wonderful ride. I now had an electric bike, so could keep up with Eamon and even pass him on the hills. We did a big loop: cycled towards Eumundi, turning left at Gold Creek Road, climbed up the range and around Mount Eerwah before flying down to Kenilworth-Eumundi Road and then on to Eumundi, where we stopped for coffee before heading back to the warehouse. Glorious. As usual we would try not to talk about work stuff, but as usual we would end up talking about it. It had been a big part of my life since 2007, and for Eamon's the year before, when he reluctantly took over his father's bicycle wholesaling business when it was on the verge of collapse.

Back inside I sat on one of the couches and was posting photos of my ride on Twitter when my phone rang. It was Michael Burge. 'Hi, Mary, I hope you're sitting down. I just wanted to let you know your book *The Serpent Rising* has won the High Country Indie Book Award. It was voted this year's clear winner by the book club members. It won't be announced until December, so you can't tell anyone yet.'

I burst into tears. *What the hell.* I hadn't thought I had any chance of winning as my book was up against some 'proper' books – Marg Hickey's *Rural Dreams*, Jessica White's *Hearing Maud*, Melissa Lucashenko's *Too Much Lip* – all published by traditional publishers. I had to ask Michael several times if he was being serious. When I told him of my bizarre petition to my mother, he laughed and said 'well, anything's possible'. Once off the phone, I yelled out to my son, 'Come here, you won't believe it.'

All the way home I had a big smile on my face. Was this a sheer coincidence or did I manifest it? That is completely New Age bullshit, but ... I then said out loud, 'Thanks, Mum, but actually that's not enough. You have to do something about Anna's book. You've got one week.'

CHAPTER 24

Goddess Justitia

When I first read the excerpt from my sister's book published in *Stuff* on 18 October 2020, I thought it was a bit strange. The writing was uneven and the language in places was odd. This is because the language is not hers. It was stolen. I stumbled upon this fact a year later by sheer chance.

A month after the bomb of that article exploded in *The Australian*, I flew to Alice Springs to launch a second edition of *Sundowner of the Skies* at the Central Australian Aviation Museum. Aside from being the youngest and most inexperienced solo aviator to reach Australia, my father was the first overseas aviator to land at Wyndham, the northernmost town in the Kimberley region of Western Australia, as well as Alice Springs and Broken Hill, the two other stops he made as he came down though the centre of Australia's vast continent. Other aviators had made landfall at Darwin, then headed southeast.

Dad was determined to fly the shortest route to Sydney, across the Great Sandy Desert to Alice Springs. No aviator had made this crossing before. It was considered more treacherous than the adjoining Tanami Desert, where in April 1929 Keith Anderson and Bobby Hitchcock had died. They had flown from Sydney to join the air search to locate Charles Kingsford Smith and his crew, who had disappeared in northwest Australia. Flying over the desert, Anderson and Hitchcock had to make a forced landing when the push rod on a valve cylinder loosened, causing a loss of power. They died of thirst a few days later, Hitchcock under the right wing of their plane *Kookaburra*, Anderson almost half a kilometre away.

My father was lucky. On 5 November 1930, after a hellish trip of almost 13 hours, he landed at 7.20 pm in a field at Alice Springs. Bonfires had been lit to guide him. At the time experienced airmen described his flight from Wyndham to Alice Springs as an amazing performance and being 'on its own'. The field where he landed is still there today, a few hundred metres down the road from the museum.

The trip to Alice Springs was uplifting and inspiring. It took my mind off Anna's book. When I returned home, not only was Katrina Casey's book *Fractured* waiting for me, but I had the idea of writing an article about my father's flight through central Australia. ('Oscar Garden: The Supreme Navigator' was published later that year in *Aviation News*.[125])

One week (yes, exactly one week) after learning *The Serpent Rising* had won an award and telling my mother to do something about Anna's book, I was sitting at my computer writing about Dad's visit to Broken Hill. I hadn't written much about this visit in *Sundowner of the Skies* and thought I'd see what Anna had written in her book. I'm not sure why I decided to check her reference, but it was one of the articles I'd used: 'Oscar Garden's Flight. Cheque for 20 Guineas Presented Last Night. Left for Sydney today', published on the front page of the *Barrier Miner* newspaper on 7 November 1930.[126] At the civic reception at Broken Hill, Dad was given a cheque accompanied by a short letter of congratulations. Anna quotes this letter, but I noticed the rest of the one-and-a-half pages of text in her book had been copied verbatim from the article, except she had changed 'Mr Garden' to 'Dad' or 'my father'.

I was taken aback. The next chapter was on his arrival and reception in Sydney. More of the same. Large sections of text copied. I was incredulous. I spent hours going through her book and discovered that most of it, except for a few pages at the beginning and the final short chapter at the end, had been simply cut and pasted with no attribution.

The extract published in *Stuff* the day before her book was released was mostly plagiarised. Here are two examples:

> When he was ready to leave, he told people what he intended to do and, naturally, they were somewhat alarmed; but he got away before they could even come to see him off or to persuade him not to make the flight.[127] (*Stuff*, 2020)

> When he was ready to leave Croydon, he told his people what he intended to do, and naturally they were somewhat alarmed; but he got away before they could even come to see him off or to persuade him not to make the flight.[128] (*Sydney Mail*, 1930)

> Something happened that might have easily put an end to the flight and to him. He didn't know how, but when he started from Munich the throttle was open wide ... When an aeroplane is started with the throttle open that is usually the end of the machine. It just starts out and wrecks itself. He realised what had happened; the aeroplane would dash around in circles.[129] (*Stuff*, 2020)

> It was here that something happened that might have easily put an end the flight and to me. I was lucky. I don't know how it happened, but when I started from Munich the throttle was open wide. When an aeroplane is started with the throttle open that is usually the end of the machine. It just starts out and wrecks itself. I realised what had happened. I knew that the aeroplane would dash around in circles.[130] (*Sunday Mail*, 1930)

As well as copying from newspaper articles, she had copied from several aviation texts. In the chapters on TEAL, she had stolen chunks from two aviation books: Ian Driscoll's *Airline* and Maurice McGreal's *A Noble Chance*, as well as Ian Thomson's Masters thesis *A History of TEAL*.[131] While she attributed the occasional sentence or paragraph, the text before or after was copied word for word. When an article or book quoted Dad, she simply left out the quotation marks and changed 'I' to 'my father' to make it look like it was her original writing. Sometimes Oscar Garden was replaced with 'Dad' or 'he', but other times not, which meant for a very uneven text. Why hadn't anyone noticed? Why hadn't I?

I began writing up a spreadsheet of examples of plagiarism, but after 15 pages and about 10,000 words I gave up. There were too many examples. Her book was a quilt of unacknowledged quotations.

I was absolutely elated. My heart and brain felt like they were exploding with gratitude. *Thanks Mum.* I knew this was the end of Anna's book.

Was this just a coincidence, one week after telling my mother she had to do something about my sister's book? I don't know, but a part of me is inclined to go with this quote of William Blake: 'In the universe, there are things that are known, and things that are unknown, and in between, there are doors.'

I managed to track down Paul McGreal, the son of Maurice McGreal (who died in 2012) and emailed him the spreadsheet. While at TEAL, Dad had employed Maurice as a pilot in 1944, and after Maurice retired he wrote three books on aviation, including *A Noble Chance*. I interviewed him while I was working on *Sundowner of the Skies*. Paul was pretty annoyed and contacted Mary Egan Publisher (who'd published Anna's book) to voice his displeasure. I was unsuccessful in locating Ian Thompson or any member of Ian Driscoll's family.

I rang my publisher, who recommended a solicitor in Auckland who specialised in intellectual property. During a lengthy phone call, the solicitor explained to me that although nothing could be done about plagiarism of other works – unless it was a group action – he thought I may have a good case for copyright infringement. I told him I'd already received that advice from a Sydney solicitor earlier in the year but it had gone no further. He said he was keen to investigate this and would get back to me after he'd read both books.

Meanwhile, I sent the spreadsheet to Anna and Robert. I was convinced they'd be mortified: Robert would regret supporting Anna and her book, realise it had been a huge mistake and Anna would feel ashamed of being found out and would offer to destroy all copies of her book. For someone reasonably intelligent, I can be quite foolish and deluded.

Robert was annoyed. 'I am sick of this saga you are carrying on with,' he said and pointed out that Anna had agreed not to do another print run, and there were hardly any copies left in bookshops. He didn't know what I was hoping to achieve. 'Save your money!!' I said that the book was still available on Amazon as an ebook and in some shops, libraries and museums, and needed to be removed. I told him a solicitor was working on the case.

I was stunned by his reply. 'Get stuffed and don't contact me again. You have so lost the plot you need help.' He'd never spoken to me like that. Of course, I had lost the plot a little bit, but I was getting help.

Very shaken, I decided I did not want to hear from him ever again. I hoped he would not contact me even if Anna got cancer or was dying. We had always been emotionally estranged, but now we were completely estranged. I felt relieved and safer.

I was sure the New Zealand media would be interested in reporting the plagiarism. Nup. I emailed scores of editors and journalists; most did not respond. I thought Steve Braunias would be interested, but he wasn't. 'I might pass on pursuing this for *Newsroom*, sorry – it's such a mess, isn't it? I hope things someday work themselves out.'

Such a mess? Things work themselves out? Did he mean we should start getting along like normal siblings? This felt like the same taboo, the same shaming around estrangement. The same exhortation of 'why can't you just get along?'. He knew there'd been a history of abuse, since in the article he'd published he took out bits about my sister being violent. Maybe he was sick of hearing from me, but I can't help but think that if it was someone else other than my sister, someone unknown to us, who'd written a book on Oscar Garden and plagiarised most of it, the media would've been interested.

The journalist who'd reviewed both Anna's book and mine for *Otago Daily Times* wasn't interested. Nor was *Stuff*. One of their news directors replied, 'I sympathise with your position, but this is not a dispute in which *Stuff* wishes to get involved.'

I was frustrated at this reply. This was not a dispute, I shot back, but plagiarism. That's the story. This was an author he promoted; it was beside the point the author was my sister. I reminded him *Stuff* had published an excerpt from her book; a quick Google search would have found my original article in the *AFR* with remarkable similarities to the piece printed.

Wasn't it a good news story? Wasn't it reasonable for *Stuff* to publish a retraction and an apology? My father was a significant figure in New Zealand's aviation history. The fact that a second book full of errors and mostly plagiarised had appeared so soon after mine, wasn't that newsworthy? Shouldn't readers be warned not to buy it, not use it for research? Was I expecting too much?

While googling plagiarism in New Zealand, I came upon the story of award-winning Māori author Witi Ihimaera's plagiarism.[132] Reviewing his novel *The Trowenna Sea* for *The Listener*, the literary critic Jolisa Gracewood had a feeling something wasn't right with parts of the text. She'd never heard of its subject, Hohepa Te Umuroa, who was convicted of rebellion and transported to Tasmania in 1846. When she looked him up on Google she found 'uncanny resemblances' to other sources. She wrote on her blog:

> As a writing teacher I'd occasionally come across a phrase or a paragraph that was somehow out of kilter with the surrounding text. It's a curiously physical phenomenon: the hairs on the back of your neck go up, and your heart sinks ... But I never expected

to encounter that feeling as a book reviewer, let alone with a major new work by a respected writer ... There really is no joy in stumbling across a story like this one.[133]

It was called the 'literary news story of the decade in New Zealand', considering Ihimaera was a professor of English and a distinguished creative fellow in Māori literature at Auckland University.[134] Ihimaera bought back the remaining stock of his book, about 1800 copies, stored them in a storage unit in Auckland and visited them every month as he could not bear the thought of destroying them. He was 'proud of them' and loved them no matter what![135]

Good news arrived from my solicitor. He had drafted a letter to Anna and Mary Egan for me to check. I was elated to read it. My knight in shining armour! At last, someone had my back. This is an extract from the letter:

> We consider that your book, *Oscar Garden: A Tale of One Man's Love of Flying* published in October 2020, is an adaption of *Sundowner of the Skies* and so infringes Mary's exclusive rights under the Copyright Act 1994. [New Zealand]
>
> We say this because it is apparent from the content and structure of the book that you used *Sundowner of the Skies* in preparing your book. You appear to admit this, saying that the impetus for writing *Oscar Garden: A Tale* was after you read *Sundowner of the Skies* in 2019. As a result, you have then taken the substance of *Sundowner of the Skies*. There are countless examples we could point to ... Given that *Sundowner of the Skies* is an original work and acted as the starting point for your book, you needed to do more than simply rewrite the book in the manner that you have. By appropriating Mary's considerable skill, effort and judgment, you have infringed Mary's copyright under the doctrine of altered copyright ... As you can imagine, Mary is deeply disappointed by your actions in infringing her copyright and your denials.

It was pointed out that Anna had used the same quotes from third-party sources and placed them in the same order, and that the majority of the photographs were not only the same, but arranged in the same order as in my book. They noted that my book was the first biography of Oscar Garden to be published anywhere in the world and it had taken me over 10 years to write.

We received responses just days later. The publisher's solicitor replied that 'purely as a pragmatic solution in what is clearly an unfortunate dispute between family members', they would cease publishing and distributing the book and undertake to not publish any reprints or further editions.

Why frame it as 'an unfortunate dispute' between family members? This suggested I was partly to blame for my sister writing her book. It felt like the same old argument used to dismiss sibling abuse or any other kind of family violence.

Anna's solicitor also agreed to cease publishing the book but denied any copyright infringement. Why give in so easily? I'd be fighting back if someone accused me of copyright infringement or plagiarism, and I knew I hadn't. They said their client was a far more experienced writer than me, had a doctorate, and had 'particular experience in writing academic content on the basis of her independent research'.

I also had a doctorate. I felt insulted by this suggestion that my sister was a more experienced writer. A year later, with a clearer, calmer head, I realised that although she'd had no experience writing for the general reader and had never had a feature article published, she did have more experience in writing academic content, albeit in the narrow field of organisational change in businesses. Rage and bitterness cloud the mind and do not allow one to see things clearly.

In response to their letter, my solicitor pointed out that in Anna's book there was plagiarism from a range of sources, including three aviation works (the ones I mentioned earlier), and it was riddled with factual inaccuracies. He suggested they provide a copy of her manuscript so a plagiarism check could be done, noting that if this offer was refused then that 'further tells against your client's denials of copyright infringement'. My sister turned down the offer of a plagiarism check but agreed to remove the book from museums and libraries.

First out of the box was Tauranga Library. Paul Cuming, the collections specialist at the library, informed my solicitor that the items were being removed, and mentioned that I was meant to speak there that month (October 2021). My trip had been cancelled due to Covid-19 – New Zealand had closed its borders.

Other libraries followed suit. I cannot describe the relief I felt to hear that my sister's books were being removed from libraries. The thought of her book sitting next to mine had made me feel nauseated, especially if I would have to give talks about *my* book at various libraries and museums.

It had been just over a year since the release of *Oscar Garden: A Tale of One Man's Love of Flying*. Just over a year since I had stood on top of that mountain in the Sunshine Coast hinterland and received the email from my cousin saying she thought 'this would be of interest' when in fact it was a grenade that blew up my life as I knew it, leaving me reeling and shell-shocked for the next 12 months, with the reverberations continuing even longer.

A few museums and libraries dragged their heels. In March 2022, after an online search, I noticed copies were still available, including at some Australian libraries, the National Library of New Zealand, Auckland Museum and MOTAT.

I decided to email MOTAT directly. The director replied that in the absence of a court order they would require written confirmation from the author and the publisher that the book contained 'false, inaccurate and/or plagiarised information', and a request that it be returned to them for destruction. In these circumstances, he said, they would expect the purchase price of the book and any other costs incurred in relation to the issue to be reimbursed.

I forwarded this response to my lawyer, who said he would ring me the following week as he needed to think this through. I'm not sure what came over me, as I'd vowed to never have contact with my sister again, *never*, but I had this strange nudging to email her. I included MOTAT's response and suggested she contact them directly, instead of wasting time dealing with lawyers and her publisher! Surprisingly, she did!

> I understand from my sister Mary Garden that you need written confirmation from the author concerning the removal from public view of my book: *Oscar Garden: A tale of one man's love of flying*. I am that author and hereby confirm that there are some inaccuracies in my book as well as some inadvertent plagiarism. There is a legal agreement with my sister that the book cannot be held in public view in libraries and museums.
>
> Please return them to me for destruction. This is not requested lightly. Without this action my sister will prosecute.
>
> Please phone me if you wish to discuss. You are welcome to seek compensation.
>
> Many thanks
>
> Annamaria Garden

MOTAT's director emailed me later that day to let me know that Anna had provided the confirmation they needed and they would be returning their two copies to her.

Over the next few days, my sister emailed me with notifications that copies had been removed from other places, including from seven Australian libraries, although she said Auckland Museum had 'flatly refused'. I decided to forward MOTAT's email to Auckland Museum, and simply wrote: 'Note, the books have now been removed from MOTAT and other libraries due to plagiarism and multiple errors.' A few days later I received a reply from the museum that they'd removed the item, adding, 'Please refrain from contacting us in the future about this book.' I felt hurt by this barb. Where was the sympathy for my position?

Later that day, I received this email from my sister: 'Auckland Museum has finally removed the book. I think that's that then?' It was the last I heard from her.

All copies of *Oscar Garden: A Tale of One Man's Love of Flying* have been removed from libraries and museums. There may be the odd one floating around in bookshops, but I purchased any I found from searching online and had them posted over to me. I have them still.

Now my sister's book was truly dead. I had killed it. There was justice at last. I'd stood up to my sister for the first time in my life, and angels and knights had swept in to help. I thought to myself, *Thanks, Mum, better late than never.*

CHAPTER 25

A Bad Habit

I had mixed feelings about my sister's extensive plagiarism. I was relieved as it meant the end of her book, but also shocked that someone who was so intelligent had resorted to such skulduggery.

And what about those who enabled her? As copyright and plagiarism consultant Jonathan Bailey points out, 'The plagiarist is responsible for the plagiarism, but when plagiarism is published, we have to at least look at the hands it passed through on the way out the door.'[136]

As no journalist seemed interested in reporting my sister's plagiarism, presumably because she was unknown in the literary world and she was my sister, I wrote my own story and called it 'A Family Matter'. In the piece, I explained the difference between copyright infringement and plagiarism.

One news site came close to publishing 'A Family Matter' and the editor sent me an edited copy, leaving out some things he wasn't comfortable with. Even then, he had reservations, as he said my story was 'totally one-sided'. A balanced story, he said, would require interviews with my sister, the publisher and copyright lawyers, and he didn't have the time to do all of this.

Were interviews with all these people required? Journalist Michael Burge didn't think so. He said this was setting up 'a false equivalence' between my sister and me, 'as tempting as the sibling rivalry angle clearly was'. As far as the plagiarism was concerned, I did not need a 'balanced' story. I had the spreadsheet of examples. What more was needed?

The term 'bothsideism', or false balance, refers disparagingly to the practice of journalists who, in their attempt to be fair, present each side of a story, even when the factual evidence is stacked heavily on one side.[137] The factual evidence was stacked on my side. The plagiarism is easily determined by checking the endnotes in Anna's book. Retired University of Sheffield journalism lecturer Jonathan Foster once said, 'If someone says it's raining and another person says its dry, it's not your job to quote them both. Your job is to look out the fucking window and find out which one is true.'[138]

A few weeks later, the news site decided against publishing my essay. The editor apologised and said he felt it needed to be something reported by a journalist: 'I am too busy and do not have staff.' All I wanted was a journalist to do a thorough investigation and write something. I wish I'd suggested paying the editor or someone else to do this. I had the money.[139] Disappointed, I told Michael Burge about the latest rejection and he said I'd probably have to wait for a plagiarism scandal. He was right. Half a year later, I finally got my say with the John Hughes scandal.

On 9 June 2022, *The Guardian* published an extraordinary story.[140] An investigation by Anna Verney had uncovered 58 similarities and identical sentences in John Hughes' book *The Dog*, nominated for the Miles Franklin Award, and the 2017 English translation of Svetlana Alexievich's non-fiction book *The Unwomanly Face of War*. In the days that followed further plagiarism was found. For example, extracts from *The Great Gatsby, Anna Karenina* and *All Quiet on the Western Front* were found in *The Dog* with no attribution.[141]

It was a huge news story and all over social media, especially Twitter. I couldn't help feeling envious. There had been not one word in the New Zealand media on my sister's extensive plagiarism. Clearly, plagiarism stories get media attention when they involve major public standing of some sort – the status of the author, the size of the publisher – or if any awards, prizes, plum jobs or public funding are involved.

At last, I had my opportunity. I wrote a piece in which I explored the John Hughes' case as well as several other notable plagiarism scandals, and mentioned my own experience thanks to my sister. I sent it to Jonathan Green at *Meanjin* and he got back to me straight away to say he was happy to publish it, saying it was a nice piece and obviously informed by my direct experience. 'Magpies & Memory'[142] was published on 18 June 2022, my birthday. It was the best present. Not only were my sister's books off the shelves but also my story on her theft was out in the world.

It is frustrating to think how much plagiarism probably slips past everyone's notice. And when someone gets caught out, it may not be the first time it's happened. I wondered if Anna had plagiarised before, in her other books, or in her PhD thesis? I didn't bother checking until a year after the *Meanjin* article was published.

I only have one of her books, *Reading the Mind of Organisation*. In this she describes a situation with TEAL after Dad left and mentions Maurice McGreal's *A Noble Chance: One pilot's life*. While not the cut and paste she resorted to in her book on our father, it comes close to quoting without attribution:

When the Sandringham flying boats were grounded in 1947 and the airline virtually brought to its knees, Roberts' [General Manager] answer was to make a vigorous 'rally the troops' ... there was a good turn up of staff in the social hall for the Boss's talk. The backdrop of the stage showed a tropical scene with palm trees and a shoreline of goldens sand with a brilliant orange sun cutting the horizon and flooding the sky with its rays ... The GM stood at the lectern ... (McGreal, p. 93)

> A new fleet had to be grounded ... and the airline was virtually brought to its knees. The General Manager decided that the answer was to rally the troops. They were all called to a big gathering in a local hall for a talk. The backdrop of the stage where he was to speak consisted of a tropical scene with palm trees, golden sand and, above, a brilliant sun perched just on the horizon with its rays flooding the sky ... The General Manager stood at the lecture ... (Garden, pp. 123–124)[143]

Perhaps it is just carelessness and sloppiness. Perhaps no one at any of her three universities showed her how to attribute properly. I think a habitual plagiariser does it because they have got away with it; it becomes a bad habit. My sister got away with shoplifting back in 1970. Perhaps this led to stealing words from books and even stealing money and food when she became ill, because she was too proud to go to WINZ and obtain income support. I didn't feel like checking her other books, as I was no longer interested. I was no longer on a crusade for justice.

There are eerie parallels between John Hughes and my sister. Anna is nine years older than Hughes but they both studied in the UK in the 1980s. Hughes attended the University of Newcastle in Australia where he won the University Medal and a scholarship for a PhD in literature in Cambridge. Both Hughes and my sister were considered 'brilliant'. In 1988, Hughes dropped out and returned to Australia, and would later complete a PhD at the University of Technology, Sydney. His first book *The Idea of Home*, a collection of autobiographical essays, was published by Giramondo in 2004 and won several prestigious awards. My sister's book, *Reading the Mind of the Organisation*, published in 2000, was also widely acclaimed, albeit in the field of business organisation.

A later in-depth examination of John Hughes and his plagiarism was published in *The Monthly* in March 2023. 'Being John Hughes' by Anna Verney and Richard Cooke describes countless instances of plagiarism in *The Dogs*, thousands of words from dozens of texts, from sentence parts to pages at a time. [144] A table, which compared Hughes' book with these books, came to 170 pages long but wasn't completed because there were too many examples.

Anna and Richard found this pattern of using passages of unattributed material began early in Hughes's literary career, and seems to have escalated, 'shedding attributions and leaning more heavily on unattributed intertextual material'. The question remains: why did someone with John Hughes's ability need to plagiarise? I asked Richard if he and Anna Verney had come close to finding a motive, or was it just a bad habit that he got away with perhaps? Richard replied: The ultimate 'why' is unknowable, but your bad habit theory is close to my own. It seems to be a technique that became a compulsion, and when the institutional safeguards around him failed it got completely out of control.'[145]

It seems that it was a bad habit my sister got away with too.

In mid-2023, I stumbled over another plagiarism story. Emeritus Professor of History and Politics at Griffith University, Ross Fitzgerald AM is a well-known figure in Australia – in 2014, he was appointed a Member of the Order of Australia for 'significant service to education in the field of politics and history as an academic, and to community and public health organisations'.[146] Author of 43 books, including memoirs, biographies and novels, his co-authored book *Going Out Backwards: A Grafton Everest adventure* was shortlisted for the 2017 Russell Prize for Humour Writing, and he was a judge for the Prime Minister's Literary Award for Non-Fiction and Australian History in 2014 and 2015. He is also an avid book reviewer. His reviews featured regularly in *The Weekend Australian* and occasionally in *The Sydney Morning Herald, Canberra Times, Quadrant* and *The Spectator*.

In June 2023, freelance writer and reviewer Joy Lawn discovered that Fitzgerald's review in *The Weekend Australian* of Carmel Bird's *Love Letter to Lola* strongly resembled her review commissioned by

Books + Publishing and published more than three months earlier. Caroline Overington, literary editor of *The Australian*, reported in her weekly column that '*The Australian* is looking into the matter', and that Professor Fitzgerald 'has offered an unconditional apology'. As soon as I read this, I rang Carmel Bird, who is a close friend of mine, and said I bet there is more. There sure was.

Over the next week, I discovered that Fitzgerald had plagiarised scores of book reviews, including his review of my book *Sundowner of the Skies*.[147] The reviews I examined had countless examples of passages plucked from previously published reviews of the same books written by other authors; publishers' promotional materials for the books in question; or the words of the authors themselves, especially the introductory and conclusion chapters of their books and even the captions of photos. Just the odd word added or changed. A bad habit he got away with over many years.

My essay 'Plagiarism, Cobbling or Accidental Inclusion' on this extraordinary saga was published in *Meanjin* on 19 July 2023.[148] Although I'd decided not to mention my sister's plagiarism, I smiled when I saw the essay published online. Towards the end of the essay, I'd written, 'It's quite straightforward to avoid plagiarism: by simply citing or adding a note acknowledging anything borrowed, copied or pasted into your work.' The new editor, Esther Anatolitis, had added these words 'As I noted in an essay on this topic for *Meanjin* last year' before 'it's quite straightforward', and included a link to my essay 'Magpies & Memory'.

Following *Meanjin's* publication of my essay, Caroline Overington announced in *The Weekend Australian* that Fitzgerald would no longer be writing for the masthead.[149] He is still reviewing for other magazines, including *Quadrant*, a conservative Australian journal.

CHAPTER 26

Unpacking Book Matters

Why did my sister write her book? What was the point?' I went round and round in circles trying to answer this question.

In an email dated 16 November 2020, she said, 'I wasn't really responding to anything specific in yours. I just wanted to write my own version.' Yet this is not the story she gave the media. Instead, she said things like, 'I disagreed so strongly with my sister's rendition of my father that I put pen to paper and wrote furiously putting together my tale on Dad', or 'Mary's book infuriated me. I felt that another version of Dad needed to be written.'

Let's unpack this. What was she so *furious* about?

In all the correspondence between us, Anna did not point out one thing I'd written about Dad in *Sundowner of the Skies* that was incorrect or exaggerated, not one thing that she disagreed with or that I'd omitted. In *One Man's Love of Flying*, however, she omits crucial things. She does not mention Mum's 'despair and distress', or 'the horror and damage from Dad', that she'd described in her letters. She leaves out Dad's violent streak, his gambling addiction and his miserliness, all corroborated by almost everyone who knew him.

In her book, Anna wrote very little on Dad's life after he left

TEAL. Apart from a few pages at the beginning of the book, it's the only other section where there's not extensive plagiarism. This is the weird thing. There is not one word in that short chapter that contradicts anything in *Sundowner of the Skies*. It took me a year to realise this, until I could read that chapter with any measure of calm. Before then, it was as if I'd locked my sister in a suitcase stuffed with rage and labelled it 'monster, fucking liar'.

Although Anna believed her book to be very different from mine – she emphasised this in that article commissioned for *The Weekend Australian* – it is not. *One Man's Love of Flying* resembles mine. It is an adaptation of *Sundowner of the Skies* but leaves out some major warts. It is a shrunken flawed version. A version full of holes. It is a hagiography.

Salmon Rushdie's father was dismissive of his son's book *Midnight's Children*, perhaps because he saw himself in the protagonist's father, who, like him, had a drinking problem. Years later, when he was dying, he told his son what he really thought: 'I was angry because every word you wrote was true.'[150] Was my sister angry about my book because every word I wrote about our father was true? That I'd told the truth, the full story – warts and all.

Perhaps she also wrote it out of revenge because I'd breached her privacy in the first edition of *Sundowner of the Skies* and had mentioned her mental illness and how she'd treated Mum. And she just made up all these other reasons as to why she wrote her book. This sort of makes sense to me.

To what extent was Anna a liar, and loose with the truth? For a long time, I thought Anna was a pathological liar and just changed her story when it suited, including dates. But the picture became clearer when I tried to unravel things, especially the exact order of events, while working on this book.

I realised, for example, that when Anna mentioned my *book* in the media, she usually meant my *manuscript*. In an email dated 16 October 2020, she had explained to me, 'As far as book/manuscript is concerned I tend to use the terms interchangeably. This is wrong so I am trying to correct it.' I had dismissed this at the time, thinking she was lying and trying to cover her tracks.

It didn't help that Robert had told me she wrote hers *after* my book was published. Perhaps he just got muddled and confused; he had not been aware of Anna's diagnosis of schizoid affective disorder. Perhaps he didn't know that Anna began writing *after* reading my draft manuscript, not my book.

From the timeline provided by her solicitor, and based on what she said – that it took nine months – I now realise Anna finished her first version in September 2018 and began submitting it to publishers. It is reasonable to assume she was trying to beat me to publication and would have done anything to get there first, even if it meant stealing. Perhaps we sent our respective manuscripts to the same publishers – say, Awa Press, Otago University Press, Potton & Burton and Exile Publishing. (I wonder if any of them received *One Man's Love of Flying* and rejected it along with mine, thinking 'how odd'.)

And perhaps she wrote her book out of envy and resentment, born from a lifelong comparison of our looks and behaviour by our relatives? Was it simply a case of one-upmanship, whipped up on a wave of mania, a bit like Dad in his Gipsy Moth *Kia Ora* taking off to Australia, except her flight crash-landed.

Regardless of the reasons she provided, and others I've come up with, there is one thing that is crystal clear. Her book essentially is an extension of her abuse of me. Anna's friend Susan Lea said:

> With her resentment toward you, I believe she could easily justify anything. She feels ownership over your father, so she asserts that ownership.
>
> When people have certain mental issues, they confuse authorship; they believe that if they think they do something, that means they did it; they confuse their identity with the identities of others, especially family members. Medication can also further confuse people.

I've always thought it was odd that in the 1970s Anna legally changed her name to Annamaria. Maria is another form of Mary. Why did she do this when she resented me so much?

Soon after Dad retired, Mum decided to leave him. She was in their bedroom packing her suitcases when Dad walked in. Somehow, she fell over one of the suitcases and they both burst out laughing. Mum told me he then looked forlorn and said, 'I just can't help it. I can't help myself.' Perhaps Anna, too, could not help herself.

It is difficult to maintain rage against someone who has a serious mental illness, but what about those who knew my sister was writing a book behind my back and did not warn me or try to talk her out of it, perhaps even encouraged her? It is very difficult not to feel furious about their silence and stupidity.

Towards the end of writing this book, I discovered my half-brother Michael and his wife Martha had known about Anna's project. My naivety astonishes me. I'm not sure why I was so affected by this, why I felt so betrayed. After all, Anna moved up from Wellington to Waiwera to be closer not only to Robert but also to them. Others knew too. Rhonda, my second cousin (who'd kept the secret of my half-brother from me for all those years) told me that Martha and Anna went up to Coromandel and spent time with some of their relatives at the old family cottage in Hannaford Bay. Anna told them she was working on a book about Dad.

And what about Robert? He knew Anna had a serious mental illness that led to her being reckless, impulsive and violent. He knew how long I'd spent labouring over my book, and that I'd gifted my collection to MOTAT, without which Anna could not have written her book. Didn't he feel uneasy about his support of her? At one point I stretched my brain and considered that maybe he thought he was doing a good thing, that Dad would be even more famous with two books out there.

The people who knew what Anna was doing secretly, behind my back, plus those involved with the publication of her book, unwittingly enabled more abuse.

There has been an army of bystanders throughout my life, people who knew of my sister's violence and did nothing, or chose to ignore or dismiss it, or worse even blame me for it. Their abandonment allowed the abuse to continue. The chief enablers were Mum and Dad, who overlooked my sister's violence, physical and emotional, from the time I was a child. Aunt Margaret further enabled the abuse, when I was staying in Remuera. New Zealand's mental health system played a part by not giving my sister the help she needed for seven long years, and by not supporting me when I was assaulted. Then when I thought I was safe at last, because after Mum and Ola died there was no longer any need to fly over to Auckland, out of nowhere came Anna's hand grenade in the form of a book, aimed directly at me.

The impact of her book was overwhelming, yet another trauma to add to my pile. As Australian author and historian Daniel Oakman poignantly pointed out, 'The inter-generational trauma you write about in *Sundowner of the Skies* is revived with the publication of your sister's book.'[151]

Should I forgive her? And those who enabled her? There is a strong pressure in our society for forgiveness in order to move forward, let go, heal. But is it only forgiveness that allows us to move on from those who have hurt us? And what does it even mean? I found this explanation on the Mayo Clinic website, and it struck a chord:

> Forgiveness means different things to different people. But in general, it involves an intentional decision to let go of resentment and anger.
> The act that hurt or offended you might always be with you. But working on forgiveness can lessen that act's grip on you. It can help free you from the control of the person who harmed

you. Sometimes, forgiveness might even lead to feelings of understanding, empathy and compassion for the one who hurt you.

Forgiveness doesn't mean forgetting or excusing the harm done to you. It also doesn't necessarily mean making up with the person who caused the harm. Forgiveness brings a kind of peace that allows you to focus on yourself and helps you go on with life.[152]

The person I really need to forgive and feel compassion for is myself. For the way I behaved during that nightmare of a year, hellbent on seeking revenge and some sort of justice over my sister's book. All my rants on social media. All the emails I sent with countless versions of various articles, hundreds of darts in the dark, fired at news outlets all over New Zealand, even Australia, and the odd one further afield, screeching 'please publish this!'

And I needed to feel compassion for little Mary, running, running, always on the run, hiding under her bed, behind bushes, up the tree with a knife in her hand. The teenage Mary bent over in the car, blood trickling down her back, the neighbour rushing her to hospital; young mum Mary devastated by her sister's letters, being ghosted, wondering what she'd done wrong; the adult Mary stumbling out of the little grey car and running up the hill in Helensville, terrified for her life, thinking her sister was finally going to kill her; and the older Mary, now a grandmother, a few years ago finding out about her sister's book, shell-shocked and wondering when it would ever end. Hadn't she had enough trauma in her life?

Home and family relationships are not safe for many people. My family home wasn't safe for me, nor were my relationships with family members after I'd left home. Mum often told me you don't have to be friends with family. She was spot on. I did not choose the family I was raised in, or the siblings I shared my childhood with, growing up on that toxic tree in New Zealand. But I chose to leave. I walked away to save myself. Do not feel sorry for me, throw your hands up in the air and say what a pity they didn't get on, couldn't work it out, what a shame it came to this.

How about saying, you are lucky to have stopped some of the damage and created a much healthier life for yourself and your own children. As that policeman at Orewa said, I was lucky to be living in Australia. 'Go back there and try to forget your family.'

My mother always said, 'Thank goodness you went away. Australia has been so good to you.'

Good on you, Mum. And thanks.

I had a dream recently. I was sitting on a bench and realised my sister was sitting next to me. I glanced at her. She was not the ogress I might have expected but she was like a little child. I felt a deep love and compassion for her. I stood up and walked away. She came running after me, and said rather anxiously, 'Do I need to apologise to you?' I looked at her and said in a strong but gentle voice, 'No, I need nothing from you.' I continued walking and did not look back.

CHAPTER 27

The End

On 17 March 2023, just weeks after this dream, I was shocked to receive an email from my brother, even though I'd told him I never wanted to hear from him again. He said Anna was in hospital. She had been admitted in late January for acute psychosis, which he said was now under control. However, they had since found out she had a neurological illness, with tests indicating she may have Creutzfeldt-Jakob disease.

'She has deteriorated quickly, can only get a few words out at a time. Just thought we would let you know,' Robert wrote.

Creutzfeldt-Jakob is a rare degenerative disease of the brain that is fatal. It destroys brain cells and causes tiny holes to form in the brain. You would not wish this disease on your worst enemy. It causes the brain to become spongy; it turns it to mush, and leads to dementia. Most sufferers die within six months.

I was stunned. I'd just finished a rough first draft of this book, writing it quickly in a few months. A week earlier I'd even sent some sample chapters to an editor for an assessment. The first line had been, 'My sister is dead, so now I can write about her.' A few days later I changed it to, 'My sister is dead to me, and now I can write about her.' I'd wondered if I might have to release this book in Australia and not New Zealand, or maybe wait until my sister actually died, which could be years away since both Mum and Dad died in their nineties. I even thought I might rewrite it as a fictional tale.

At first, I wasn't going to reply to Robert. He had never apologised to me for his part in issuing a legal threat and his cruel words of 'Get stuffed and don't contact me again. You have so lost the plot and need help' but a day later I swallowed my bitterness and thanked him for letting me know.

A part of me wondered if I should fly over to Auckland but I thought better of it after I read up on the disease and learnt that some patients can become violent. What if Anna attacked me? Also, I would not be welcome there, I was sure. I was the monster who had dared to take legal action against her *own* sister. Instead, I sent flowers from Auckland's Botanist Florist, which provides unconventional and eclectic flowers. I chose the deluxe size Bright Bouquet, and on the card put, 'We are all thinking of you. Sending you love and peace, from Mary, Eamon and Natalya.' The nurse I spoke to told me Anna had lit up and smiled when these flowers arrived.

I received this comforting message from Susan Lea:

I absolutely adored Anna. She had many persons who respected and admired her, and she had many in love with her. She doesn't mean to harm others. I have forgiven her.

Thanks for all you did for Anna. She will no longer be able to interfere with your life.

And, despite being combative with you, Mary, your sister, Anna, struggled in her life, and your compassion for her made you a better person. You were strong enough to give birth and raise children. Anna suffered. She attended church often. She prayed. She was kind to me when my 'friends' wanted nothing to do with me.

During those first few days after learning of Anna's illness, when I was lurching from grief to relief, I thought of that old leather suitcase of

Dad's – the case I'd sent over to Anna in a moment of weakness, after she had told me I'd got her illness wrong in my book.

Hesitantly, I asked Robert if I could possibly have the suitcase back, as it was very precious to me and I'd promised it to Natalya. 'Yes,' he said, 'For sure.'

Epilogue

Anna lasted longer than we expected. She died peacefully at Northhaven Hospital, Whangaparāoa, Auckland, on 19 August 2023 at 1:35 am. There was a small funeral held a week later. I was not told about it. My brother assumed that I would not be interested. I would have liked to have been given a choice.

Two weeks before her death, I dreamt that Anna and I were on holiday together. We were having a wonderful time, talking and laughing. I knew she was dying, and at one point I said, 'I'm sorry if anything I've said has hurt you.' She said, with a smile on her face, 'Maybe you need more therapy.' I thought to myself (in the dream): that is a weird thing for her to say as she doesn't believe in therapy. And she's the one who needs therapy!! And why was I apologising?

Afterwards, lying there awake, I felt a deep calm, there was a warmth in my heart, I felt love towards my sister – it was as if she was there in the room with me. I realised that despite her lashing out at me, her attacks, we had been very close as children and teenagers, much closer to each other than to Robert, and we shared a bedroom for all those years. We were best friends for almost half our lives. I had the feeling she was leaving us soon.

And she did.

*

Although I'd planned to keep *this* book a secret from Robert, in the end I came clean, told him I was writing a memoir and there'd be a section on Anna's book. I sent him some questions with things I sought clarification on and said, 'Take your time with your responses, as I may end up quoting you!' His replies came in minutes later.

I'd asked him about *that* legal letter, which threatened me with defamation if I published my article, 'The Hagiography: Why My Sister's Book feels Like a Stab in the Back', even though I'd just written the truth of what had happened to me. I said I was curious why he took that action as apart from extracts from some of his emails he was hardly mentioned in the article, except for the paragraph in which I'd said that if our father's abuse didn't affect him that was great, some children are more resilient than others. But I'd added, 'People who suffer trauma can consciously try to suppress their recollection of painful events and over time the forgetting becomes automatic.'

I asked if he had taken offence to that paragraph, or was he just supporting Anna? He replied:

> I never felt there was abuse and looking back I think Dad's parenting was common for that era. I do take offence with that sentence implying that I did suffer trauma and am suppressing it – I am completely at peace with my upbringing.

He said he supported Anna because I was going way over the top with my actions and it was going to cost Anna quite a lot of money, plus mental stress. No argument there. As I've said, I was quite deranged and not well. But what about my mental stress and the money it cost me?

I also asked about his response after I discovered that Anna's book was mostly plagiarised in which he had said I should just accept what had happened, move on and save myself money. And that he had found it hard to believe it had been 'hugely traumatic'. I explained that I had come close to having a breakdown over Anna's book and the betrayal, and that my doctor had sent me to one of Queensland's best psychiatrists, who concluded that it *would* have been a major trauma for me.

> Now that time has passed, do you see how it could have been so distressing for me? Or do you think I should have just accepted it all, that perhaps you thought it was good to have two books on Dad out there, so more people came to know about him? Perhaps you thought it would sell better than mine as it didn't have the warts like mine.

He replied:

> I truly did not think this would be traumatic and am surprised it has been so bad. I would have accepted it all. I never have had an opinion of which book would sell better and it didn't matter. For me to have both books is a real plus so I always have great accounts of his story.

A short time later, this arrived: 'I know how much you did for Anna and sorting out Mum's and Ola's affairs which was brilliant.' I did not reply.

*

In January 2022, I moved to Castlemaine in central Victoria to be closer to Natalya and her partner and their two daughters. I am on Dja Dja Wurrung Country, which despite its beauty still bears the scars inflicted during the gold rush. This area is not lush and green like South-East Queensland; rather, it is rocky with box-ironbark and dry sclerophyll forest.

I love it here. I feel grounded and very much at home. I bear scars from my rocky life, but I believe that the violence which threaded through it has ripped open my heart to make me more empathic and understanding.

Across the road from my lovely sustainable house is a national park, and up behind me bushland. There is a myriad of walking tracks. I walk them often, Ivy scampering ahead, waving her tail with joy. I usually try to walk mindfully, do the Zen thing.

This area is also wonderful for cycling. I cycle alone and with new cycling friends. As well as cycle paths there are lots of gravel roads with little traffic. These roads, many built during the goldrush of the mid-nineteenth century, are a joy to ride along. They traverse the Castlemaine Diggings National Heritage Park, Australia's first National Heritage Park. The Castlemaine area was one of the richest goldfields in the world, and is one of the best-preserved. There is a special magic cycling through this area, past stone ruins of huts, fences and even water wheels (used to drive mining machinery).

I have much to be grateful for. For being in this place. For having friends and family who I can be myself with. People who do not tolerate bullying or abuse, people who have my back.

As for this book, writing it in my new home has helped me heal and get rid of lifelong feelings of shame. What a miracle.

At first my brother could not find our father's suitcase. While Anna was dying, he and his partner began cleaning out her unit but could find no sign of it even though he said they checked thoroughly. I asked him to check under her bed. 'There's no way in the world she would have got rid of it. Has someone taken it?' A week later he emailed: 'Found the suitcase today. It was under some other junk.' I told him to chuck away the stuff inside – folders and so forth – as I had no need for them, and to send it over to me.

The suitcase arrived safely back in Australia. Somehow it had lost its leather handle on its time away from me, although one end had come loose when it had been in my possession. I'd never got around to repairing it. Apart from a plastic bag containing brass buttons from Dad's TEAL uniforms, from when he was the Boss of that burgeoning company, the suitcase was empty.

The Forgotten Abuse

Sibling abuse is the most common form of violence in the family. It occurs four to five times as frequently as spousal or parental child abuse.[153] Our society has not recognised this form of family violence, let alone looked at ways to prevent it or to try to rectify its harmful impact on victims. It remains the hidden or forgotten abuse.

The three main types of sibling abuse are:

- **emotional abuse:** insults, contempt, manipulation, threats, derogatory taunts, excessive teasing
- **physical abuse:** being held down, punching, choking, kicking, slapping, biting, hurting with toys or weapons
- **sexual abuse:** touching, masturbation, intercourse, being forced to watch pornography.

In Australia:

If you or someone you know is experiencing or at risk of any kind of family violence, call 1800RESPECT 1800 737 732.

If you or someone you know needs support, you can contact Lifeline 131 114 or Beyond Blue 1800 512 348.

If you have experienced childhood trauma, you can speak with a Blue Knot counsellor by calling 1300 657 380.

In New Zealand:

Helplines for abuse and family violence include Shine 0508 744 633 and Lifeline 0800 543 354.

For support with trauma and PTSD, you can contact Manaaki Tāngata Victim Support 0800 842 846 or Barnardos NZ What's Up 0800 942 8787.

Notes

Author's Note

1   John Caffaro 2022, 'Sibling abuse of other children', in R. Geffner, J.W. White, L.K. Hamberger, A. Rosenbaum, V. Vaughan-Eden and V.I. Vieth (eds), *Handbook of Interpersonal Violence and Abuse Across the Lifespan: A Project of the National Partnership to End Interpersonal Violence Across the Lifespan (NPEIV)*, Switzerland: Springer, pp. 1295–1322.

2   Victorian Government 2016, *Royal Commission into Family Violence*, p. 153, <rcfv.archive.royalcommission.vic.gov.au/MediaLibraries/RCFamilyViolence/Reports/Final/RCFV-Vol-IV.pdf>, accessed 18 January 2024.

3   Ibid.

Chapter 1: Going West

4   'Queensland Compared, Census 2016', Queensland Treasury, <https://www.qgso.qld.gov.au/issues/3221/qld-compared-census-2016.pdf>, accessed 19 January 2024.

5   Georgina Fuller, 2015, 'The serious impact and consequences of physical assault', *Trends & Issues in Crime and Criminal Justice*, No. 496, Canberra: Australian Institute of Criminology, <https://www.aic.gov.au/publications/tandi/tandi496>, accessed 19 January 2024.

6   B. Cook, F. David and A. Grant 1999, *Victim's Needs, Victim's Rights: Policies and Programs for Victims of Crime in Australia*, Research and Public Policy series no 19. Canberra: Australian Institute of Criminology,

<https://www.aic.gov.au/sites/default/files/2020-05/rpp019.pdf>, accessed 19 January 2024.

Chapter 2: A Lot of Running

7 On their first mention, I've spelt out the correct pronunciation for place names in New Zealand. Many non-Māori people, especially Pākehā, white New Zealanders (including myself), have butchered te reo Māori. For example, mispronouncing Tauranga where I spent my childhood years Towel-Wronger. It is Toe-rrrung-ah. Thankfully, there has been a push in recent years for New Zealanders to use the correct pronunciation, to honour Māori culture and the deeply personal meanings of these words.

8 Mary Garden 2019, *Sundowner of the Skies: The Story of Oscar Garden, the Forgotten Aviator*, Sydney: New Holland.

9 Alison Jones 2020, *This Pākehā Life: An Unsettled Memoir*, Wellington: Bridget Williams Books.

10 Susan Kedgley 2021, *Fifty Years A Feminist*, Palmerston North: Massey University, p. 60.

Chapter 3: A Violent Streak

11 Maurice Gee 2018, *Memory Pieces*, Wellington: Victoria University Press, p. 327.

12 Meera Atkinson 2018, *Traumata*, Brisbane: University of Queensland Press, pp. 66–7.

Chapter 5: The Hut

13 John Caffaro and Allison Con-Caffaro 2005, 'Treating sibling abuse families', *Aggression & Violent Behaviour*, Vol. 10, Issue 5, p. 606.

14 Amani Hayder 2021, *The Mother Wound*, Sydney: Pan Macmillan, p. 45.

15 Ibid.

16 Robyn Davidson 2023, *Unfinished Woman*, London: Bloomsbury Publishing, p. 30.

17 Ibid. p. 75.

18 Talia Marshall 2020, 'My lucky, unlucky book', *Verb Wellington*, <https://www.verbwellington.nz/essays/my-lucky-unlucky-book>, accessed 19 January 2024.

19 Karla Elliott, Jane Fitz-Gibbon and Jane Maree Maher 2020, 'Sibling violence: Understanding experiences, impacts, and the need for nuanced responses', *British Journal of Sociology*, Vol. 71, pp. 168–82.

20 Darlene Lancer 2020, 'Sibling bullying and abuse: The hidden epidemic', *Psychology Today*, February, <https://www.psychologytoday.com/au/blog/toxic-relationships/202002/sibling-bullying-and-abuse-the-hidden-epidemic>, accessed 19 January 2024.

Chapter 6: The Stab in the Back

21 Phillip Matthews 2018, 'Maurice Gee on his mother's thwarted writing career, his messy adolescence and how he met the love of his life', *Stuff*, 6 August, <https://www.stuff.co.nz/entertainment/books/107203619/maurice-gee-on-his-mothers-thwarted-writing-career-his-messy-adolescence-and-how-he-met-the-love-of-his-life>, accessed 19 January 2024.

22 'The Beatles in New Zealand', Ministry for Culture and Heritage, <https://nzhistory.govt.nz/culture/beatles>.

23 Margaret McClure 2016, 'Auckland places – Central suburbs: Parnell to One Tree Hill', *Te Ara: the Encyclopedia of New Zealand*, <www.TeAra.govt.nz/en/photograph/16192/remuera>, accessed 19 January 2024.

24 Blake Morrison 2023, *Two Sisters*, London: The Borough Press, p. 92.

Chapter 7: You Want the Whole World at Your Feet

25 Susan Kedgley 2021, *Fifty Years A Feminist*, Palmerston North: Massey University, p. 48.

26 Louise Matthews 1993, 'Beauty business boomer!', *New Zealand Women's Weekly*, 12 July, p. 18.

27 Personal email, 5 April 2023.

28 Susan Kedgley 2021, *Fifty Years A Feminist*, Palmerston North: Massey University, pp. 46–47.

29 Sharon Verghis 2004, 'Reclusive writer Janet Frame dead', *Sydney Morning Herald*, 30 January, <https://www.smh.com.au/entertainment/books/reclusive-writer-janet-frame-dead-20040130-gdi98k.html>, accessed 19 January 2024.

30 Andrea O'Neill 2015, 'Porirua Mental Hospital Ahead of its times', *Stuff*, 8 August, <https://www.stuff.co.nz/dominion-post/news/70912254/porirua-lunatic-asylum-ahead-of-its-times---150-years-of-news>, accessed 19 January 2024.

31 Corinna Tucker and Tanya Whitworth 2023, 'Sibling aggression and abuse go beyond rivalry – bullying within a family can have lifelong repercussions', *The Conversation*, 2 March, <https://theconversation.com/sibling-aggression-and-abuse-go-beyond-rivalry-bullying-within-

a-family-can-have-lifelong-repercussions-199247>, accessed 19 January 2024.

32 Darlene Lancer 2020, 'Sibling bullying and abuse: The hidden epidemic', *Psychology Today*, February.

33 *RNZ* 2022, 'The Rise and Fall of Counterculture in Aotearoa', *RNZ*, 20 August, <https://www.rnz.co.nz/national/programmes/saturday/audio/2018854515/nick-bollinger-the-rise-and-fall-of-counterculture-in-aotearoa>, accessed 19 January 2024.

34 Margareta and Maurice moved to Nelson in 1973, where they brought up their two children, Abigail and Emily, and relocated to Wellington in 1989. I was in India for much of the 1970s, and bringing up my own children in the 1980s, but I have fond memories of visiting them in Wellington and in Nelson after their children had left home.

35 Mervyn Dykes 1971, 'Commune folk seek truth down by the riverside', *New Zealand Weekly News*, 4 January, pp. 1–8.

36 National Library of New Zealand, <https://natlib.govt.nz/photos?text=Curious+Cove>, accessed 19 January 2024.

37 Encounter groups were a method of psychotherapy developed in the 1960s in which members were encouraged to be honest and open, and emotionally expressive.

Chapter 8: Turning East

38 Sue Middleton 2010, 'Ashton-Warner, Sarah Constance', *Te Ara: The Encyclopedia of New Zealand*, <teara.govt.nz/en/biographies/6a1/ashton-warner-Sarah-constance>, accessed 19 January 2024.

39 Judith Herman 2022, *Trauma and Recovery: The Aftermath of Violence from Domestic Abuse to Political Terror*, New York: Basic Books.

40 Janet Frame 1990, *The Complete Autobiography*, London: The Women's Press, p. 188.

41 Shannon Redstall 2023, 'Gloriavale was built "on the backs of young women", court told', *Stuff*, 30 March, <https://www.stuff.co.nz/business/better-business/131656167/gloriavale-was-built-on-the-backs-of-young-women-court-told>, accessed 19 January 2024.

42 Ros Lewis 2019, 'Ros Lewis was sexually assaulted by James K Baxter', *Stuff*, 20 April, <https://www.stuff.co.nz/national/111980198/ros-lewis-was-sexually-assaulted-by-james-k-baxter-at-jerusalem-she-wasnt-the-only-one>, accessed 19 January 2024.

43 Ibid, p. 40.

Chapter 9: Estrangement

44 Stacey Colino 2022, 'How to deal with sibling estrangement', *Psycom*, 10 November, <https://www.psycom.net/relationships/sibling-estrangement?s=09>, accessed 19 January 2024.

45 Mary Garden and Annamaria Garden 2021, 'Daddy dearest: Sisters in full-flight book battle', *The Weekend Australian*, 9 July, p. 18.

46 Ibid, p. 605.

47 Alexander C. Jensen and Susan McHale 2015, 'What makes siblings different? The development of sibling differences in academic achievement and interests', *Journal of Family Psychology*, 29 (3), pp. 469–78, <https://www.ncbi.nlm.nih.gov/pmc/articles/PMC4460605/>, accessed 19 January 2024.

48 Wasim Kakroo 2022, 'Comparison among siblings: an open invitation to mental health issues', *Kashmir Observer*, 15 April, <https://kashmir observer.net/2022/04/15/comparison-among-siblings-an-open-invitation-to-mental-health-issues/>, accessed 19 January 2024.

49 The British Association for Psychological Type, <https://www.bapt.org.uk/about-bapt/>.

50 Fern Schumer 2022, 'The anguish of not knowing why a sibling cuts off from you', *Psychology Today*, 20 December, <https://www.psychologytoday.com/au/blog/brothers-sisters-strangers/202212/the-anguish-of-not-knowing-why-a-sibling-cuts-you-off>, accessed 19 January 2024.

51 Kipling Williams 2007, 'Ostracism: The kiss of social death', *Social and Personality Psychology Compass*, Vol 1(1), 5 September, pp. 236–47. <https://compass.onlinelibrary.wiley.com/doi/10.1111/j.1751-9004.2007.00004.x>, accessed 19 January 2024.

52 Robyn Davidson 2023, *Unfinished Woman*, London: Bloomsbury Publishing, pp. 174–5

53 Research tour funded with a grant from the Sunshine Coast Council: Regional Arts Development Fund.

54 Andrew Anthony 2015, 'Writing is a way of getting rid of shame', *The Guardian*, 1 March, <https://www.theguardian.com/books/2015/mar/01/karl-ove-knausgaard-interview-shame-dancing-in-the-dark>, accessed 19 January 2024.

55 Nikki Gemmell 2023, 'Throne of the wolves', *The Weekend Australian Magazine*, 6 May, p. 10.

Chapter 10: Unravelling

56   Karla Elliott, Jane Fitz-Gibbon and Jane Maree Maher 2020, 'Sibling violence: Understanding experiences, impacts, and the need for nuanced responses', *British Journal of Sociology*, Vol. 71, pp. 168–182.

57   Darlene Lancer 2020, 'Sibling bullying and abuse: The hidden epidemic', *Psychology Today*, February.

58   Alison Croggon 2021, *Monsters: A Reckoning*, Melbourne: Scribe.

59   Lucy Blake 2015, 'Hidden voices: Family estrangement in adulthood', Centre for Family Research, University of Cambridge, <https://www.slideshare.net/NoamShemer/hiddenvoicesfinalreport-58625784>, accessed 19 January 2024.

60   Genevieve Shaw Brown 2016, '7 signs it's time to cut toxic (family) ties', *ABC*, 28 December, <https://abcnews.go.com/Lifestyle/signs-time-cut-toxic-family-ties/story?id=27278012>, accessed 19 January 2024.

61   Blake Morrison 2023, *Two Sisters*, London: The Borough Press, p. 273.

Chapter 11: Days of Anna's Life

62   Annamaria Garden 2000, *Reading the Mind of the Organization: Connecting the Strategy with the Psychology of the Business*, Aldershot: Gower.

63   Warwick Brunton, 'Mental health services', *Te Ara: the Encyclopedia of New Zealand*, <https://teara.govt.nz/en/mental-health-services/print>, accessed 19 January 2024.

64   Jay Neugeboren 1997, *Imagining Robert: My Brother, Madness, and Survival*, New York: William Morrow and Company, Inc., <https://archive.nytimes.com/www.nytimes.com/books/first/n/neugebor-robert.html>, accessed 19 January 2024.

65   The address hung on my wall for many years. In 2020, I gifted it to Strathnaver Museum, near Tongue, Scotland. <https://www.johnogroat-journal.co.uk/news/plaque-gift-inspires-strathnaver-museum-to-ask-the-public-to-celebrate-local-heroes-204196/>, accessed 19 January 2024.

Chapter 12: Saving My Sister's Life

66   'Can stress cause dementia', Alzheimer's Society, www.alzheimers.org.uk/blog/can-stress-cause-dementia, accessed 19 January 2024.

67   New Zealand Government 2018, *Pathways to Wellness. November 2018: Government Inquiry into Mental Health and Addiction*, <https://www.

mentalhealth.inquiry.govt.nz/assets/Summary-reports/He-Ara-Oranga.
pdf>, accessed 19 January 2024.

Chapter 13: Temporary Truce

68   Annamaria Garden 2015, *The Roles of Organisation Development*, Surrey,
     England: Gower Publishing Limited.
69   Centre for Public Impact 2019, 'Piri Pono – a peer-led acute residential
     service', <https://www.centreforpublicimpact.org/case-study/piri-pono-
     peer-led-acute-residential-service-new-zealand>, accessed 19 January
     2024.
70   Annamaria Garden 2017, *Organizational Change in Practice: The Eight
     Deadly Sins Preventing Effective Change*, London: Routledge.
71   Jean Bartunek 2018, 'Book Review: Annamaria Garden *Organizational
     Change in Practice: The Eight Deadly Sins Preventing Effective Change*',
     Organization Studies, Vol. 39, pp. 143–50.
72   Annamaria Garden 2018, *Burnout: The Effect of Jungian Type*, London:
     Freedom Press, Scholar Select.
73   Annamaria Garden 2018, *How to Resolve Conflict in Organizations:
     The Power of People Models and Procedure*, London: Routledge.
74   Annamaria Garden 2021, *Burnout and the Mobilisation of Energy*,
     London: Austin Macauley.
75   Chris Reed (McCauley Publishers) 2021, 'Burnout and the mobilization
     of energy', *NZ Booklovers*, <https://www.nzbooklovers.co.nz/post/
     burnout-and-the-mobilisation-of-energy-by-annamaria-garden>,
     accessed 19 January 2024.
76   *Hibiscus Matters* 2021, 'New burnout book providing tools for recovery',
     21 September, <https://www.localmatters.co.nz/health/new-burnout-
     book-providing-tools-for-recovery/>, accessed 19 January 2024.
77   Hal Arkowitz and Scott Lilienfeld 2011, 'Deranged and dangerous:
     When do the emotionally disturbed resort to violence', *Scientific
     American Mind*, 1 July, <https://www.scientificamerican.com/article/
     deranged-and-dangerous/>, accessed 19 January 2024.
78   Andrew Anthony 2023, 'The Best Minds Review: Rich examination of
     madness and the way the West deals with it', *The Guardian*, 16 April,
     <https://www.theguardian.com/books/2023/apr/16/the-best-minds-
     jonathan-rosen-review-rich-examination-of-madness-and-the-way-
     the-west-deals-with-it?CMP=Share_AndroidApp_Other>, accessed
     19 January 2024.

79   Owen Jacques 2023, 'Man charged with alleged stabbing murder of 69yo Conondale man Christopher Gwin', ABC, 15 May, <https://www.abc.net.au/news/2023-05-15/christopher-gwin-murder-man-charged-on-sunshine-coast/102345414>, accessed 19 January 2024.

Chapter 14: My Lost Half-Brother

80   Daryl Higgins 2011, 'Unfit mothers ... unjust practices? Key issues from Australian research on the impact of past adoption practices', *Family Matters*, No. 87, pp. 56–67.

81   'Hello and goodbye', Ministry for Culture and Heritage, <https://nzhistory.govt.nz/war/second-world-war-at-home/hello-and-goodbye>, accessed 19 January 2024.

82   Forces War Records, *Ancestry*, <https://uk.forceswarrecords.com/memorial/619466285/john-riley-1907/facts>, accessed 19 January 2024.

83   'Yankee boys, Kiwi girls', Ministry for Culture and Heritage, <https://nzhistory.govt.nz/war/us-forces-in-new-zealand/yankee-boys-kiwi-girls>, accessed 19 January 2024.

84   Alice died on 22 July 2023. I spent time with her in Nelson, in September 2022, while I was touring the South Island to give some talks on *Sundowner of the Skies*. It was her birthday, and she looked across the table and said, 'This will be the last time you will be seeing me, Mary.'

85   Michael Neilsen 2019, 'Body of missing rugby league stalwart Mike McClennan believed to have been found', *New Zealand Herald*, 22 October, <https://www.nzherald.co.nz/nz/body-of-missing-rugby-league-stalwart-mike-mcclennan-believed-to-have-been-found/VZIH5UTZXNSUKNLWUBSZO7VMHQ/>, accessed 19 January 2024.

86   Caroline Williams 2019, 'Hundreds gather to farewell "cheeky, determined, rugby league icon" Mike McClennan', *Stuff*, 26 October, <https://www.stuff.co.nz/sport/league/116948298/hundreds-gather-to-farewell-cheeky-determined-rugby-league-icon-mike-mcclennan>, accessed 19 January 2024.

Chapter 15: The Mad Gardens

87   Marina Jones 2014, 'The Madness of Sir Isaac Newton', *Futurism*, 28 March, <https://futurism.com/the-madness-of-sir-isaac-newton>, accessed 19 January 2024.

88   Ross Fitzgerald 2019, 'A Journey of Discovery', *The Weekend Australian*, 24 August, p. 19.

89 Australian Institute of Health and Welfare 2022, 'Mental Health: Prevalence and Impact', 10 November, <www.aihw.gov.au/reports/mental-health-services/mental-health>, accessed 19 January 2024.

Chapter 16: To Cut or Not to Cut

90 Buzz Bissinger 2007, 'Ruthless with Scissors', *Vanity Fair*, January, <https://www.vanityfair.com/news/2007/01/burroughs200701>, accessed 19 January 2024.

91 Jane Friedman 2020, 'How to and (Especially) How Not to Write About Family', *Jane Friedman Blog*, 9 June, <https://janefriedman.com/write-about-family-memoir/>, accessed 19 January 2024.

92 John Myrtle 2018, Review of *Charles Ulm*, *Honest History*, 20 August, <https://honesthistory.net.au/wp/myrtle-john-charles-ulms-vision-and-determination-made-him-a-pioneer-of-australian-aviation/>.

93 Elaine Forrestal 2018, 'Not an untold story', 30 December, *Elaine Forrestal Blog*, <https://elaineforrestal.com.au/2018/12/30/not-an-untold-story/?amp=1>, accessed 19 January 2024.

94 Denise Newton 2021, 'Magnificent (and flawed) men and women in their flying machines', *Denise Newton Writes*, 2 November, <https://denisenewtonwrites.com/?p=3282>, accessed 19 January 2024.

95 2019, 'Oscar Garden, New Zealand's forgotten aviator', *New Zealand Herald*, 21 July.

Chapter 17: Te Riri Pākehā: The White Man's Anger

96 Vincent O'Malley 2021,' Remembering raupatu: A forgotten anniversary', *The SpinOff*, 3 December, <https://thespinoff.co.nz/books/03-12-2021/remembering-raupatu-a-forgotten-anniversary>, accessed 19 January 2024.

97 Moana Jackson 2021, 'Facing the truth about the wars', *E-Tangata*, 17 September, <https://e-tangata.co.nz/history/moana-jackson-facing-the-truth-about-the-wars/>, accessed 19 January 2024.

98 'Tauranga school apologises for child removal', *Sunlive*, 30 October, <https://sunlive.co.nz/news/255112-tauranga-school-apologises-child-removal.html>, accessed 19 January 2024.

99 Kate Wells 2019, 'Tauranga's "forgotten aviator" honoured with mural', *Sunlive*, 12 August 2019, <https://sunlive.co.nz/news/217664-taurangas-forgotten-aviatorhonoured-mural.html>, accessed 19 January 2024.

Chapter 18: Have You Seen Stuff?

100 State Library New South Wales 2020, *Sundowner of the Skies*, General History Prize, 2020 – Short-listed, <https://www.sl.nsw.gov.au/awards/general-history-prize/2020-shortlisted-sundowner-skies>, accessed 19 January 2024.

101 Annamaria Garden 2020, Extract from *Oscar Garden: A Tale of One Man's Love of Flying*, *Stuff*, 18 October. <https://www.stuff.co.nz/entertainment/books/300126101/oscar-garden-a-tale-of-one-mans-love-of-flying>, accessed 19 January 2024.

102 Mary Garden 2005, 'Sundowner of the Skies – Mary Garden takes flight with her father', *Weekend Financial Review*, 24–8 March, pp. 6–7, Review section.

103 Todd Thatcher 2019, 'Can emotional trauma cause brain damage', Highlands Springs Specialty Centre, 4 February, <https://highland springsclinic.org/can-emotional-trauma-cause-brain-damage/>, accessed 19 January 2024.

104 Annamaria Garden 2000, *Reading the Mind of the Organization: Connecting the Strategy with the Psychology of the Business*, Aldershot: Gower, pp. 123–4.

105 Kelly Dennett 2020, '"I think he'd be very proud of Air NZ": Daughter's book about flight pioneer father Oscar Garden,' *Stuff*, 18 October, <www.stuff.co.nz/travel/300128519/i-think-hed-be-very-proud-of-air-nz-daughters-book-about-flight-pioneer-father-oscar-garden>, accessed 19 January 2024.

Chapter 19: We Act for Your Siblings

106 My publisher in New Zealand retired in 2022. He organised the release, publicity and distribution of *Sundowner of the Skies* separately from the Australian publisher, based in Sydney.

107 *NZ Booklovers* 2020, 'Interview: Dr Annamaria Garden talks about Oscar Garden.' Note, the original interview was posted on 19 October 2020. On 15 November I emailed my sister and told her that some of the statements in the interview were defamatory. She agreed to remove several sentences and a revised version was posted the following day: <https://www.nzbooklovers.co.nz/post/interview-dr-annamaria-garden-talks-about-oscar-garden>.

108 Jennifer Robinson and Keina Yoshida 2022, *How Many More Women?* Crows Nest: Allen & Unwin, p. 383.

Chapter 20: I'll Bags It

109 Doug Bishop, Lindsay Cregan, Bryony Dewar-Leahy and Rose Kinnear 2022, 'Self-redress when you are defamed – your right of reply to an attack', *Clayton UTZ*, 1 September, <www.claytonutz.com/knowledge/ 2022/september/self-redress-when-you-are-defamed-your-right-of-reply-to-an-attack#:~:text=When%20you%20can%20reply%20to,not%20 be%20liable%20for%20them>, accessed 19 January 2024.

110 Janet Frame 1990, *The Complete Autobiography*, London: The Women's Press, p. 198.

111 Hayden Donnell 2020, 'Sudden shutdown for New Zealand largest magazine publisher', *Media Watch*, 2 April, <www.rnz.co.nz/national/ programmes/mediawatch/audio/2018741194/sudden-shutdown-for-new-zealand-s-largest-magazine-publisher>, accessed 19 January 2024.

Chapter 21: Smash Hit

112 Oscar Garden Collection: Manuscript, pictorial and object collection which includes aviator Oscar Garden's licences/certificates, passport and pilot/engine/aircraft log books; photograph album and loose photographic prints showing Oscar's involvement in aviation and the Garden family; newspaper clippings related to the flying career of Garden; correspondence relating to the Garden family; and a medal presented to Garden in November 1930 by the citizens of Wellington. <https://collection.motat.nz/objects/106337/oscar-garden-collection>, accessed 19 January 2024.

113 *The Sun*, 5 November 1930, p. 13.

114 Eleanor Black 2016, 'Authors beware: scam publishers are charging up to $15k for shoddy work', *Stuff*, 15 September, <www.stuff.co.nz/ entertainment/books/84274470/authors-beware-scam-publishers-are-charging-up-to-15k-for-shoddy-work>, accessed 19 January 2024.

115 Mary Egan Publishing, 'Services', <https://www.maryegan.co.nz/ services>.

116 Jim Sullivan 2021, 'Oscar Garden: One man's love of flying, *Otago Daily Times*, 1 February, <https://www.odt.co.nz/entertainment/books/oscar-garden-tale-one-mans-love-flying>, accessed 19 January 2024.

117 Garth Cameron 2021, 'Review *Sundowner of the Skies: The Story of Oscar Garden, the Forgotten Aviator* and *Oscar Garden: A Tale of One Man's Love of Flying*', *Aviation News*, March, p. 16.

118 Annamaria Garden 2020, *Oscar Garden: A Tale of One Man's Love of Flying*, Mary Egan Publishing, pp. 237–8.

119 Mary Garden 2021, 'Why my sister's book is a stab in the back', *Newsroom*, 5 April, <https://www.newsroom.co.nz/sister-vs-sister>, accessed 19 January 2024.

Chapter 22: Another Betrayal

120 Daniel Joyce 2021, 'Christian Porter's defamation action threated to further chill public interest journalism', *The Guardian*, 16 March.

121 Blake Bailey 2015, 'David Sedaris talk about surviving the suicide of a sibling', *Vice*, 2 June, <https://www.vice.com/en/article/7bdvdg/remarkable-messes-0000671-v22n6>, accessed 24 January 2024.

122 Caroline Overington 2021, 'Daddy Dearest: Sisters in full-flight book battle', *The Weekend Australian*, 9 July, p. 18.

123 Soon after the article was published, one of these men began stalking me on social media and harassing me. It was terrifying. He'd send bizarre emails threatening me with defamation and attaching scores of screenshots of general tweets I'd made. He also sent emails to my son, urging him to take me to 'a shrink'. Each time, I'd report him to the police, but they could not locate him. This went on intermittently for two years, until I discovered his whereabouts and went to court to obtain protection.

Chapter 23: Mum to the Rescue

124 Charlotte Grimshaw 2021, 'From fiction to fact: how writing a memoir changed my brain', The 18th Annual Frank Sargeson Lecture, 13 October, <https://charlottegrimshawauthor.com/columns-and-reviews/from-fiction-to-fact>, accessed 19 January 2024.

Chapter 24: Goddess Justitia

125 Mary Garden 2021, 'Oscar Garden: The supreme navigator', *Aviation News*, November, pp. 24–5.

126 *Barrier Miner* 1930, 'Oscar Garden's Flight. Cheque for 20 Guineas Presented Last Night. Left for Sydney today', 7 November, p. 1, <https://trove.nla.gov.au/newspaper/article/46537139?browse=ndp%3Abrowse%2Ftitle%2FB%2Ftitle%2F53%2F1930%2F11%2F07%2Fpage%2F3360176%2Farticle%2F46537139>, accessed 19 January 2024.

127 Annamaria Garden 2020, 'Oscar Garden: A tale of one man's love of flying', *Stuff*, 18 October, <www.stuff.co.nz/entertainment/books/300126101/oscar-garden-a-tale-of-one-mans-love-of-flying?cid=app-iPad>, accessed 19 January 2024.

128 *Sydney Mail* 1930, 'Oscar Garden's solo flight from England', 12 November, p. 17, <https://trove.nla.gov.au/newspaper/article/159660194?searchTerm=%22oscar%20garden%22%20garden%27s%20solo%20flight%20from%20england>, accessed 19 January 2024.

129 Annamaria Garden 2020, 'Oscar Garden: A tale of one man's love of flying', *Stuff*, 18 October, <https://www.stuff.co.nz/entertainment/books/300126101/oscar-garden-a-tale-of-one-mans-love-of-flying?cid=app-iPad>, accessed 19 January 2024.

130 *Sunday Mail* (Brisbane) 1930, 'Two sides of flying, Oscar Garden, who flew from England tells of crash in darkness and how he ate 20 eggs', 9 November, p. 4, <https://trove.nla.gov.au/newspaper/article/98213510?searchTerm=%22oscar%20garden%22>, accessed 19 January 2024.

131 Ian Driscoll 1979, *Airline: The Making of a National Flag Carrier*, Auckland: Shortland Publications; Maurice McGreal, 1994, *A Noble Chance: One Pilot's Life*, Wellington: McGreal; Ian Thomson 1968, *A History of TEAL*, Masters thesis, University of Canterbury.

132 Yvonne Tahan 2009, 'How Witi was found out', *New Zealand Herald*, 7 September, <https://www.nzherald.co.nz/nz/how-witi-was-found-out/UH5S67GLHNBVHZ3Z3QNKHVRIIA/?c_id=1&objectid=10607862>, accessed 19 January 2024.

133 Jolisa Gracewood 2009, 'A good read', *Public Address*, 6 November, publicaddress.net/busytown/a-good-read/, accessed 19 January 2024.

134 Scott Hamilton 2009, 'What Witi Ihimaera could learn from Eliot', *Scoop*, 23 November, <https://books.scoop.co.nz/2009/11/23/what-witi-ihimaera-could-learn-from-eliot/>, accessed 19 January 2024.

135 Kim Knight 2000, 'The unforgiving sea', *Stuff*, 21 November, <https://www.stuff.co.nz/sunday-star-times/features/4366622/The-unforgiving-sea>, accessed 19 January 2024.

Chapter 25: A Bad Habit

136 Jonathan Bailey 2019, 'Nora Roberts sues Cristiane Serruya, wins injunction', *Plagiarism Today*, 30 April, <www.plagiarismtoday.com/2019/04/30/nora-R.s-sues-cristiane-serruya-wins-injunction/>, accessed 19 January 2024.

137 Liz Spayd 2016, 'The truth about false balance, *New York Times*, 10 September, <https://www.nytimes.com/2016/09/11/public-editor/the-truth-about-false-balance.html>, accessed 19 January 2024.

138 Lauren Simpson 2018, 'Trust in the Media: a conversation with former journalism professor Doris Schmidt', Allianz for a Better Utah, 25 July, <https://betterutah.org/trust-in-the-media-a-conversation-with-former-journalism-professor-doris-schmidt/>, accessed 19 January 2024.

139 I'd lifted myself up from being a single mum, battered and bruised after a few disastrous relationships and struggling on a pension, to being reasonably well-off, but that's a long story. In short, it was mostly through real-estate. Like Dad I moved a lot, not quite as frenetically as he had done. Unlike Dad I made money each time I sold a house. I bought beautiful unusual houses and put my imprint on them; I had a flair for home improvement and decoration. Plus, I was still employed, even though I had reached retirement age.

140 Anna Katherine Verney, 'Miles Franklin-nominated novelist apologises for plagiarising Nobel laureate "without realising"', *The Guardian,* 9 June.

141 Alyson Miller 2022, 'Plagiarism, John Hughes' *The Dogs* and the ethical responsibilities of the novelist', *LSJ Media*, 14 July, <https://lsj.com.au/articles/plagiarism-john-hughes-the-dogs-and-the-ethical-responsibilities-of-the-novelist/>, accessed 19 January 2024.

142 Mary Garden 2022, 'Magpies & memory', *Meanjin*, 18 June.

143 Annamaria Garden 2000, *Reading the Mind of the Organization: Connecting the Strategy with the Psychology of the Business*, Aldershot: Gower.

144 Anna Verney and Richard Cooke 2024, 'Being John Hughes', *The Monthly,* March, pp. 34–48.

145 Direct Message, Twitter, 11 April 2023.

146 'Recognition in Queen's Birthday Honours', Monash University, 11 June 2014, <https://www.monash.edu/news/articles/recognition-in-queens-birthday-honours-1>, accessed 19 January 2024.

147 Ross Fitzgerald 2019, 'A Journey of Discovery', *The Weekend Australian*, 24 August, p. 19.

148 Mary Garden 2023, 'Plagiarism, cobbling or accidental inclusion', *Meanjin*, 19 July, <https://meanjin.com.au/blog/plagiarism-cobbling-or-accidental-inclusion/>, accessed 19 January 2024.

149 Caroline Overington 2023, 'Come Writers and Critics', *The Weekend Australian*, 22–23 July.

Chapter 26: Unpacking Book Matters

150 David Remnick 2023, 'The Defiance of Salman Rushdie', *The New Yorker*, 6 February, <https://www.newyorker.com/magazine/2023/02/13/salman-rushdie-recovery-victory-city>, accessed 19 January 2024.

151 Email to me, 16 February 2021.

152 Mayo Clinic Staff 2022, 'Forgiveness: Letting go of grudges and bitterness', Mayo Foundation for Medical Education and Research, 22 November, <https://www.mayoclinic.org/healthy-lifestyle/adult-health/in-depth/forgiveness/art-20047692>, accessed 19 January 2024.

Appendix

153 John Caffaro 2022, 'Sibling abuse of other children', in R. Geffner, J.W. White, L.K. Hamberger, A. Rosenbaum, V. Vaughan-Eden and V.I. Vieth (eds), *Handbook of Interpersonal Violence and Abuse Across the Lifespan: A Project of the National Partnership to End Interpersonal Violence Across the Lifespan (NPEIV)*, Switzerland: Springer, pp. 1295–1322.

Acknowledgements

Deepest gratitude to everyone who has played a part in this story, especially those who supported me through the trauma of my sister's book. You know who you are, even if I do not name you.

Special thanks to:

Peter Van Beek, who first suggested I write a book about sibling abuse, although I dismissed the idea at the time. Michael Burge and Carmel Bird, who have been champions of this book from the outset. Johanna Winchcomb, who read various drafts and provided honest and perceptive feedback. Samantha Miles and Kirstie Innes-Will for their superb editing. Helen Christie for the elegant text design and Alex Ross for creating such a perfect cover. Tom Cleary of Chapman Tripp, a heroic lawyer who stood up for me. Melanie Webley of Flourish Psychology for her help over many years. My cousin Gillian MacColl who has always had my back. Lastly, fellow-survivors of sibling abuse who have shared their stories with me.

And of course, writers, readers and booksellers everywhere. Good books can change the world.

Permissions

Grateful acknowledgement is made to the following for permission to reprint extracts from previously published material:

Atkinson, Meera 2018, *Traumata*, reprinted with permission of University of Queensland Press, Brisbane.

Davidson, Robyn 2023, *Unfinished Woman*, reprinted with permission of Bloomsbury Publishing Plc, London.

Gee, Maurice 2018, *Memory Pieces*, Victoria University Press (now Te Herenga Waka University Press), Wellington, reprinted with permission of the author.

Haydar, Amani 2021, *The Mother Wound*, Pan Macmillan, Sydney, reprinted with permission of the author.

Kedgley, Susan 2021, *Fifty Years A Feminist*, reprinted with permission of the author and Massey University Press, Palmerston North, New Zealand.

McGreal, Maurice 1994, *A Noble Chance: One Pilot's Life*, Wellington: McGreal, reprinted with permission of Paul McGreal.

Morrison, Blake 2023, *Two Sisters*, The Borough Press, London, reprinted with permission of the author.

Robinson Jennifer and Yoshida Keina 2022, *How Many More Women?* reprinted with permission of Allen & Unwin, Crows Nest, Australia.

About the Author

Mary Garden is an author and journalist, with a PhD in Journalism (USC). Her work has appeared in many publications, including the *Australian Financial Review*, *The Weekend Australian*, *The Guardian*, *Meanjin*, *The Humanist*, *New Zealand Geographic*, *Newtown Review of Books*, *Newsroom* (NZ), *Crime Magazine* and *Northern Times* (Scotland), as well as scores of aviation magazines.

Her memoir *The Serpent Rising: A Journey of Spiritual Seduction*, first published in 1988, recounts her years in India in the 1970s where she fell under the spell of several gurus who led so-called 'spiritual' groups that were in fact sex cults. It has had enduring appeal and won the High Country Indie Book Award 2021. Her biography *Sundowner of the Skies: The Story of Oscar Garden, the Forgotten Aviator*, a warts and all account of her father's extraordinary but troubled life, was short-listed for the NSW Premier's History Award 2020 for a work of international significance.

She is a keen cyclist and works in her family's bicycle business, KWT Imports. She writes when she can.

marygarden.com.au